A PASSION FOR

STEAM

A PASSION FOR
STEAM

PATRICK WHITEHOUSE and
DAVID St JOHN THOMAS

WHSMITH
EXCLUSIVE
·BOOKS·

PAGE ONE
Paris – Vichy Express.
P. B. WHITEHOUSE

FRONTISPIECE
Last of a long line. An ornate
Chinese locomotive, a QJ 2–10–2,
one of the most modern in the world,
still exudes the feeling of power and
majesty. The slogans on the front are
those provided by the 'prize crew'
men (three to a footplate, two sets to
an engine) who use it as their own
and care for it accordingly.
P. B. WHITEHOUSE

ACKNOWLEDGEMENTS

This book has been consolidated and made to live by help from a number of experts; this is not only acknowledged, but also greatly appreciated. In addition to the two main authors', work has been contributed as follows. *On the Old Lines*, Sir Peter Allen; *Great Locomotive Builders, A Night in a Steam Depot, Steam Pioneers, A Day in the Life of an Engine Driver*, A. J. Powell; *Some of the World's Mightiest Engines*, Basil Cooper (part); *Enthusiasm for Steam*, F. Harrison; *Horseshoe Curve*, Trains Magazine; *Beyond the Scrapyard Gates*, David Wilcock. Others have kindly contributed to the snippets and are credited at the end of these. The authors would also like to pay tribute to the photographers who have so kindly looked out some of their best pictures. With a book covering such diverse subjects it has been impossible to collate the text without referring to many learned magazines and others works: to these and to many others too numerous to be able to list here, the authors and publishers extend their thanks.

This edition published exclusively for
W H SMITH LTD
by David & Charles Publishers plc

British Library Cataloguing in Publication Data

Thomas, David St. John
    Passion for steam.
    1. Steam locomotives, to 1980
    I. Title   II. Whitehouse, Patrick
    625.2′61′09

    ISBN 0-7153-9419-3

Printed in Portugal by Resopal

CONTENTS

1
OPEN REGULATOR

OF all man's inventions, the steam locomotive is perhaps the most romantic and has done the most to change the world in which we live.

You wait by the lineside on a rough day, every sound drowned by the wind, until you think you hear a distant – very distant – whistle. Before your ears can confirm it, your eyes catch a glimpse of steam rising over a fold in the hills through which the railway comes. You catch a few further glimpses and then hear the unmistakable beat of a locomotive working flat out hauling an express passenger up the grade. The magic sound (and for many it is pure music) gets louder and closer until you cease to be a mere onlooker and get absorbed into the scene and feel warmth from the fire of the vibrant machine whose crew wave their hands as naturally as though you were their close relative.

Throughout its journey, almost every steam locomotive that has ever travelled has had people watch and hear her – yes, always her – progress, noting it perhaps subconsciously with the reassurance of a punctual pattern, setting their watches or waking up or setting out to school by her passage, or just looking up in admiration. Most steam locomotives are awe-inspiring mobile power houses, and you would have to be very dull not to notice them. Imagine their impact before the days of high tech or even motor cars.

There are of course many ingredients in their romance. For example, while most of them in fact have a great deal in common, using the same almost simplistic basic technology, their variety as well as their size has been (and still remains) enormous. A steam engine is a steam engine, yet how diverse their wheel arrangements, their design concept, their sounds and smells. And their finish and the care or not bestowed on their appearance varies just as much (often giving a hint of ethnic origin) from the machine of clean, curved lines topped with sparkling brass fittings that is as pleasing to the eye as a painting, to the down-at-heel grimy, uncared-for engine which even in its maker's original paintwork would have looked ungainly, its 'innards' crudely displayed to the world. In Britain and some of her former colonies the first naturally carries a nameplate, itself perhaps a thing of art, the name evocative; the latter nobody would name affectionately and you probably have difficulty in deciphering the working number.

Next, nearly all steam locomotives share two vital points. Maximum power is not simply obtained by turning a handle, but by understanding, careful calculation and movement of the controls, indeed by coaxing, creating a partnership between man and machine that petrol and diesel-driven vehicles generally lack. Just as different locomotives of identical design and building behave differently, for each is a living creature with her own personality, so you can tell the very character of the driver struggling to keep his heavy train on the move up a steep incline in adverse conditions. Coupled with that, the steam engine is unique in not merely creating its own power but in keeping a stock of it, so that for a period it can actually use more than is being made. Getting up a head of steam is a phrase that has passed into everyday language, but locomotive men do it literally, not merely before setting off but on the move, perhaps deliberately going easy so as to build up the head of steam for later use.

With all its achievements and foibles, all its variations on a simple theme, there is no wonder that the steam locomotive has been more written about and discussed than any other of man's inventions. For over a century and a half, great crowds have flocked to the lineside to note the latest arrival or modification or traffic challenge, or in more recent days nostalgic occasion. Even where steam has disappeared from regular service, preserved locomotives attract audiences that those offering many types of entertainment can only dream of, while the conveyance of enthusiasts to distant parts where the regulator is still opened as an everyday matter of carrying the traffic is another big business. As is told in later pages, workaday steam is declining but by no means dead or in some places even dying.

And wherever you find locomotives, there will be the men of steam, members of one of the world's greatest fraternities. Often their conditions are dismal, the work hard not to mention dirty, the hours unsocial. They may literally be too hot on one side and too cold on the other, but east and west, north and south, they nearly all love it. No

In the beginning. An early print of a London & Birmingham Railway train leaving Primrose Hill tunnel north of London.
MILLBROOK HOUSE COLLECTION

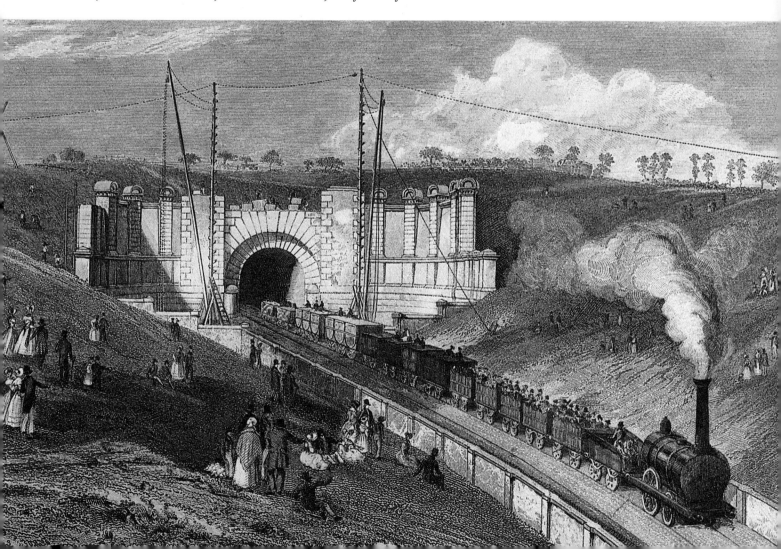

workers have followed their fathers and grandfathers into the same job as eagerly as the footplate men. Few get so much exhilaration from their everyday exertions or have been more reluctant to retire. Early on the diesel salesmen of course pointed to the better working conditions their machines provided, along with greater hours in service because of lower maintenance needs, and they were right. Sitting at the controls of a diesel is better in every way; in theory. It is just that men do not become so passionate about diesels. 'It is a job and you can do it or not, but steam is a way of life,' is one way in which it is often put. And it says much

By Train to the Indus

A warm afternoon saw a handful of us (young officers) at Dedali joining the all-stations to Manmad Junction, where we would pick up the *Frontier Mail* for a two-day journey to Rawalpindi. The all-stations train ran to seven coaches, hauled by a British-built D4 4-6-0 of early 1920s vintage. The Maharashtra countryside of the Province was flat, dry and dusty, and after about three-quarters of an hour and three stations the journey started to become boring and tiresome. So at the next stop onto the engine!

The driver, a stocky Indian with a flaming red beard, beamed a welcome; the fireman's assistant polished the inspector's seat on the tender front. Red letter day – a sahib riding on their engine. (Most Indian engines carried a fireman, who did the actual firing, and an assistant who worked the injectors, got coal down in the tender and kept the footplate clean.) Across the plain the driver started to explain the controls. I cut him short: 'That's all right, thanks. I know. I used to build these things back in England.' So he got off his seat, motioned me to it and moved to the inspector's seat. Strange locomotive, strange route, no knowledge of the time-table, nothing!

The driver had been using full regulator, so I did the same. The engine had a pull-up regulator handle, with a screw clamp on the quadrant to hold it open (which the assistant operated – too menial
continued overleaf

about that way of life that the men of steam were not only generally revered in their community but in many parts of the world their children were expected to do better at school than those of other workers.

They were doing one of the most important jobs of their day, the steam locomotive often being the most sophisticated thing that worked in the local community. And they had to do it round the clock, in all weathers and conditions, as part of a great team of railwaymen running the system controlled by a rich variety of signalling methods and other rules, yet often for hours at a time completely out of touch conversation-

Early sophistication in steam. A reproduction of a Currier and Ives print showing a typically ornate American 4-4-0 of the 1880s on the Hudson River Railroad. In the background is an equally typical artefact of river navigation: a stern wheeler paddle steamer. Each represents the most sophisticated form of travel around at the time.
MILLBROOK HOUSE COLLECTION

continued
a task for the driver). The screw reverse was straightforward, as was the vacuum brake. We ambled along without exceeding about 45. The stations loomed up on the horizon as low buildings, no platforms to speak of, the odd clump of trees for shade beyond a tall distant signal. The assistant knew the road; as each distant came in sight he would unclamp the regulator, put on the blower, and leave me to judge when to shut off steam. Start braking gently at the distant and stop in the platform. Hordes of people descend and climb on at the same time. A wave of the flag, a toot on the whistle, and off we would go again. – A. J. Powell

wise with anyone but their footplate mate. Even on the footplate, conditions were often so tense and noisy that the driver or engineer and his fireman communicated with the minimum of words or in sign language. Each understood yet checked the other's skill, the fireman skilfully building his fire so as to have the greatest heat to make the most steam when the hardest work came, while always avoiding waste of fuel, the driver perpetually monitoring gauges and controls as well as keeping an eye on the road ahead and deciding speed through the combination of cut off, regulator and brake. Even in the days before radio was common, it came as a great surprise to many who had reached the top of their profession in other walks of life to realise that even in fog and driving snow the footplatemen had to judge all, including the vital knowledge of just where they were at any given moment, through sight and sound; and that once they started on a non-stop journey of say four hours, there was no means of communicating with the conductor or guard in the train.

It was called responsibility.

The world over, footplatemen lived up to it, with only the rarest instances of oversights or positive misjudgements, though inevitably these sometimes led to death and disaster on the grand scale. Electric light signalling with powerful colour-beams, and even automatic train control (such as a bell or gong relaying the state of the signal ahead and where appropriate the brake being applied) began to make conditions easier on some routes in the later days of steam in some countries, and from the footplates that were totally open to the elements on the earliest machines there was a steady progression to more enclosed cabs and working conditions. But such was the trust placed on the locomotive crew that most railways did not even provide them with a speedometer to tell the speed.

If things went wrong, they generally had to fend for themselves, immediate technical assistance seldom being available. But it was one of the saving graces of the steam locomotive that it seldom failed completely out on the road; many railways had to learn the painful way with diesels how disruptive a total breakdown can be out in the country. A hundred and one things could reduce the steam locomotive's performance. Sometimes a pause was needed to get up steam. Usually at least a passing loop could eventually be reached to avoid totally disrupting the following traffic. The footplatemen naturally had to gauge when they should halt or summon up assistance; at many locations at the foot of inclines they had discretion whether or not to call for an extra machine to be added.

Most actions and decisions became instinctive, the driver and his mate who sometimes worked together for decades understanding each other's thought processes as they uniquely understood the potential and limitations of their locomotive. What happened out on the road would frequently depend on how well maintenance was done in shed, whether the locomotive had been properly prepared for that particular run, what the quality of coal was like. Keen footplatemen naturally vied with each other for the best. And even the best needed constantly checking up.

At the great termini stations, the starting train would normally be brought in by a small shunting locomotive, probably a tank locomotive without separate tender. The process went like clockwork. Until the

FACILITIES

FETERIA & BUFFET

3 - BUFFET

46146

powerful train engine had set back on to the stock, and hooked on, the shunting locomotive stayed attached at the other end, supplying steam to heat it in winter. The actual coupling and uncoupling might be done by the fireman, or by a shunter, depending on local practice. The conductor or guard would come up to give the driver the details of the load and any special instructions, for he it was, not the driver, who was in charge of the train. Then back to the rear to carry out the brake test, to make sure that the shunting engine had been uncoupled, and to oversee the final loading of parcels and mail traffic. Meanwhile the fireman would be giving final attention to his fire and washing down the footplate, and the driver might well have time to walk round his engine, the familiar oil can in one hand and rag in the other, giving a last drop of oil to slide bars or big ends. That was the part that the public saw, if they were interested enough to look; but the footplatemen had booked on duty up to two hours before, to check late notices of speed restrictions or water shutoffs, prepare their engine, and top up with coal and water if necessary before leaving the depot.

Terminus. An interior shot of Euston station London in April 1962 and nearing the last days of its original form. In the platform, at the end of its journey from the north, is rebuilt Royal Scot class 4-6-0 No 46146 The Rifle Brigade. The engine is in BR express locomotive green whilst the coaches in their second livery since nationalisation in 1948 approximate to the old LMS colours. J. B. SNELL

11

Right. No problems with Shap Fell. Stanier's Duchess class Pacific No 46228 Duchess of Rutland *shows no difficulty in moving a heavy train up this notorious incline very much as described in the snippet by O S Nock (pages 13–14).* DEREK CROSS

Heartland of Canadian steam. A study of steam on the Canadian National Railway at Turcott roundhouse Quebec in 1943 – the height of World War II and a busy time for North American railroads. On the turntable is 4-8-4 No 6205, one of the engines used on principal passenger trains including the transcontinentals. Note the 'switchers' with their dual steps forward of the buffer beam. MILLBROOK HOUSE COLLECTION

Something of the character of steam depots large and small is caught in the following pages. Always remember they were the places where the elite of workers went to report for duty, at all times of day and night. Each depot had its individual character; all had that familiar reek of steam, smoke, coal and oil. Tons of soot were sent up into the atmosphere from the largest of them, making washday a hazardous affair for housewives in pre washing-machine days. But then even within the great roofed passenger stations of Europe and America, and a few even in the southern hemisphere, there might be twenty or thirty locomotives in various states of animation, all inevitably polluting the air.

Writing from a western perspective, inevitably the past tense creeps in . . . and correctly so even where steam makes regular appearances on tourist and other special occasions, for we will never again see or hear leave alone breathe the great mass of steam that once made civilisation move. Great would be the shock if the grime of yesteryear reappeared, serious enough though the pollution of the internal combustion engine is in many places. Yet, as again these pages tell, even daily mass-produced steam should not be described wholly in the past tense, for

there are pockets where you can still see a score of working locomotives. And where there is such activity, as in China, undoubtedly the men of steam still hold a special place in the esteem of their community.

What of steam's historic role? The simple fact is that it was the steam locomotive that first carried man at a speed faster than that of an animal. Not merely that, but it had a virtual monopoly in speed as well as the carriage of great loads over land for several generations.

Built by their tens of thousands in the great locomotive works – among the world's largest and most progressive factories of their time – the machines conquered every kind of terrain and in the five continents to knit the very essence of civilisation together. Of course, there were other parts to the railway than the steam locomotive, but without it the railway did not exist in the sense we understand it. It was the steady improvement and increased power of the locomotive that forced the pace of other developments, such as the quality of rails and track, bridges, viaducts and tunnels, signalling and safety, stations and (not least) passenger and freight rolling stock. The steam locomotive and the railway were synonymous.

In Britain they resulted in the generation 1830–60 seeing greater changes to society than have ever occurred since or are likely to happen again. When George Stephenson's famous *Rocket* and sister machines started work on the world's first public passenger-carrying steam railway, the prototype of today's Intercity routes, Britain, like the rest of the world was a series of largely self-contained and inevitably self-reliant communities. Only a few of the wealthy could afford the legendary stage coaches. Perhaps only one in twenty citizens ever travelled on a horse or even in a horse-drawn vehicle. Horizons were limited to the distance that could be walked. Buildings were made of local materials, food grown locally so that the cities of the early Industrial Revolution had to keep farms within them to supply daily milk. The British Navy could only communicate with its various depots during the Napoleonic wars

Rescued at Crewe

It was in the transitional period between steam and electric traction on Britain's West Coast main line, and I was riding the down *Midday Scot* to increase my knowledge and experience of the diesels, already used on the principal trains. We were brought to a stand at the last signals before entering Crewe station and held so long that the fireman climbed down to telephone the signal box. It was a good job he did, for he noticed that the diesel's water tank was leaking. When we ran into Crewe, the platform inspector was not amused. 'A nice time to tell us you want a fresh engine,' he snorted. But Crewe is deservedly famed for getting things done in a hurry, even to producing a substitute engine for a 245-mile top-link express run at a moment's notice; and while the failed English Electric Type 4 was coupling off someone on the platform said 'he's giving you 6228'.

The fresh driver laughed, sensing a leg-pull; obviously it was D228 that was coming down for us. But even as we spoke a red 'Duchess' came backing down from the shed.

Our fireman, who had come on duty prepared for nothing more strenuous than the tending of a steam-heating boiler, now faced the task of shovelling some six tons of coal in the space of 4½ hours. But it was very soon evident that no half-hearted attempt was to be made to deal with the emergency. A knotted handkerchief replaced his uniform cap and he commenced to dig. By the time all was ready we were 18 minutes late away, with a load of 12 coaches, 455 tons behind the tender. Although the driver started very quietly, taking the measure of the engine, it was soon clear that *Duchess of Rutland* was in good condition. At express speed she rode as though a considerable mileage had been
continued overleaf

Early locomotives. The early American Tom Thumb *from the Smithsonian Museum and the National Railway Museum's working replica of George Stephenson's* Rocket *on the turntable at Sacremento in May 1981.* K. P. LAWRENCE

continued
worked since last general over-haul, but no one minds a bit of hard riding if the engine will go, and from Winsford Junction to Moore we averaged 76mph for 12½ miles on end. By Wigan, so rapid was our progress and so wonderfully clear the road that the situation of an emergency was receding, so far as I was concerned, and I realised I was clocking some of the fastest running I have *ever* recorded over the route – by steam, of course.

Preston was passed within even time; we skated across the North Lancashire plain at 75–77 mph, and passed Carnforth, 78.3 miles from Crewe, in 76¾ minutes. We went magnificently up to Shap, despite drizzling rain, and covered the 31.4 miles of ascent, in which the train had been raised almost from sea level to an altitude of 915ft, in 35¼ minutes with Shap Summit, 109.7 miles breasted in one second under 112 minutes from the start at Crewe.

With a smooth run down we clocked into the Citadel station at Carlisle, 141.1 miles, in 141½ minutes from Crewe, 9½ minutes less than schedule. My footplate authority did not extend into Scotland on this occasion, but I recorded the further fine work of the driver and fireman, and on arrival in Glasgow I was able to congratulate them again on a memorable run. Quite apart from the dramatic circumstances in which it started, it was one of the finest I have ever made with a steam locomotive over the West Coast Route. – O. S. Nock

by someone on horseback or by messages sent painfully slowly by a semaphore signalling system spread along the south coast.

Only thirty years later, at the end of a period of great upheaval often nicknamed 'creative destruction', the basic railway system was virtually complete, unifying the country now served by national newspapers and standardised building materials and foodstuffs, brand names famous even today seizing the market opportunities the steam trains provided. Street lighting became standard, gas being made from coal the trains brought, while crops could be grown in the best areas and sent rapidly to the centres of population – and the whole enlightenment brought about by the greater movement of people and goods resulted in the fastest period of social reform ever experienced. For example, with better lit streets came the demand for proper sanitation systems, and an attack on diseases such as cholera that generally died out as the railway system expanded. Medicine, the political system, education, all were reformed with the creative urge the railway unleashed.

Everywhere the arrival of the railway was a watershed in social consciousness and attitude – starting with the adoption of railway or standard time, replacing local time according to the sun. Such was the boost to enlightenment that many people thought that once the steam locomotive had become universal war would be impossible.

Railways were largely Britain's gift to the world, and building them in much of South America, the Orient, Australia and large parts of

Africa gave Britain great wealth and prestige. The United States naturally had the strength and determination to go its own way – its own way to conquer the continent. America was indeed unified as the whistle of the steam locomotive could be heard spreading across the Prairies and through the Rockies until the journey from coast to coast could be finished in a few days. Not even world wars have been met with greater response than that given to the building of America's railroads, in some cases the tentacles of the great main lines being extended by several miles a day. Every rural community fought to have its short line so as properly to participate in the national progress.

The steam locomotive made it all possible, such as politicians visiting different parts of the nation, the harnessing of the great grain crops of the Prairies, the integration of business and social life on the national scale with the great cities specialising in different industrial tasks, Chicago claiming to be the railway capital of the world. Today it may seem quaint that businessmen and politicians had to spend several days from East Coast to West, but it was the steam locomotive that made possible the lifestyle we know today. The internal combustion engine has merely polished off the task.

German Pacific. One of the West German (DB) class 01 4-6-2s in full cry with a heavy express in the later 1960s. Although steam is now finished on the DB a number of locomotives including some 01s have been kept in private preservation and can be seen on special excursions from time to time.
MILLBROOK HOUSE COLLECTION

Just An Ordinary Day

It is the fifteenth of December, 1959, a day of chilly breeze and lowering cloud in Glasgow. Soon after 8.30 we emerge, replete with bacon, egg, fried bread, and a vast mug of sweet tea under our belts, from the cheery company and dingy walls of the enginemen's hostel in Inglefield Street. We have a fifteen minute walk to Polmadie shed, past decaying sandstone tenements and the Queens Park works of North British Loco. 'We' consists of my old friends driver Albert Eccles and his fireman, Jack Ridgway from Newton Heath, plus myself as observer.

At the foreman's office, Eccles books them on and is told '70052, up 7'. Ridgway turns on his heels and makes for the stores for bucket, tools, shovel and oil, while his mate casts an eye over the late notice case. They will spend the next hour preparing *Firth of Tay* for the 10.50 Glasgow Central to Liverpool and Manchester, but I have pressing business with the shedmaster meantime.

Come 10.15, I find them near the head of a queue of engines ringing off, and climb aboard. 70052 looks smart, and is in good fettle as befits an engine only two and a half months off general repair at Crewe. Ridgway has a medium fire on, level with the bottom of the firehole but built well up in the back corners of the wide grate, though I would be happier to see some good Yorkshire in the tender instead of the Scottish cobbles, which are too swift for comfort.

Our turn comes, a yell to the bobby as we pass, '10.50 Manchester', and we roll gently back to Central and hook on in No 1. Steam heat on, the guard comes up to advise '10 on, 340 tons', and goes back to do the brake test, leaving us simmering gently, waiting for the signal and the right-away.

Spot on time we are off with a couple of slight, grumbling slips,
continued overleaf

Across the border, British Columbia only agreed to become part of a unified Canada against the guarantee of the speedy completion of the Canadian Pacific. Steam literally made the nation possible.

Each country had its own style. While the British Raj adopted a very British way of doing things along with the machines largely shipped out of Glasgow, most of the larger European civilisations became self-contained and developed a rich variety of technical tradition, in which the French generally held the lead, followed by the Germans. The Australian states, jealous of their individuality, determined that the steam locomotive's conquering power would be limited through the deliberate non-adoption of a national gauge.

Most of the world, including North America and most of Europe, adopted the standard gauge of 4ft 8½in which George Stephenson used for the Stockton & Darlington following earlier private coal-carrying lines in Britain's North East, the cradle of railways. It just happened, the distance between the wheels no doubt having been the conventional one for coal-carrying road vehicles. Not everybody thought the automatic adoption of this gauge was wise. One of Britain's most colourful engineers, Isambard Kingdom Brunel, builder of the Great Western Railway, decided on 7ft, and there is no doubt that that gave greater stability and for a time ran the world's fastest trains. Later in history, a wider gauge than 4ft 8½in would undoubtedly have been welcomed by the locomotive engineers ever trying to squeeze out more power for heavier loads and greater speeds. Many countries like Britain staged a challenge to the standard, but ultimately even the Great Western had to give way since technical superiority was less important than the pragmatic matter of having a standard for through working. And powerful indeed are the best of the machines packed into the 4ft 8½in, such as the QJ class 2-10-2s still being built in China in 1988. In the United States, the ultimate in power was the Big Boy. It perhaps gives a more understandable feel for its sheer volume to say that a scale model built for a track only 7½in wide measures 24ft in length.

To start, some engineers doubted if the steam engine with smooth metal wheels on smooth metal track would gain sufficient adhesion. One pioneer designed a perpetual cog as a way round the difficulty. Over the years many locomotives have indeed slipped to a standstill, but steadily machines became surer footed as the loads they carried increased. An enormous body of technical knowledge and experience was applied by locomotive designers, often among their countries' most famous citizens, to adopt wheel arrangements and sizes through which the power could be reliably transmitted. And to this day vast machines convey heavy loads through some of the world's hardest terrain on gauges much narrower than the standard 4ft 8½in. The 3ft 6in gauge conquered Japan, New Zealand and much of Africa, while the metre gauge climbs mountains in many parts of the world. Because of space limitations, many industrial concerns the world over used a narrow gauge for their internal transport systems; remember that when steam was universal, it had to be used to transport items even within a large works, or from mine and quarry. Many of the most original if not individualistic

Left. Firth of Tay *goes south. BR standard Pacific No 70052 heads a heavy train out of Carlisle in the mid 1950s.* ERIC TREACY

Unification. The completion of the first transcontinental railroad joining the Central Pacific and Union Pacific companies at Utah on 10 May 1869. One of the world's most historic railway occasions. ASSOCIATION OF AMERICAN RAILROADS

continued

gently across the Clyde bridge and then Eccles begins to open her out and make sweet music at the chimney. We are doing 51 by Rutherglen, but then get hauled down for a 30 mph subsidence slack at Newton, which nobbles us for the sharp climb from Uddingston to Motherwell. One minute down there, but at least the station staff are awake and save half a minute on the stop.

Away again against the distant, on full regulator and 38 per cent to lift the train away on the 1 in 116 grade: but to no avail, for we are stopped dead at Flemington Station while we watch Shieldmuir Junction put a ballast train across in front of us! Hard things are said of signalmen in general, and this one in particular, for there we are with nearly 10 miles of unrelenting climb ahead of us, much of it at 1 in 100, to Craigenhill.

Ridgway is making his shovel ring on the firehole shield as Eccles gives her full regulator and 42 per cent, gradually pulling her up to 32 per cent, and *Firth of Tay* is shouting to the chimney tops. Speed climbs to 41 at Law Junction and the slight easing past Hallcraig box brings it up to 48. By now cutoff is back to 25 per cent, and we clamber over the top at a minimum of 43, with pressure just 10-lbs. below blowing off. But alas, Carstairs are not ready for us – probably pre-occupied with getting the Edinburgh portion across – and again we are stopped outside. 31 minutes from Motherwell instead of the booked 27, and we are 4½ down.

continued overleaf

Canadian Transcontinental. One of the Canadian Pacific Railway's huge 2-10-4s No 5903 at the foot of the Rockies in British Columbia. The locomotive and tender are jointly over 98ft long and weigh 336 tons – over 80 times that of Stephenson's Rocket.
COURTESY RAILWAY WONDERS OF THE WORLD

continued

5 minutes to attach the 3-coach Edinburgh section on our tail is too optimistic, and they take 6½. So we are 6 late as we lift 13 bogies, 438 tons away – only 12 tons under our limit to Beattock Summit – and Eccles hammers her hard to get some speed for picking up 1100 gallons of water on Pettinain troughs, only a mile out. But in the dip to the Clyde bridge at Lamington, we are up to 72, and the characteristic hard, rattly ride of the 'Britannias' is very evident in the cab. Thence to the Summit we are on full regulator and 23-25 per cent, and despite a slight slack beyond Crawford we are by Summit in 27½ minutes (28 allowed). Then a bit of high speed coasting down to Beattock, with frequent slight brake applications to prevent her exceeding 80 on the Greskine curves. By Beattock station we are doing 86, and Eccles gives her a breath of steam to keep her at it on the gentler grades to Wamphray.

But trouble now strikes. First the exhaust injector steam valve handle and extension spindle comes off the valve in front of the cab, due to the intense vibration at speed, and steam is shut off briefly until Ridgway makes a temporary repair. Then signals are on at Nethercleugh – they are probably refuging a freight at Lockerbie and he is taking his time – and after some more 80 mph running they are on again at Gretna, and finally we come into No 4 platform at Carlisle on the call-on and crawl the length of it behind the late-departing *Waverley*. Now we are 9¾ down.

The water column gives us new strength, but parcels handling loses us another minute, and just to add to the fun there is a nasty bit of drizzle on the rail and the fire shows signs of caking rather solid under the door and needs the pricker in it. However, 70052 holds her pressure and water well

continued opposite

machines were designed for such lines, and happily many have been preserved as mementoes of the age when anything more than a few tons going any distance over land was of necessity pulled by steam on rails.

Ahead of the car builders, the locomotive manufacturers were the first to develop huge markets, on the international scale. With its early start, Britain employed a large workforce making steam engines for itself and

Europeans in Peru. A German built (Henschel 1951) 2-8-2 No 104 double heads a British (Hunslet 1936) 2-8-0 No 107 on the 3ft 0in gauge line en route from Huayancayo to Huancavelica in the high Andes in 1979.
COLIN SCHROEDER

continued
while slogging up to Southwaite: Ridgway by this time has dug his way back into the tender somewhat, and thinks the coal pusher would save his back. But alas, it is partly jammed, and stalwart efforts by the three of us – well, 2½, because a watchful eye has to be kept on the road – are needed to ease it. Meanwhile the fire has not been touched for five minutes or so, despite full regulator and 25 per cent, and pressure has fallen to 200lbs. by the time coal is moving again. All the same, we pass Plumpton in 22 minutes, one under schedule, and things are looking brighter until we get a double yellow approaching Penrith, which pulls us down to 39. Then away smartly from that, only to get a 20 mph relaying slack at Clifton.

So our approach to Shap is perhaps noisier than it might have been, with 30 per cent on the reverser and the regulator against the stop, to fight back to 35 before Shap station and 36 at the Summit box: our passing time is 4 minutes better than schedule, but would have been 7½ better without the two checks.

Coasting down to Tebay, brakes holding speed to little over 70, we scoop 1400 gallons on Dillicar troughs, run easily through the Lune gorge and the Low Gill – Grayrigg curves, and drop down Grayrigg bank, twice touching 80, to make the Oxenholme stop just 6½ late.

Only 2 minutes allowed there, but 13 on means drawing up
continued overleaf

numerous countries. Four works were found within a square mile in the Glasgow suburb of Springburn. Among the famous British names were the North British, Hunslet of Leeds (specialising in machines for industrial systems) and Beyer Peacock of Manchester (makers of the famous Garrett articulated locomotives, effectively two machines in one with a central boiler and cab). But American salesmen were not slow off

Broad Gauge. A replica of Brunel's 7ft 0in gauge Iron Duke *4-2-2 running in Hyde Park London to celebrate the hundred and fiftieth anniversary of the Great Western Railway in 1985.* K. P. LAWRENCE

A 3ft 6in gauge Berkshire. South African Railways class 24 2-8-4 No 3601 takes coal from the massive wooden stage at Sydenham shed Port Elizabeth on 31 January 1979. These North British Locomotive Co machines have a modern cast steel locomotive bed (or chassis). P. J. HOWARD

continued

twice, and by now I am standing on the adjacent siding to catch the rightaway on the sharp right-hand curve. But it is four minutes instead of two when we get it, then full regulator to get the train up to 81 by Milnthorpe and 73 over the Yealand hump. We are into Lancaster comfortably in 19½ minutes – another minute regained, but half of it is dissipated by station overtime.

Now the drizzle comes sneaking in from the sea, and the rail up to No 1 box is treacherous indeed. Eccles gives it to her hard – you cannot lift 13 from a standing start up a mile of 1 in 98 without – but even with sanding on continuously she is touchy on her feet and we breast the top of Lancaster No 1 at only 17. So despite a sustained 73 at Brock, *continued overleaf*

the mark, and works such as those of Baldwin in Philadelphia helped equip the railways of countries as diverse as Ecuador, Peru, Chile, Angola and Manchuria. Eventually American manufacturers dominated in Japan. Germany also developed an extensive locomotive export business, while France and Belgium also made their considerable mark in such places as North Africa and Turkey.

The story of steam is that of ingenuity, mass production and individualism, of faith and experimentation, of people of all races carrying just about everybody and everything – all based on the simple principle of boiling water to make steam to force through the cylinders that propel the driving wheels. Here we examine some of the many variations and refinements and catch something of the passion past and present that has made steam not just a vast industrial process but that unique way of life.

Standard or narrow gauge, whatever the colour or religion of the men of steam, whatever the country that built the locomotive, whatever the load, there is the magic moment when the conductor, guard or whatever he is called in local parlance (in some places it is the stationmaster who ceremoniously clangs the station bell) gives the right of way and the driver or engineer gently eases the regulator to allow the first steam into the cylinders. All watch and listen to note whether the judgement is correct for the circumstances, and whether the wheels move steadily followed by barks of exhaust as a sure, accelerating grip is obtained. With a multitude of such daily starts – usually accompanied by a blast from the whistle to mark the occasion – life as we live it today was brought into being.

It is hard to exaggerate what the steam locomotive has achieved. Yet affection for it goes beyond logic!

Baldwin engines. A 2-8-0 (No 68) and a 4-6-0 (No 41) of the now preserved section of the Rede Ferroviaria Federal SA from Sao Joao del Rei to Tiridantes leaving the latter town in November 1986. This superb 2ft 6in gauge line has always kept its engines (all Baldwins including two 4-4-0s) in pristine condition. ALAN WILD

Foreigner in France. One of France's most successful mixed traffic types the 141 R class 2-8-2. Built by American and Canadian manufacturers to fill a gap caused by World War II devastation these fine machines could be found countrywide on almost any kind of train. This photograph was taken on the locomotive depot at Nantes in 1966. P. B. WHITEHOUSE

continued

we should drop nearly 2 minutes at Preston: as it is, we get pulled down to a crawl by signals at No 5 and drop 3 minutes altogether.

Whistles blow under the station roof as we ease back, split the buckeyes to drop the Liverpool portion, and ease forward again. Now we are only 4 on for Manchester, 130 tons, and we get the green light just 9 late. Eccles offers me the driving, and stands behind catching the signals: Ridgway has finished his serious labours now. With this light train we go streaking up to Euxton Junction with the exhaust inaudible, brake for the turnout, and are promptly pulled down to 15 by signals at Chorley. Off again towards the flat mosses of Blackrod, brake for Horwich Fork, and give her plenty of steam for the mile up to Hilton House. Then down to Dobbs Brow with just a sniff of steam, brake to 40 for the junction, and pull her down to 30 for the subsidence beyond Daisy Hill. Off we go again on a light rein to Pendlebury, coast down to Pendleton, and we pick up yellows to guide us over to the slow line at Windsor Bridge No 3. After that it is all squeal from the flanges on the Salford curves and I brake her to a stand in Manchester Victoria at 4.6, just 2 minutes late.

Hook off, light engine up to Thorpes Bridge, and on to one of the coaling plant roads at Newton

continued opposite

Modern German express power. An East German 02 class Pacific No 03 2236.2 at Leipzig in the late 1960s. These modern locomotives have remained in service until very recent years with some Pacifics running on passenger services well into the mid 1980s. LA VIE DU RAIL

A scene in 1965 inside the roundhouse once belonging to the GWR at Tyseley Birmingham showing final GWR/WR designs for express and mixed traffic locomotives. From the left are No 7029 Clun Castle, *the last of its class and fitted with a double chimney, a Grange class 4-6-0 No 6853* Morehampton Grange *and Hall class 4-6-0 No 6947* Helmingham Hall, *both mixed traffic types. All were withdrawn by the end of the year.*
P. B. WHITEHOUSE

continued
Heath. The fire is burnt low, there are some clinker patches showing, and *Firth of Tay* looks a little travel-stained. 224 miles she has brought us, and 9000 gallons of water have been turned into steam to do it. Ridgway's supple back has moved something like six tons of coal, and you can hardly ask more. So he and Eccles climb down, tired, glad to be home, and leave the disposal to a shed set. They call in the outside foreman's office to report on 70052, and then into the lobby to make out a repair card for the coal pusher – which will be endorsed 'forward home depot' – and the injector steam valve.

Away they go up the slope to Dean Lane and home. They walk at that time-honoured pace of enginemen everywhere, with quiet conversation and an occasional grin that tells me they are satisfied with their day's work. Just an ordinary day . . . – A. J. Powell, *Trains and Railways Magazine*

On The Old Lines

One of the evocative books written about the joy of railways and their steam power was *On The Old Lines*. The author was (Sir) Peter Allen, eventually chairman of Britain's large Imperial Chemical Industries, and the book, published in 1957, describes many of the world's exotic lines he had been able to visit if not exactly 'on business' then at least as the result of many years of extensive business travel. Here are a few extracts which capture something of the character of steam in its dying days of serving diverse communities in very different lands:

I must say that to my eye the steam engine of the post-war years looks very good, though I suppose that, here at home at any rate, 1913 was the high-water mark for looks and maintenance, compared with which the often filthy machines of British Railways look deplorable, but things were slipping here before 1948 and I can remember many dirty engines before World War II, when a shortage of engine-cleaners could not be offered as an excuse. But abroad things have always been rather different, and standards of cleanliness and maintenance have been higher to the observer's eye than here. I must say, too, that the last flowering of steam abroad has been its golden age, whereas it was not so on the railways of Britain, and the final products of the USA and Canada, of Australia, of Spain and France, and some of our products for export have to my taste been very fine and handsome engines indeed.

But all this talk envisages just the new and the great in the world of locomotives, whereas so much of the pleasure of railways is to be found among the ancient, the modest and the remote, in what I might call the research side of the hobby. This involves the discovery of little obscure lines, often those of narrow gauge, which so often have the most heterogeneous and attractive rolling-stock, for such lines are usually on the edge of bankruptcy and can rarely afford to scrap old equipment and buy new. In these out-of-the-way places the most pleasing things can be found, often completely surprising, for, while there is a very considerable railway literature for the enthusiast, it inevitably deals most with giant expresses and modern equipment and seldom describes the elderly, the recondite, or the humble aspects of railwaying. There is thus no means of knowing what you will find at, say, the junction of Mataporquera in northern Spain until you go there – and when I did go there, what a rich harvest of interest and pleasure there was. But then, Spain is the most wonderful mine of treasure for the railway observer interested in this kind of research.

As for engines, then, I just take pleasure in watching them, in eyeing them, photographing them, sizing them up, and once in a while, if I can fix it, riding on them.

★   ★   ★   ★   ★

A steam engine without a chimney in the conventional position is a strange sight and takes a lot of getting used to. Looks are, of course, a matter for argument, and one man's view is as good as another's. If 'I know what I like' is the last ditch of the diehard, perhaps I can put it the other way round and say 'I know what I don't like,' and I am afraid that I don't like this Italian engine with the Franco-Crosti boiler and no chimney at the front end. To be sure, the heat-recovery principle which they employ is a sound one and is a valiant attempt to remove one of the greatest defects of the steam engine, its low thermal efficiency. It would be wrong, of course, to try to adjust the design of a heat-recovery system to allow the exhaust steam to escape in the conventional position merely for the sake of looks, and certainly the Italian design makes no such compromises nor attempts to evade the effects of taking the exhaust away just ahead of the cab. The British Railways design using the Crosti boiler differs from the Italian, as it has only a single heat-recovery drum, and that below the boiler drum proper, and incorporates a vestigial chimney in the conventional position for lighting-up purposes only. This, while it does not to my eye result by any means in a handsome locomotive, does avoid the incongruous appearance of the Italian machines.

★   ★   ★   ★   ★

Up in the north of Spain in the bleak moorlands backing on to the Cantabrian mountain chain is the longest of all the Spanish metre-gauge lines, the Ferrocarril de La Robla, which covers a distance of no less than 335 kilometres, starting from Bilbao and weaving over the mountains south-westwards to León with an eleven-kilometre branch to La Robla itself. This quite considerable railway, which owns sixty-seven steam engines, has fascinated me ever since, early one morning, on my way north to Santander on the RENFE main line, we overtook a freight train on the metre-gauge line parallel to us as we left the junction of Mataporquera – which, incidentally, means 'Kill the swineherd's wife'. I determined then that as soon as I could I would go back and have a look at this line. Accordingly on a freezing cold mid-May day, as cold as Cromer beach in a February east wind, I spent a most profitable half-hour, starting off with a 2-8-0 built by the Swiss Locomotive Company of Winterthur in 1904 which had the unique feature, as far as I was concerned, of a *green* buffer beam. Originally this engine worked on the Rhaetian Railway in Switzerland. The next locomotive to come in view was the outside-cylinder 0-6-2 tank called *El Esla*, built locally in 1907, which seemed to me to have a pure Great Western chimney. This engine marshalled her small freight train and chuffed off into the mountains towards Bilbao. Then a big freight came in from the east, headed by a 1931 Garratt from Babcock & Wilcox of Bilbao, called *José Mª de Basterra Ortiz*, a name which seemed appropriate to the engine's extreme length. She came off

Classic 0-6-0. Although the last years of steam produced large and powerful locomotives whose very mass evoked a feeling of awesome splendour they were not always aesthetically as attractive as those of earlier design. Perhaps the best looking engines came from later Victorian and Edwardian days – certainly those prior to World War I. This charming scene, taken at Waterford in Ireland in 1946 shows off a whole series of railway classics – the standard inside cylinder 0-6-0 (an ex Great Southern & Western J15 class originating in 1863 but built up to 1903), a mixed train of modern and old six-wheeled stock and an island platform with a typical canopy roof.
SIR PETER ALLEN

From north Africa to northern Spain. One of the joys of this 335km long metre gauge railway was the use of redundant ex Tunisian Pacifics on the longer distance passenger trains. F-R No 182 waits at La Yecilla on 14 May 1960. L. MARSHALL

Home built Spaniard. La Robla metre gauge 0-6-2 tank No 280 El Esla built locally in 1907.
SIR PETER ALLEN

at Mataporquera and her place was taken by a brand-new 2-8-2 tank engine with a sharp brass-bound chimney, a really big engine built as recently as 1953 by Babcock.

*   *   *   *   *

Taking photographs got me arrested in Belgrade. Walking into the station on a fine summer evening I took a few pictures and then approached the red-hatted stationmaster for leave to walk down to the running-shed. Goodwill was evident, but lack of English and French on his part and of Serbo-Croat and German on mine prevented a meeting of minds, and eventually I was led into the stationmaster's office to explain my wishes on the telephone to somebody, unknown, with a know-ledge of French as limited as mine but with different shortcomings. The unknown interpreter then spoke to the stationmaster, who looked at me and continued to smile; I said 'OK?': in an interrogative tone; he shrugged his shoulders, so, a nod being as good as a wink to a blind horse, I walked out and down to the shed. Here I got some excellent pictures, but immediately afterwards a busy man came out of the office whose manner at once put him down as a foreman. My German was enough to identify the word 'verboten' in his speech of welcome, so I politely bowed and withdrew.

Arrived back at the platform, I was straightway picked up by a uniformed policeman and I was made to understand with great civility that it was a case of 'cummerlongermee'. Marvelling how a few words of schoolboy German can return under stress, I was vaguely able to explain that this sort of thing was quite all right in England, that my passport was at the hotel, that I belonged to the Railroad Photographic Club of America – and here was my card to prove it – and that I was a railway amateur. The same explanations to a fat uncom-promising plain-clothes man in the guard-house led him to a lot of telephoning and to writing out a detailed report on a buff form with a vile pen, and then, inexplicably, after forty minutes, to a wave of the hand and freedom.

*   *   *   *   *

'And how did you leave Edmonton?' asked my chairman with kindly interest. 'Sir', I replied, 'on the footplate of CPR Pacific No 2351,' which was the truthful reply, though not perhaps the one expected. And so indeed I had, by the kindly indulgence of the local Canadian Pacific officers, with a permit to ride to Wetaskiwin forty-two miles down the line towards Calgary.

It was a memorable ride in many ways, not the least because this train, called *The Stampeder*, really got a move on and, although light, averaged nearly 50mph for the 194 miles from Edmonton to Calgary with twelve stops, one of them, at Red Deer, of five minutes. The locomotive was willing, though not recently shopped, and the movement of the footplate was lively, to say the least of it, especially as the crew, like crews the world over, wanted to show off the 'old hoss' to the best advantage in front of a guest and whacked her up to 76mph, at which speed the noise, dust and movement reached a new level of uproar in my experience.

The CPR colour scheme for its express passenger engines is splendid: basically black, the tender, cab and running-boards are relieved with big crimson panels and yellow lettering and lining, while the boiler and cylinder casings are grey russia iron or grey-painted. As each engine comes off duty it is hosed down with an oil-water mixture containing a detergent and then is hand-cleaned before it returns to duty, down to cleaned spokes and whitened tyres. I once complimented a CPR shed foreman on the appearance of his engines and his reply was one we might ponder here; he said, 'We would be ashamed to send them out in any other condition.' It will be a sad day indeed when all the fine and magnificently kept steam engines on the CPR have gone.

*   *   *   *   *

The last flowering of the steam engine in the United States was in many ways the finest, and some of the engines built in America at the end of the era of steam were the most powerful and attractive of all. One can quote the streamlined T_1 class of 4-4-4-4s on the Pennsylvania built in 1942, although streamlining had by then largely gone out of fashion, the beautiful clean-lined 300 class of 4-8-4s on the Delaware & Hudson dating from 1943, some excellent 4-8-4s of the Union Pacific and the immensely powerful and majestic Niagara class of 4-8-4s on the New York Central of 1945. Now the steam engine has disappeared entirely along the Hudson and the Mohawk valleys, by the shores of Lake Champlain, and in New England too.

The Delaware & Hudson for many years was my favourite among the railroads of America, and they produced a fine succession of graceful and efficient locomotives as well as a group of experimental high-pressure engines. European influence or at least some of the European graces of appearance were apparent both in rebuilds from early designs and in new locomotives. A small group of 4-4-0s, originally 'camelbacks' with the driver's cab forward of the firebox and the fireman's abaft it, were converted into a handsome 'Anglo-American' class; so also were a group of 4-6-0s of later date. Then, too, the 600 class of 'Pacifics' were cleaned up and 'Europeanised' with flanged chimneys and side-sheet exhaust deflectors, and uncommonly fine they looked. After that came the three 'Pacifics' of the 651 class with a boiler pressure as high as 325 pounds per square inch. Then in 1940 came some 4-6-6-4 Mallets, which at least looked as good as such engines can look, and at last in the mid-years of the War the 300 class, where American power and European grace were, I think, about evenly matched.

*   *   *   *   *

Opinions can certainly differ about which is the most spectacular railway in the world, but my vote would go to the Central of Peru if only because it does the most spectacular things and the most prodigious climbing, all on the standard gauge.

Starting from the Pacific coast at the port of Callao, the Central runs inland to Lima the capital, and then turns towards the great mountain barrier of the Andes, which it attacks by way of the precipitous Rimac River valley. Between Callao and Chosica, thirty-three miles, the line has climbed from sea-level to 2,820ft, nothing very much, but from then on the work begins in earnest until the summit of the main line is reached in the Galera tunnel, seventy-three miles from Chosica at the tremendous height of 15,694ft, an average climb over this stretch of 1 in 33.

To do this the railway has to climb for miles on end at 1 in 25 and 1 in 24, gaining height up the side wall of the valley by a series of thirteen zigzags up which the engine alternately pulls and backs the train. Once over the top the line runs down to the fertile Huancayo valley, to its terminus at Huancayo 10,700ft up and 215 miles from the sea. Not content with this main line performance, the Peruvian Central reaches its highest point and the absolute world's record height for the standard gauge at 15,805ft at La Cima on the Morococha branch near the junction of Ticlio on the main line, just twelve feet short of the world's record height for any gauge held by the Antofagasta & Bolivia Railway. The steam engines, like the railway company, are British mainly in the form of sturdy green-painted 2-8-0s built by Beyer Peacock and known as the 'Andes' class. Because of the steep grades and in particular, the lengths of the stubs at the switchback ends, trains are comparatively short, the consistency being four passenger cars and up to half a dozen boxcars.

* * * * *

The most attractive and spectacular trip which the Argentine Railways can offer is undoubtedly the railway journey over the Andes from Mendoza, where the broad gauge of the San Martín Railway ends, and the metre-gauge Transandine Railway runs over to Los Andes in Chile. In about 150 miles the Transandine rises from 2,518ft at Mendoza to the summit in the tunnel near Las Cuevas at 10,450ft and then descends to 2,667ft at Los Andes. Frequently the railway has been damaged by floods and whole sections have been washed away, but during my visit to South America in December 1952, the line was working and we enjoyed an unforgettable day in transit from Mendoza to Santiago de Chile. We were lucky enough, too, to have fine weather for it, and until late in the afternoon the great mountains were free from cloud. We, therefore, got a sight of Aconcagua, the highest mountain in all the Americas, 23,080ft, just after leaving the station of Puente del Inca.

We had left Mendoza early in the morning behind a wheezy old 2-8-2, which took us across the lower foothills towards the great mountain wall. Then at Blanco Encalada we took on a big 2-6-0+0-6-2 Beyer-Garratt and got down to some real climbing which took us up to Punta de Vacas at a height of 7,850ft. Here the real haul began, and we went up to the division point at Las Cuevas past Puente del Inca on the rack, on a ruling grade of 1 in 16.

On the Chilean side there is another spectacular section on the rack, where the gradient runs as steep as 1 in 12½, and has many miles of 1 in 14 and 1 in 15. At Rio Blanco we changed over from electricity to steam again, to a most attractive old American narrow-gauge 'Mikado' built by Baldwin around the turn of the century, with all the fittings – cow-catcher, headlight and bell and a wonderful great chime whistle. All of this added up to a long day, as we had been up since dawn, and by the time we got to bed in Santiago it was twenty-three hours since we had got up in Mendoza.

Jugoslav narrow gauge. Sir Peter Allen was not alone in crossing the paths of the guardians of the people's liberty in Jugoslavia – most photographers who were able to photograph the superb 750mm narrow gauge railway from Belgrade on to Sarajevo and Dubrovnik had similar (or considerably worse) problems! But it was well worth it as this was one of the most fascinating lines in Europe. This photograph relates to Sir Peter's story and is taken at Belgrade. The engine is an 85 class 2-8-2 No 85.007.
SIR PETER ALLEN

2
GREAT LOCOMOTIVE BUILDERS

Right. Wheel lathe at work. Still in use today is ex LMS Bescot shed's wheel and axle turning lathe but now it is doing the same job for a new purpose – keeping preserved locomotives in fit condition to run on Britain's main lines. The machine is installed at the Birmingham Railway Museum, Tyseley, and is seen here with a pair of ex GWR pannier tank wheels.
BIRMINGHAM RAILWAY MUSEUM

Inside the firebox. Retubing the boiler of a modern British steam locomotive firebox, that of ex LMS 4-6-0 No 5593 Kolhapur, a Jubilee class three cylinder engine built by the North British Locomotive Co in Glasgow for the LMS Railway.
BIRMINGHAM RAILWAY MUSEUM

THE table of the big vertical boring machine carries a new driving wheel tyre, its as yet unmachined exterior a mixture of rust and grey mill scale. It has been rough bored, as the blued steel chips round the clamp pedestals confirm. Now the operator adjusts his finish boring cut and sets the machine in motion. It is tough stuff, tyre steel, with an ultimate tensile strength of 50–5 tons per square inch (nearly twice that of mild structural steel), but the heavy carbide-tipped tool takes a 15thou finish cut at 600ft a minute. The swarf comes off like effervescent, glittering wire wool, which the operator continually rakes clear of the toolholder. The finished bore has a wellnigh mirror-smooth surface, devised to inhibit the development of fatigue flaws.

Along in the boiler shop, the din of riveting is incessant. On a large marking-out table, boilermakers are busy producing a drilling template for the stay and rivet holes in the Belpaire firebox wrapper sheet of a Pacific boiler. It is a complex piece of development, for the ½in thick nickel steel plate will have a top slope, taper from front to back and be rolled to a continuous curve at radii varying from 6½in to 40ft, yet the drilling will be done on the flat. And that is not all! The corresponding

Beardmore engine. After World War I Great Britain suffered from an acute locomotive shortage which could not be dealt with in the confines of the railway companies own workshops and some work was put out to private manufacturers. For example Beardmores of Clydeside constructed some Prince of Wales class 4-6-0s for the London & North Western Railway. One of these engines was LMS 5825 seen here with a train on the West Coast Main Line.
MILLBROOK HOUSE COLLECTION

copper inner firebox wrapper plate, ⅝in thick, will be similarly drilled and rolled, and then when assembled the stay holes will correspond precisely and a long screw thread tap run through the holes in both plates *must be at right angles to the plate surfaces.* There are something like one thousand eight hundred stays, and they cannot be laid out entirely in nice straight lines.

If ever there was a job calling for great skill and years of experience, this was it. The year is 1935. Such work is regarded as routine, high technology by the standards of the time, as it always has been since the founding of the great locomotive works in the early days of steam. Though in itself the steam locomotive is not self-evidently a particularly sophisticated machine, it has traditionally been built in some of the world's finest engineering establishments. Machine tools and other equipment were steadily replaced in a search for reduced production costs and greater reliability. Nations at war were grateful for the sophisticated fabrication and machining that they have been able to undertake. But let it be admitted at the same time that because of their long ancestry, some old, outdated practices lingered on in dark corners and out of the managerial gaze. In one Southern Railway workshop in Britain, an Armstrong-Whitworth screwing machine of 1865 vintage was in use for seventy years! But, then, locomotive works were by no means unique in this respect.

32

Steam locomotive building works easily divided into two groups. On the one hand was a profusion of private firms, usually specialising in locomotives to the exclusion of everything else, and catering for specific markets. On the other – and it was a phenomenon almost, but not entirely, confined to Great Britain – were the workshops of the railway companies, the users. For these latter works, the building of new locomotives was always a minority occupation; their prime function was the overhaul of locomotives taken out of traffic due to wear and tear, and even when, in the 1920s and 30s, new building was concentrated at a limited number of works, it seldom constituted more than 10 per cent of their overall workload.

To earn the description of a 'great builder' something much more than high standards of manufacturing technology was needed. Any fool could build a locomotive in accordance with someone else's drawings. Well, no, that is not quite true. One recalls that after World War I, when there was an acute locomotive shortage, certain firms switched from arms production into the potentially lucrative field of locomotive building. Beardmores, on Clydeside, was an example. At first the ninety *Prince of Wales* 4-6-0s which they built for the LNWR were so 'tight' that hot bearings were frequent and running in was prolonged. The same applied when Woolwich Arsenal assembled SR 2-6-0s of Maunsell design: they required overhaul *before* they went into traffic. If a builder was to be reckoned 'great', he surely had to have not only the manufacturing capability to produce sound engines at a competitive price, but also to have a full design organisation to translate the user requirements – which could not always be fully specified – into ironmongery. Over and above that, the top-flight builders could sometimes be in a position to offer the purchaser a machine to do the job more efficiently than had been

Crewe works in the 1930s. Few railway companies in the world built their own locomotives – this was a phenomenon almost, but not entirely, confined to Great Britain. This photograph shows the construction of a Princess class Pacific No 6207 Princess Arthur of Connaught *in 1935.*
D. S. M. BARRIE COLLECTION

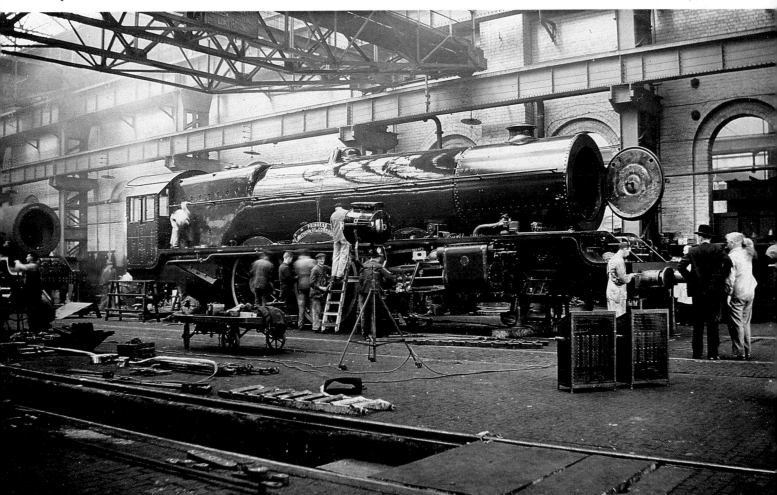

envisaged; the use of Garratt locomotives in Africa was an example of railways being led by the builder, to their mutual advantage. This design capacity could be a very expensive 'overhead', but could be of benefit in that standard major components could be used in designs for various railways. Even complete designs could be sold to more than one customer: why should not the Portmadoc, Beddgelert & South Snowdon Railway purchase a locomotive from Hunslet (the 2-6-2 tank *Russell*) in 1906 to a basic design supplied to Sierra Leone in 1898 if it fulfilled requirements?

Much depended on follow-up of locomotive designs in service, both for performance and for maintenance. In large markets close at hand, the incentive to give excellent service was obvious. But a builder producing new locomotives for Chile or Mozambique was in a more difficult position. Some managers spent a considerable proportion of their time on such missions to all corners of the globe; Cyril Williams of Beyer Peacock was an outstanding example, ever expensively on the trot in days before quick air travel.

Of the railway-owned building works in Britain, the really big names were undoubtedly Swindon and Crewe; by comparison, Derby, Doncaster, Darlington, Horwich and Stratford trailed behind, with the remainder well down in output.

First in the new building field was Crewe; the works opened in 1843, by transfer from Edge Hill, Liverpool, and produced its first new locomotive later that year. From then until the end of the LNWR in 1923, it produced a veritable torrent of locomotives to a steady tradition of simplicity, even crudity in some cases, and instantly recognisable as Crewe-built. Highlights along the road were Webb's 2-4-0 Jumbos, and a variety of three- and four-cylinder compounds which only their designer could love; the Whale Precursors and 0-8-0s; and in superheater days the George the Fifth and Claughton classes. Crewe's growth over the years left it an organisational nightmare which was only resolved with the completion of its new, very fine erecting shop in 1927 and the rationalisation which this permitted. Its standards of workmanship and finish were not always of the highest and it took the arrival of William Stanier as CME to start an improvement when he saw his first Princess

Split Duty

In most trades the world over, split hours of duty have always been deservedly unpopular. But when it came to taking trippers to the beach, enjoying several hours on the sands themselves and booking back on for the return journey home, there were always enthusiastic takers.

South Wales had one of the world's most intensively used railway systems, the rival lines often crowded into the same valley normally largely devoted to taking coal from pit to port. On summer Sundays and Bank Holidays, however, every available locomotive was pressed into service to take miners and their families to the sea.

The drivers and firemen often spent the day with their own families who travelled behind them at privilege fare. To save money, the railways left a score or more locomotives gently simmering in the charge of a single crew at the beach terminus between arrival in late morning and departure in early evening.

Pacific completed. The works will always be associated with the superb Duchess Pacifics and the BR standard Britannias.

Though Swindon opened as repair workshops a few months before Crewe, it was three years before it turned out its first new locomotive; thereafter it took very special circumstances to cause the Great Western to buy elsewhere. It had to approach the traumatic gauge change (which was completed in 1892) with duplicated erecting shops to handle broad- and narrow-gauge locomotives. Once the change was over, there was argument about whether to develop Swindon to overcome its inadequacies or to move the emphasis to Wolverhampton works. Swindon won by a short head, and as a result the magnificent new A erecting shop was built. The works had a justifiable reputation for fine workmanship; for many years from 1933 it was the sole user of the Zeiss precision optical alignment equipment for the accurate setting up of frames and cylinders when others were using taut piano wire or string. The very mention of Swindon conjures up images of glossy green engines, brasswork setting off the paintwork to an accompaniment of staccato exhaust beats and strange trumpeting and chomping noises from vacuum-brake equipment. Saints, Stars, Castles and Kings, and many other classes, continue to have their devoted adherents. Nor should one forget the BR standard 2-10-0s of which the very last (and the final steam engine for BR) No 92220 *Evening Star* was built there; it just had to have a copper-capped chimney!

Derby started building new in 1851 but always bought a considerable proportion of its engines from contractors. Some would say that it was so busy rebuilding older engines that it lacked the time to build from scratch: but many of its rebuilds were to all intents and purposes new. Horwich was laid out on a green field site to open in 1887, and within two years was building new 2-4-2 tank engines. From that date the Lancashire & Yorkshire never bought another engine from an outside contractor. New building ceased in 1930, but resumed in 1946 and continued intermittently for another ten years. By contrast, St Rollox (Glasgow) was never fully master of the Caledonian's new build requirements, and fed the Scottish building firms with steady orders.

On the LNER, Doncaster ('The Plant') always regarded itself as the premier works, with Darlington as runner up. Both built over two thousand two hundred new locomotives, though when it needed, Doncaster could always out-produce Darlington, thanks to a separate New Erecting Shop opened in 1891. Darlington steadily took over from the cramped but still useful Gateshead works. After World War I the North Eastern Railway had plans for major improvements there, but only a new boiler shop and office block materialised before the project was halted. Doncaster in particular will forever be associated with Gresley's Pacifics and Green Arrows, and for the brave attempt – only partially successful – at an express passenger 2-8-2, *Cock O' The North*. Both continued building, latterly mainly of the smaller BR standard classes, until 1957. Gorton Works ('The Tank') had ceased building soon after World War II, while Stratford (London) and Cowlairs (Glasgow) felt the chopper within a year of the LNER's takeover. In spite of all this building capacity, the LNER placed steady contracts – in one or two cases for very large numbers – with the private builders.

Giants of Speed and Power at A Century of Progress.

The Royal Scot
Famous London-Glasgow-Edinburgh flyer of the London, Midland & Scottish Ry.
1st class corridor brake coach
1st class sleeper coach
3rd class sleeper coach
Lounge car and brake
1st class corridor vestibule coach
Electric kitchen car
3rd class vestibule coach
3rd class corridor brake coach

The Burlington Train
A composite train made up of equipment from regular Burlington trains.
U. S. Railway Post Office car
Reclining chair car (Aristocrat)
Dining car (Black Hawk)
Salon-bed room Pullman (Black Hawk)
14 Section Pullman (Aristocrat)
Lounge car (Ak-Sar-Ben)

The Pride of the Prairies
Engine 35 . . . vintage of 1882. Behind it is a reproduction of the first railway car in which U. S. Mail was assorted in transit, (1862) and thus the actual starting point of today's extensive Railway Post Office service.

The Southern had three building and repair works, at Eastleigh, Brighton and Ashford. Eastleigh was a new works laid out in green fields as late as 1910, using much of the plant from the closed Nine Elms; the result was serious obsolescence by the 1930s and substantial re-equipment proved necessary. Brighton was a works on a difficult site but with a fine erecting shop. Ashford had its limitations. As a result, much of the Southern's new building was a co-operative effort of the three works, making parts for erection at one or other of them. It seemed to work reasonably well on the moderate scale called for in producing Lord Nelsons, Schools and, of course, the controversial Bulleid Pacifics.

Some thirty private locomotive building firms were active in Britain. Some of these unashamedly concentrated on small, mainly shunting locomotives, usually for industrial use. There was a middle group, picking up a variety of orders wherever they could; two of them, Beardmore at Dalmuir and Armstrong-Whitworth in Newcastle-upon-Tyne, came into locomotive building in 1919–20 with the drying up of arms orders after World War I and had short and only occasionally busy lives. Several of the others went to the wall in the slump of the thirties. And then there was the 'big three', North British Locomotive Co in Glasgow (which from its formation by amalgamation of three Glasgow builders in 1903 built well over 11,000 steam locomotives), the Vulcan Foundry at Newton-le-Willows, which produced over 6,000 locomotives from its augury as Charles Tayleur & Co in 1833, and the Gorton Foundry of Beyer Peacock & Co with nearly 7,800 steam locomotives to its credit.

Glory of the 1930s. In 1933 the LMS 4-6-0 No 6100 Royal Scot (in fact No 6152 in disguise) was sent on exhibition to the USA and Canada. It is seen here with two American sisters at the Burlington World's Fair. A contrast in locomotive types. Some of the Royal Scot class were built by the North British Locomotive Co at Hyde Park works in Glasgow.
MILLBROOK HOUSE COLLECTION

37

Bulleid Pacific. A West Country class 4-6-2 No 34020 Seaton *in its original condition leaves Yeovil on a stormy day.* P. M. ALEXANDER

North British was the biggest building facility outside of the US. Its three works from its amalgamation, Hyde Park (ex-Neilson, Reid), Atlas (ex-Sharp, Stewart) – both these in close proximity in Springburn – and Queens Park (ex Dübs) in Polmadie, were capable of prodigious output of the very largest locomotives. In one year, between them they produced no less than 577, ranging from mere 3ft 6in-gauge engines for Africa to 5ft 6in-gauge giants for India. Many of these larger engines by virtue of gauge or height, could not be taken by rail to Stobcross Quay for export, and locals often had the stirring sight of an engine on a low loader, hauled by two steam traction engines, setting off down the Springburn Road, in some cases with rubber sheeting over chimney, dome and cab roof lest they came in contact with the overhead tram wires. Orders for one hundred locomotives at a time were commonplace – class 15F 4-8-2s for South Africa, class XD 2-8-2s for India. There were also Gresley Pacifics for the LNER, Royal Scots for the LMS, even, as a last fling in 1957, a dozen South African 4-8-2+2-8-4 Garratts sub-contracted from Beyer Peacock. But by this time the writing was on the wall for steam almost worldwide, and the firm was tardy in entering the diesel field. Now it has all gone, though Springburn Museum continues the memory.

Vulcan Foundry, at Newton-le-Willows, was one of the earliest builders of steam locomotives, having been associated with Robert Stephenson in the 1830s. It had a very long history of supplying Indian railways, as well as evincing a brief interest in the Fairlie-type locomotive about the turn of the century. When the Indian Railway Board produced preliminary designs for a new standard range of broad- and metre-gauge locomotives in the early 1920s – the well-known X and Y series – it was Vulcan that was charged with preparing the working drawings. They also got the first contract to build but thereafter other builders came into the picture, working from Vulcan drawings. Other notable Vulcan products were the big 4-8-4s for the Chinese National Railways in 1934–5, an example of which is now preserved in the National Railway Museum in York, and the postwar Liberation 2-8-0s for European rehabilitation.

Lastly there was Beyer Peacock, on a rather cramped 23 acre site at Gorton, Manchester (opposite the Great Central's works) from which, paradoxically, in later years it produced some of the largest locomotives in the world. It built its first new locomotive in 1855, and quickly established a reputation for good looks as well as sound, forward looking design in its products. But it really came into its own with the taking up of the H. W. Garratt patent for an articulated locomotive, which proved to be just what was needed for many colonial applications. From the first example for Tasmania in 1908, Beyer Garratts were built (some under licence by other builders for the firm often had a bulging order book) for virtually all gauges from 2ft to 5ft 6in. They ranged from lightweight 2-6-2+2-6-2s for the South African 2ft 0in-gauge lines, weighing no more than 36 tons and with axleload restricted to 3¾ tons, up to the awesome New South Wales 4-8-2+2-8-4s supplied in 1952, which turned the scale at just over 264 tons. On the way mention must be made of the 186 ton metre-gauge 59 class 4-8-2+2-8-4s of East

Beyer Peacock Garratt. One of the huge 4-6-4 + 4-6-4 articulated engines built in Manchester for Rhodesia Railways (now National Railways of Zimbabwe) at Victoria Falls station. P. B. WHITEHOUSE

Problem Replica

Last year, Mr. Henry Ford, of motor-car fame, requested Messrs. Robert Stephenson & Co of Darlington, to build an exact replica of George Stephenson's celebrated *Rocket* as built by the same firm in 1829. The request was simple, concise and straightforward; yet it presented the world-famous firm of locomotive builders with a problem which, in a very short while, came to be regarded as almost, if not quite, impossible of solution! The original drawings and specifications of the *Rocket*, if ever they existed, have long since been lost, and existing drawings, notes and other information concerning the old engine were found, on being carefully scutinised, to be somewhat conflicting and unreliable. True, we still have the *Rocket* with us, preserved at the Science Museum, South Kensington, but the engine is known to have been extensively modified by George Stephenson himself between 1830 and 1836, so that the engine, or rather, what remains of her, at South Kensington is of very little use to anyone who wishes to discover exactly what she was like in her original condition. Her original appearance is known, near enough, from many illustrations that were published in various journals at the time she won her fame; but the solution of many problems of design and construction, not to mention details of materials used in the original engine, was found only after many months of intensive and patient research, and the very careful testing of each item of evidence that came to light.

Even now, all that can be claimed for the replica is that it represents fairly accurately the *Rocket* as she was turned out by Robert Stephenson and Co in 1829, when the firm's factory was at Newcastle. The actual methods of manufacture in use a hundred years ago have been employed,
continued overleaf

African Railways and the 192 ton GMAM class of the same wheel arrangement in South Africa on 3ft 6in gauge, one of which is now preserved in the Greater Manchester Museum of Science & Industry. It should not be thought that the Garratt was a low-speed freight engine; the Central of Aragon in Spain had big 4-6-2+2-6-4s in passenger service, while in Algeria perhaps the ultimate development of the Garratt in this direction was tested at up to 82mph. Beyer Peacock had a certain 'je ne sais quoi' with the Garratt; when, during World War II, the Australians tried to design and build 4-8-2+2-8-4 Garratts for the 3ft 6in-gauge independently of Gorton the result was an absolute disaster, some examples never being fully assembled and others going straight from the builders' works to the scrapheap. Beyer Peacock then built engines of the same wheel arrangement in 1951 for Queensland Railways, which were an outstanding success. Curiously the very last Garratts to be built, in 1967–8 were constructed not in Europe but in South Africa for domestic use – a batch of eight 2-6-2+2-6-2 2ft 0in-gauge beauties by Hunslet Taylor.

On the Continent of Europe, almost all countries had their own locomotive building industries, many of which exercised a strong degree of design autonomy in dealing with their national railway systems. In practice, countries in Eastern Europe tended to lean towards Germany in design matters, where the lead was taken by Henschel, Borsig, Krupp, Berliner Maschinenbau and Hanomag, who were also actively in competition with British builders in the export field. The name of Krupp may be reviled for its work in the armaments field, but to set against this one remembers the splendid streamlined three-cylinder 4-6-4s built in 1938 for the fast Berlin–Hamburg services. By contrast, the French railways (amalgamated into the SNCF in 1938) exercised a strong design 'presence' in placing orders, and contracts for French colonial railways seldom strayed from French builders. The principal firms were Société Alsacienne, Fives-Lille, Franco-Belge and Schneider. In Switzerland, despite the rapid erosion of any steam base in the face of electrification, the firm of SLM Winterthur merits mention, particularly in the field of specialised mountain locomotives.

And then there was the United States and Canada. Those in Britain whose experience of North American steam locomotives never stretched beyond the wartime Austerity 2-8-0s or the Southern's little USA 0-6-0 shunting tanks gained very limited knowledge of the genre. During the twentieth century the American locomotive developed from relative crudity into highly sophisticated machines of tremendous power – and this happened largely by the response of the principal manufacturers to intense competition.

The steam locomotive-building industry in North America can only be described as immense, catering not only for the enormous domestic market but also exporting all over the world. Central and South America, Europe and Africa, India, China and Australasia all received substantial numbers of US-built locomotives, ranging in size from big Mallet-type articulateds down to narrow-gauge midgets for sugarcane plantations. Before World War II in those parts of the globe coloured red (except Canada) the American builders seldom managed to get very far in the door, the handling of contracts through the Crown Agents for the Colonies organisation in London saw to it that British builders took the lion's share, unless they were so hard pressed that delivery dates were too distant. It was under just such circumstances that in England the Midland, Great Northern and Great Central went to America for 2-6-0 power to the tune of eighty locomotives as the century opened. But wartime needs gave US builders an enhanced opportunity.

In the twentieth century the big three builders were (in order of output) Baldwin, Alco and Lima. Matthias Baldwin was in the field from 1832, and his works in Philadelphia Pa grew to the point where further expansion was blocked. It moved out of the city to a new site at Eddystone in the first decade of the century, and ultimately covered an area of no less than 500 acres. In its lifetime the firm built a total of about 59,000 steam locomotives. The American Locomotive Co was formed in 1901 as a merger of nine building firms. The main constituent was the Schenectady (NY) Locomotive Works, on which all production was gradually concentrated; it had started production in 1851, and by the time steam locomotive production ceased in 1949 no less than 46,300 had emerged from its doors. Lima Locomotive Works was not on this

Lima Engine. A modern Nickel Plate Line Berkshire No. 759 (1944) stands alongside a Western Maryland Co-Co No 7470 at Hagerstown Maryland on 6 August 1971. This modern 2-8-4 is now operated by the Fort Wayne Railroad Historical Society in the eastern USA.
RON ZIEL (MILLBROOK HOUSE COLLECTION)

continued
wherever practicable, in the production of the replica. For example, the boiler, which is made of iron plates ¼ in. thick, was rivetted together with wrought-iron rivets *by hand*, a method practically unknown in boiler shops at the present time. Again, steel was not known in George Stephenson's day; consequently, no steel has been used for any of the details in the replica. Iron, wood, copper and brass are the only materials which have been used. The boiler tubes presented one of the principal difficulties in that absolutely no evidence is forthcoming as to how the original tubes were made, exactly; not one of the original tubes can now be found, otherwise this tube problem might easily have been solved. The replica tubes were made from copper sheet rolled to shape and hand-brazed; as there are 25 of them, each 3 in. in diameter and 6 ft. long, the coppersmith must have had a nice job! – J. N. Maskelyne in *The Model Railway News*. 1929

heroic scale, only starting conventional engine construction in 1901 and building some 4,800 steam locomotives until the last came out in 1949, but stands comparison with the other two by the pioneering excellence of its designs. An interesting feature of all three companies was their diversification into other products such as machine tools, excavators, hydraulic presses, even cars and lorries in Alco's case. Alco also owned the Montreal Locomotive Works in Canada which turned out over 3,600 engines.

A look at US steam-engine design and production in the twentieth century reveals intense competition in bringing in important design innovation as between Baldwin and Alco, though Lima also was quick to capitalise on winners. In the field of articulated Mallet-type locomotives, for instance, Alco introduced the breed for yard and trip work in 1903–4, and Baldwin was in the lead in adapting it for main-line service from 1906, both with compound propulsion. The first simple expansion articulated, for the Pennsylvania RR, came from Alco in 1911; Baldwin produced the first Triplex articulated 2-8-8-8-2 for the Erie in 1914, while Alco netted the first really big order for simple articulateds, forty-five 2-8-8-2s for the Chesapeake and Ohio in 1924. Alco continued in the initiative with the first 4-6-6-4s (with 69in drivers) for Union Pacific fast freight service in 1936; Baldwin was quickly off the mark with similar but larger machines for the Denver & Rio Grande Western two years later. Alco bounced back in 1941 with the incredible Big Boy 4-8-8-4 for the Union Pacific, perhaps the ultimate development; 300lb pressure, a grate area of 150 square feet, tractive effort of 135,400lb and a total weight for engine and tender of 539 tons, a mobile powerhouse of great length.

Lima has not featured in this articulated saga, though they were no strangers to the concept. The firm really made their indelible mark in 1925, when they built the first 2-8-4 bought by the Boston & Albany. The two-axle radial trailing truck was adopted to support a massive firebox – in this case with a grate of 100 square feet – to step up boiler power significantly. This particular design had 63in drivers, which suited many lines, but two years later Alco trumped this by increasing wheel diameter to 70in. Between these limits was produced what became the archetypal US fast freight locomotive, which stood the test of time. When steam locomotive building ceased in 1949, the last products of Alco (for the New York Central) and Lima (for the Nickel Plate) were such 2-8-4s. Some of the thinking behind these big freight engines also manifested itself in the postwar 2-8-2s for the SNCF (class 141R) which came from more than one builder, though Alco was in the initiative. They were highly regarded by their users.

Before steam locomotive construction finally succumbed to the march of the diesel electric, thoughts turned to the possibilities of the non-Stephensonian locomotive and focussed on the steam turbine. The Union Pacific led the field with an experimental two-unit condensing turbo electric locomotive from General Electric in 1938, though its very complexity ultimately killed it. Baldwin now entered the arena, first with a large 6-8-6 geared turbine locomotive for the Pennsylvania in 1944 (similar in concept to Stanier's LMS Turbomotive of 1935) and three years later with three 2-D+2-D-2 non-condensing turbo electric

A German on the Railway of Death. A Swartzkopff 2-8-2 of 1936 on the metre gauge Madeira Mamore Railway in eastern Brazil, close to the Bolivian border. Built originally to help move rubber from the area to the Madeira River and hence down the Amazon to the sea, malaria and yellow fever were said to account for one man for every sleeper laid. P. B. WHITEHOUSE

machines for the Chesapeake & Ohio. These Baldwin machines all used conventional locomotive boilers, but though devoid of complex and automated controls the Chessie locomotives were so heavy at 383 tons that utilisation was inevitably a problem. Baldwin's last attempt in this field was *Jawn Henry* for the Norfolk & Western, a more modest-sized machine with turbo electric drive by Westinghouse and a watertube boiler by Babcock & Wilcox. It was ordered in 1949, but was overtaken by events and never entered service.

Unlike their British counterparts, very few US railroads built their own locomotives, preferring to buy their power from the established 'big three'. Three railroads did, however, build a proportion of their locomotives themselves, particularly when they were pushing design frontiers beyond the contemporary wisdom. The Baltimore & Ohio in the twenties and early thirties went through a phase of experimental boiler design, initially linked to compounding. It culminated, after several one-offs, in 1935 with *George Emerson*, a four-cylinder simple non-articulated 4-4-4-4 with watertube firebox working at 350lb. This handful of advanced engines was built at the company's Mount Clare shops.

Curiously, this concept of the four-cylinder non-articulated took root for some years in the Juniata shops of the Pennsylvania RR, which had

Alco engine. A typical North American ten wheeler. Chicago and North Western Railway No 1385 (Alco/Schenectady 42187/1907) at North Freedom, Wisconsin on 14 February 1986. This night photo session of the Mid-Continent Railway Historical Society took place in temperatures of –40°F but paid big dividends.
THOMAS R. SCHULTZ

Charly

I was sitting, one afternoon, on the terrace of a nice little restaurant in the old city of Luxembourg, overlooking the famous Pont Adolphe bridge, when I saw to my surprise a trim little 2-6-0 tank engine and a rake of bogie carriages running along the tramlines, my introduction to Charly the train.

The Luxembourg Government, at about the turn of the century, decided to construct several narrow-gauge railways, to develop areas not covered by the standard gauge 'Les Chemins de fer Guillaume Luxembourg' or 'Les Chemin de fer Prince Henri'. Charly started running to Echternach on 12 April 1904, and took his name from Charly Rischard, the minister largely responsible for its construction. Starting from the street outside the main station, the tracks ran up the Avenue de la Liberté, over the Pont Adolphe bridge and into the old part of the town, where there was a station at Le Parc. The line then ran partly on private track and partly at the side of the road

continued overleaf

West Bengal Pacific. One of the WP class 4-6-2s (No 7310) built at India's Chittaranjan Works from 1953 shunts at Lucknow shed with another modern Indian class a WG 2-8-2 (No 10323) on 23 November 1984. HUGH BALLANTYNE

continued
to Eich via Rollingergrund. After crossing the main line to Liège at Dommeldange, where there was a sizable station, we were out of the town and able to enjoy the smell of the huge pine forests and the fields, which in September, would be purple with the autumn crocus. Wine is plentiful and cheap in the Grand Duchy, the vineyards are everywhere to be seen. The line follows the contour of the land twisting and turning, there is the odd tunnel but few earthworks. The huge masts of Radio Luxembourg come into view near Junglinster, which is almost half way, and the only town of any size on the journey. Echternach is reached, and the train terminates outside the 'voie normale' station. The whole journey has taken just over two hours and we have travelled 30 miles!

There was much opposition to the running of Charly through the principal streets, and so from September 1928, the municipal tramways, 'Tramways de la Ville de Luxembourg', took over the running of trains from the main station to Dommeldange.
continued overleaf

started building some of its requirements during World War I. The Pennsy was not really an articulated system, though Juniata had built Mallets in 1918. It took up the non-articulated formula with some enthusiasm, and four variants of the type, using two two-cylinder engines on a rigid bed carrying a big 300lb boiler, were built there between 1938 and 1944. The 6-4-4-6 and 4-6-4-4 types were singletons, but the 4-4-4-4s and 4-4-6-4s of 1942 were multiplied to fifty and twenty-six examples respectively. They were very much state-of-the-art machines, and were immensely powerful – a 4-4-6-4 produced some 8,500 indicated horsepower at 57mph on the Altoona test plant – but on the road soon revealed their Achilles heels, virtually uncontrollable slipping of the separate engines. Overall they could only be branded as very disappointing.

Not so the products of the third railway builder, the Norfolk & Western RR at Roanoke, Va, which probably reached the zenith of *operational* success as part of a policy of maximum utilisation and sophisticated servicing facilities; this enabled the N&W to resist the siren calls of the diesel salesmen longer than any other major US railroad. Roanoke's star performers were the streamlined J class 4-8-4s which ran the principal passenger services until the 1950s, and the impressive A class 2-6-6-4s for fast freight service, both featuring roller bearings throughout in axleboxes and motion. North of the 49th parallel, only the Canadian Pacific was into the building business at its Angus shops; they built about seven hundred locomotives in all.

One firm which exercised a profound effect on the US steam locomotive (not excluding exports) must also be mentioned, even though it never built a locomotive. The traditional bar frame construction of US locomotives had reached its limit by the time of World War I, and was becoming increasingly difficult to maintain. Into the breech stepped the General Steel Castings Corporation, first with one-piece castings for trailing trucks about 1915, and then with a quantum leap to a one-piece cast steel locomotive bed (or chassis) in 1925. The first examples retained separate cylinders, but within a year or two these also were incorporated in the casting. The result was a rigid bed which was almost maintenance free and was essential to the successful use of roller-bearing axleboxes. The writer recalls seeing modest examples of these castings, fully machined and weighing about 10 tons in transit in 1950 to North British Locomotive Co in Glasgow for an order for one hundred class 24 2-8-4s for South Africa; they were magnificent examples of the pattern makers' and foundrymen's art.

If everything which has been said so far has necessarily been in the past tense, it is at least possible to close on a more cheerful note. The steam locomotive, simple and rugged, was in many ways ideal for railways in countries with indigenous supplies of cheap fuel, be it coal, oil or wood, with plenty of cheap labour and without a broad technical industry base. Many railways in Africa and elsewhere which accepted the diesel salesman's blandishments have had bitter cause to remember this in later years. But in Asia, where such prerequisites were abundantly available, two countries saw a longer-term future for steam and set up their own domestic industries to build modern steam locomotives, drawing on foreign expertise. In India a large new locomotive factory

46

was built at Chittaranjan, in West Bengal, to produce class WP 4-6-2s and WG 2-8-2s as well as spare boilers for existing classes. It started in 1953 with British assistance which gradually tapered off until the works was self sufficient. Production of steam locomotives has now ceased. But in China, the large scale new works at Datong, built with Russian support before relations between the two countries cooled, was still turning out new QJ class 2-10-2s at a rate of nearly one a day, until the end of 1988. They are thoroughly modern locomotives incorporating plenty of latterday American design. The works at Tangshan also continues to build smaller locomotives. Both Chittaranjan and Datong have also supplied components to other countries to keep steam locomotives in service.

Apart from small machines for railways catering purely for pleasure

Roanoke's star performer. One of the superb Norfolk and Western RR J Class 4-8-4s which ran the road's principal passenger services until the 1950s heading a train along New River, Virginia. One of these locomotives has been preserved in working order and today hauls trains over the tracks of the Norfolk & Southern Railroad on special occasions.
NORFOLK & WESTERN RAILROAD

rides, steam locomotive production has now (with the exception of Datong) ceased throughout the world. The great building firms have either embraced the diesel engine or disappeared without trace. The railways which they supplied are in many cases in decline, too. The future lies with a different brand of engineering, of greater sophistication, new skills. But there are many parts of the world which are not ready and able to provide the environment in which such machines can thrive. Already, Zimbabwe has completed a refurbishment programme for withdrawn Garratts rather than buying new diesels. Recently in the Sudan, where inability to keep its modern diesels in service produced catastrophic problems, a programme to bring steam locomotives back into service has been instituted with British help. We may yet see other countries take steps to reinstate this most versatile of machines.

continued
Passengers were required to change from the steam train into two powerful electric cars which were quite capable of hauling several trailers or a string of goods wagons through the town.

In 1940 Luxembourg was invaded and Charly was absorbed into the Deutche Reichsbahn and continued running until 1944, when, during an American air raid on the railway yards, both electric cars became war victims. Charly began to run again through the streets from which he had been banished in 1928; as the tracks were also used by the town tramcars a special car (No 36) always ran just in front of the train to operate the contactors on the overhead which controlled the points and signals.

Unfortunately all good things come to an end, and Charly seemed almost too good to be true, for in August 1954 the Chemin de fer Luxembourgoise substituted diesel buses. I shall miss the clang of the bells on the little tank engines and the smell of the dirty coal they used, as they passed the rows of shiny American cars.

A Night In A Steam Depot

The pubs are beginning to turn out, and little knots of people gather noisily in the brightly lit street. A late bus growls past and a courting couple stroll along the gritty path, arms interlocked, happily oblivious of their drab surroundings. House lights go out; a solitary cat pads silently into an alley on its nocturnal occasions. But on the other side of the dark sleeper fence, each timber with its three-hole patterns, there is an oasis of semi-darkness; inadequate light bulbs under enamelled reflectors, twenty feet up on wooden poles, cast little pools of brightness on the near-black ground, and a pattern of windows show light through the grime. There is a brief deep rumble of falling coal, a distant clang of metal on metal and a cascade of dull red fire, the occasional hiss of steam – the locomotive shed is about its business as the world prepares to sleep.

Seen in broad daylight it is a medium-sized shed of twelve dead-end roads with outbuildings, dominated by a tall concrete coaling plant. A steel-framed ash hoist presides over the two ashpits, fed by tip trucks on rails in the pits and alongside. A line of water columns across the front of the shed marks the preparation pits, surrounded by brick walkways. Otherwise it is a flat expanse of thin soil and decades of ash, carved up by indifferent permanent way and relieved only by the turntable in its pit, vacuum hosepipe carried like a pennant, and the occasional fringe of struggling grass and willowherb. But the darkness and localised lighting changes all this into a world of shadows in which blackened engines appear and disappear, seemingly without purpose or pattern.

In fact it is a shed of mixed duties, and thus of engine power. On the passenger side, there is a handful of mainline 4-6-0s, but rather more in the way of big tank engines for suburban work. These are all back on shed by midnight, and stay there until demand begins to pick up about six next morning. There are long- and medium-distance freight turns, handled by mixed traffic and 2-8-0 engines, which are mainly overnight: engines for these jobs begin to go off the shed from about six at night, and they or their opposite numbers come back in time for breakfast, though a few are active during the day. Then there are the veterans, mostly superannuated 0-6-0s, pottering about on yard-to-yard transfer trips and pickup freights and spending many daytime hours not getting very far from sight of the town hall clock. Lastly, four 0-6-0 tanks are engaged more or less round the clock shunting the terminal station, the extensive goods shed, and the small marshalling yard; some of these come home only at weekends, crew relief being at the place of work and coaling being done from a small stage by the men themselves.

By the time that the pubs close, the two men who will run this operation until six o'clock have already settled in, got the measure of the power and repair position and set their staff to their tasks. The atmosphere within the shed has cleared from the yellow sulphurous cloud while the day's washout engines were being lit up: their fires have brightened and they are beginning to make steam. The night shift running foreman has inherited an ongoing situation of engines arriving on the shed for disposal. As drivers report in by phone from the shed inlet and indicate the condition of their engines, he will provisionally allocate them to the first duty next morning. In doing so his mind is taking in the need to distribute them to stabling roads in his dead-end shed so that they can emerge in time order, while ensuring that any late starts – from enginemen coming late on duty or last-minute repairs – do not block engines in behind them. If there are delays in disposal, or if the examining fitter finds defects not reported by the incoming driver, he may find himself forced to redistribute engines and perhaps shunt one or two shed roads to clear the offender. So there may be alterations to the engine arrangements board in the lobby.

Meanwhile, alerted by his timekeeper assistant if necessary, he has to see that his rostered enginemen turn up to time; if they are late or absent, he will need to cover their work either by his few spare men (provided they have the requisite route knowledge) or by juggling men with unexpired time in their working day. All this will need to be done in conjunction with control – who may be prepared to cancel a freight trip if traffic allows – and in compliance with strict staff agreements on seniority and time availability.

The other key man is the chargehand fitter, working from the mechanical foreman's office. He has got a handful of fitters dealing with the run-of-the-mill repairs reported by drivers; it is mostly routine stuff – sanders not working, brakes to adjust, or reblock, minor steam leaks, and the like. If it is anything bigger, it may well have to be held over for the day men, or deferred if this is practicable. There is also an examining fitter doing the daily exams of the passenger and fitted freight engines. The chargehand is also working to the list of the next day's washouts. These engines have to have any residual steam blown out of them when they have been stabled and then the boilers must be cooled down ready for washing out and internal inspection by the day-shift boiler staff. One road in the shed is allocated for this task. A boilerwasher, glistening in waterproof overalls, clumps about in clogs in the patchy light, dragging long hoses to couple the floor hydrants to the injector overflow pipes. The boilers are flooded with vast quantities of cold water; it pours from washout plug holes and splashes into the pit drains, a process taking several hours.

Meanwhile, the trickle of engines arriving at the end of their duties are being disposed, in some cases by their

own crews and in others by full-time disposal men. Fill up the tender tank (not forgetting the one which has troublesome injectors which suggests that the tender water sieves need cleaning, so leave the tank almost empty) and then move under the coaling plant to fill the bunker, setting the tender two or three times to get a reasonably level top without undue spillage or overloading. (A lump of coal falling off at 70mph does not exactly thrill a bystander!) Then on to one of the ashpits to clean the fire. Here the fireman must first separate the remaining clean fire from the clinker and ash, and get started on up to an hour of hard, hot and unpleasant labour. Depending on the type of engine and the inclination of the man, and assuming the engine does not have a rocking or drop grate (in Britain the great majority did not) the fireman may lift four or so firebars, using very heavy tongs, and rake the clinker down the resulting hole into the ashpan. He then has to rake the contents of the ashpan out into the pit through the damper doors. Alternatively, he may paddle the clinker out through the firehole doors with a long-handled steel shovel. Then there is the smokebox to empty of char, a combined rake and shovel job while perched on the front platform. Trip over one of the lamp irons and he will finish up in the pit! Ah, the joys of servicing the unmodernised steam locomotive!

Now the engine can be turned if necessary, stabled and the tools taken to the stores. Henceforward it will be in the care of the steamraiser, who will visit it at regular intervals to make sure there is water in the boiler and a nucleus of fire to hold 50–80lb/sq in pressure ready for when it is to be prepared again.

As dawn approaches the trickle of enginemen booking on duty for the morning's work begins to grow. The running foreman now finds himself tied nearer to the drivers' lobby rather than touring the shed keeping an eye on coal supply, the state of the ashpits, the sandhouse, general progress. There are instructions to be given to particular drivers, signatures for weekly notices to chase up, complaints to deal with, a discipline form to hand to a driver as he books off, last minute panics to sort out, the log book to write up. The emphasis has now changed to getting engines off the shed and onto the trains on time.

There is a steady movement of engines inching out of the shed on to the preparation pits. The zinc-covered stores counters see a procession of enginemen collecting spongecloths, engine tools and cans of cylinder and axlebox oils, and filling lamp cisterns. There is the usual odd moan about the condition of firing shovels and coal picks. At each engine the driver oils round the external points with his feeder, subconsciously checking corks, while often leaving his fireman (after first levelling off his fire and putting the first few shovelfuls on) to fill up mechanical lubricators and sandboxes. He may or may not – according to his physique and inclination – do any oiling between the frames, where access to inside motion can be both difficult and dirty. Whoever does it usually keeps a spare overall coat for such work. The fireman begins to make up his fire and, inevitably, a pall of smoke begins to show over the shed. He is looking for a good, burned-through core which will quickly ignite the fresh coal fired nearer departure time. He tests both injectors and checks that the smokebox door is tight shut – and also that the disposal men have swept the char off the front platform. The last thing they want is an eyeful of that when they get going. A final brush and swill of the footplate, a wipe of the faceplate and cab windows, and they move up the shed yard and ring off.

It has been a relatively uneventful night. No derailments to call out the breakdown crew for, no lighting failures to plunge areas into darkness, no jams in the coaling plant. So when the early turn running foreman comes on duty at six, the handover is quick and not fraught. The depot emerges from the darkness and settles in for another day.

3
STEAM PIONEERS – ANCIENT AND MODERN

THE British National Railway Museum's preserved Duchess No 46229 *Duchess of Hamilton* dates from 1938 when she was completed at Crewe. Look at her, and the impression is of a thoroughbred. Moving with ease, in command of her work. See her – and hear her – blasting up to Blea Moor with a big train behind her, and the impression is awesome, yet almost every feature of her design, her whole evolutionary process, can be traced back to the ideas of pioneers stretching back to one hundred and ten years before her birth.

Pioneering has always been a hazardous pursuit. Those who practise it, confident that they know something outside the perception of others, may well succeed in pushing forward the frontiers of knowledge in a way which becomes future established practice. Equally, they may find that they have built on sand and their pioneering has produced a monumental flop. Steam locomotive development has given us a fair sprinkling of both extremes and all shades between. The names of the successful may be household words: the others are long forgotten.

As technology has advanced, the nature of the pioneer has changed radically. One hundred and fifty years ago, when railways were in their first formative stage, men arose – seldom engineers in the true modern sense, rather intelligent mechanic/managers – whose understanding of the new transport mode and whose vision put them head and shoulders above the pack. Such men were seen as masters of the new 'science'. They produced results which fascinated their fellow men; their works were in full view before their customers and anyone else with time to stand and stare – and marvel. Small wonder that, even before the days of mass communication, they should acquire fame. Single handed they had laid down what was to be done, and brought it to fruition.

But engineering developments have long outstripped this simplistic arrangement. They are now the product of many disciplines, of considerable complexity, of interlocking systems, of eliminating human involvement. Committees examine their concept, design teams do the technical evaluation, project groups oversee their construction, commissioning teams work them up to commercial operation. Who pioneered Concorde? Who designed the High Speed Train – or the APT of diminishing memory? The QE2? No single name arises as linked with any of them. They are faceless, lacking a handle. The linkage with Stephenson's *Rocket* and the like has gone.

Yet it took the thinking of a strong-willed pioneer to get the steam locomotive on the road at all. Consider the use of steam power at the end of the eighteenth century. Its main application was the drainage pumping of mines. Cornwall is littered with its remains; brick-built engine houses partially enclosing crude engines, with huge timber beams

Automatic Warning
In the later days of steam, automatic warning systems (AWS) (giving the engine crew notice of the signal indications ahead) were in use on many of the main lines. But it was far from the case on most of the world's railways.

The AWS idea had been pioneered by Britain's Great Western Railway prior to World War I. It used electrical impulses transmitted via a ramp between the tracks set ahead of the distant signal and a shoe on the locomotive. Thus a bell rang in the cab to give 'road clear' while, if no electric current flowed because the distant was at caution, the locomotive shoe tripped the vacuum brake and a siren sounded.

But sophisticated signalling was a luxury denied even to the great Transcontinentals of North America during steam days. Indeed even today, over tens of thousands of miles of trackage in the second and third worlds, trains rely for their safety on the *continued opposite*

rocking about central trunnions. Boilers were large in relation to their output, working at pressures little above atmospheric, and getting their limited draught from tall brick chimneys. Because condensing was effected by spraying water into the large cylinders, their operating speed was as low as two working strokes a minute. What possible scope for transport could such a machine offer, except perhaps for a short-distance rope haulage?

Such was the climate in which **Richard Trevithick**, son of a Cornish mine manager, produced the first moving steam 'locomotive' in 1801, a road vehicle reported to have caused utter panic amongst those who saw it on its first excursion. Three years later he built a locomotive for use on an industrial plateway at Pen-y-Darren, near Merthyr in South Wales. His boiler worked at a pressure which alarmed Boulton and Watt, the doyens of the stationary-engine field. He mounted it on four wheels, attached a cylinder whose piston was coupled to the wheels by an ingenious linkage, and hauled a number of coal 'tubs' to win a wager for his Welsh industrialist sponsor. His pioneering machine was the first breakthrough in harnessing steam to rail transport.

This boiler, and those of early locomotives which followed it, had a small grate within a large single or return flue in the boiler. In almost all (including the Pen-y-Darren engine) the exhaust steam was turned up the chimney to 'brighten the fire', but the draught was quite soft in order not to pull the fire to pieces. It took **Timothy Hackworth,** the Locomotive Superintendent of the Stockton & Darlington Railway, to develop this into the idea of a blastpipe, central to the chimney and with a reduced orifice, which was first applied in 1827.

The name of **Robert Stephenson**, son of the even more famous George, now comes to the fore. To him falls the credit for recognising

continued
dispatcher at each end of a single line section and written train orders carried in the cab and by the guard or conductor. In the case of the least sophisticated lines safety may still depend on God and the telephone.

Railways also varied over the amount of other information they provided their locomotive drivers. Some countries like France were extremely strict over speed limits and restrictions, so a sealed recorder was fixed in each engine cab. Generally limits were around 70mph and woe betide any crew who were caught out when the paper roll was monitored in detail on their return to their home depot. But from the days of Stephenson until the decline of steam in recent living memory, most drivers had to estimate their own speed, the provision of a speedometer being regarded as an unnecessary luxury. Then, for the first half century of steam it was unusual to provide enginemen even with a cab to shelter them from the elements.

the shortcomings of the large-flue boiler and producing the first multi-tubular boiler with separate firebox. Others were thinking along the same lines – Marc Seguin patented such a boiler in France in 1828 – but Stephenson was the first to produce it in the famous *Rocket* in 1829. It was a major factor in the engine's success in the Liverpool & Manchester Railway's Rainhill trials of that year.

In America the real railway pioneer, regarded as the 'Father of American railroads', was **Colonel John Stevens.** In 1826 he had built the first steam engine to run on rails there, an experimental machine on a small circular track on his own land in Hoboken, NJ. It was never put to practical use, and Stevens subsequently veered towards railway promotion rather than engineering. The next name to arise was that of **Horatio Allen**, the engineer building the Delaware & Hudson Canal Co, who ordered the first real locomotive to run on American rails – though not for long; it came from the English firm of Foster, Rastrick & Co of Stourbridge. Very much in the contemporary Stockton & Darlington mould, it weighed 7 tons on its four wheels and was named *Stourbridge Lion*, presumably by the builders. But it quickly proved too heavy for the crude track, and was relegated to stationary use. Three other locomotives were ordered at the same time, two from Foster, Rastrick and one from Robert Stephenson. Not much is known about their work, but the Stephenson engine was a four-wheeler similar to the 1828 'Lancashire Witch' for the Bolton & Leigh Railway.

The first locomotive to haul an American train in regular service was to a most unusual design, and began service in January 1831. This was the *Best Friend of Charleston*, designed by **E. L. Miller** and built in a New

Walschaerts valve gear on ex Nord Railway of France 4-6-0 No 23.628 now in possession of the Science Museum and preserved in working order on the Nene Valley Railway. P. J. HOWARD

Duchess in full flight. The National Railway Museum's Stanier Pacific No 46229 Duchess of Hamilton *(originally streamlined) is thoroughly in charge as she climbs to Ais Gill summit on the Settle – Carlisle line on 29 October 1983.*
HUGH BALLANTYNE

York foundry. It ran on four wheels, had a vertical multi-tubular boiler and weighed 4½ tons. It achieved particular fame when, five months into its life, it was wrecked by a boiler explosion after a helper tied down the safety valve because the hiss of escaping steam annoyed him!

But it was the entry of **Matthias Baldwin**, sometime watchmaker, toolmaker and machinist, into the railroad industry which got it moving steadily in the right direction. From a poorly equipped workshop he built his first locomotive for public service, the 5½ ton 2-2-0 *Old Ironsides*, in 1832. She was successful, remaining in service for more than twenty years, and proved the spur for its builder to inaugurate the Baldwin Locomotive Works, which over the next one hundred and twenty years was such a powerful force in its field. His second locomotive, the 4-2-0 **E. L. Miller** for the Charleston & Hamburg RR, pioneered the leading four-wheel bogie and was a model for construction for many years. This engine was notable for having driving wheels cast in bell metal (brass). The design was developed, as train weights grew, into the 4-4-0, patented in America in 1836 by **Henry R. Campbell**, chief engineer of a railroad in Pennsylvania. So popular did the arrangement become within the continent that it was dubbed the 'American'.

All these early engines used various mechanisms based on the simple eccentric to move the valves and thus control the admission and release of steam in the cylinder. By 1843 the Stephenson valve gear in the form in which it became the most commonly used, having two eccentrics

From the Log Book
One of the most interesting journeys in my first log book occurred returning to London after the summer holidays in 1923 by the Aberdeen express then due in Euston at 7.30pm. After the addition of the Whitehaven coaches at Preston, it became a heavy load of 420 tons, and from Crewe southwards we had one of the recently built 'Claughtons' piloted by a 6ft 6in 'Jumbo', No 2180 *Perseverance*. At that time it was not unusual for one of these old 2-4-0 engines to be used for assisting top-line expresses, and several of them were kept at Camden shed, in first-class condition specially for the purpose.

We fairly sailed up Madeley bank, touched about 77mph on descent to Stafford, and were again going like the wind across the Trent Valley line when signals delayed us.

One of the most remarkable engine performances in my log books, and remaining so more than sixty years after it was recorded, was on the 5.8pm Great Western express from Newton Abbot to Paddington on a Saturday evening in late July 1925. At Newton Abbot the train was made up to thirteen coaches, but there was no time to see the engine, which from my rear-end scrutiny I saw was a 'Star'. The friendly guard noticed I was stopwatching, but on that Saturday what with signal checks and other hindrances there was not much to record as far as Taunton.

There I was watching as three coaches were being backed on to the rear, through portions from Minehead and Ilfracombe to Paddington and the slip coach to be detached at Newbury. The guard came up exclaiming: 'Sixteen, and no bank engine!' I asked: 'Who's your driver' 'Oh, Walter Springthorpe, the finest fellow on the road, we'll be all right.' I gathered later that this driver was a son of the Old Oak
continued opposite

whose motion was combined in a slotted link, had been invented by **William Howe.** Variants of the arrangement were produced by a number of engineers with only passing popularity. But it was a Belgian engineer, **Egide Walschaerts**, who expressed his dissatisfaction with the need for two eccentrics by inventing a new valve gear in which the valve derived its motion from a single eccentric on the axle and also from the piston crosshead. An improved layout first saw application on a Belgian locomotive in 1848, but its adoption was slow in coming. No British engine carried the Walschaerts valve gear until 1881, when a single tank engine entered service on the small Swindon, Marlborough and Andover Railway. It made no impact, and a further eleven years elapsed before it appeared again, on narrow-gauge tank engines for the Belfast & Northern Counties Railway. It did not really take off in Britain until the twentieth century, when by the 1920s it had become all but universal for engines with outside cylinders.

Most railways from their first development used coke as locomotive fuel, in order to minimise smoke emission; the Stephensonian boiler provided little combustion space for the gases from a coal fire. But coke was expensive by comparison with coal for the same heat output, and many minds were directed towards adapting the locomotive to burn coal smokelessly. Some of their devices were elaborate and expensive, bringing serious maintenance problems. The simple solution, whose use became universal, was arrived at by a relative unknown, **Charles Markham**, working under the direction of Matthew Kirtley on the Midland Railway. It was he who devised the refractory firebrick arch built across the firebox below the boiler tubes in 1859. This both lengthened the path of the combustion gases and, by virtue of its incandescence, initiated their burning before entering the tubes.

In the world of steam outside the railway industry, compound engines were in wide use for marine and stationary applications, thereby obtaining improved economy. Could the steam locomotive benefit also? The first attempts to do so began in 1878 when the Frenchman **Anatole Mallet** exhibited a two-cylinder compound tank engine at the Paris Exhibition. Among those influenced by this machine was the great **Francis W. Webb**, Locomotive Superintendent of the UK's London & North Western Railway, who in 1879 modified a small locomotive on the same principle. It was the beginning of a long association between Webb and compounds, in three- and four-cylinder versions, which lasted until his retirement in 1903. They were a mixed, often unpredictable bunch, unloved by the footplate staff, and his successor quickly set about scrapping or rebuilding them as simple engines.

The really successful compound locomotive, developed over the years into a highly sophisticated machine, especially in France, can only be attributed to **Alfred de Glehn**, Chief Engineer of the Société Alsacienne though British born. The firm built its first prototype in 1886, but the concept came into its own in 1891 with two 4-4-0s for the Nord Railway. His machines invariably had four cylinders, the two high-pressure ones outside. Under driver's control various modes of operation could be selected in addition to compounding, four-cylinder simple and two-cylinder simple using either high-pressure or low-pressure cylinders. The system was enthusiastically adopted in France, and with skilled

56

handling stood the test of time until World War II. Other names were also linked with forms of compounding, notably in Britain W. M. Smith in his system of three-cylinder compounding used principally on the Midland Railway from 1901, but these were directed more to simplifying the handling than to maximising efficiency.

In the second half of the nineteenth century railway tentacles spread widely through colonial territories. Many lines were built on the cheap in sparsely trafficked or inhospitable country and light construction, severe gradients and sharp curves were often the rule. The conventional rigid-framed steam locomotive was soon reaching its limits on such railways. Into the breech stepped Mallet once more; in 1884 he took out a French patent for an articulated locomotive. This covered specifically two sets of driving wheels, the rear set rigidly integral in the frames and the front set mounted in a radial truck free to swivel, each with its own cylinders and motion; the front end of the boiler carried by a saddle bearing on the front truck; and four cylinders in compound form, the two low-pressure ones being on the front truck. The first Mallet – on the narrow gauge – was built in 1889, the first standard-gauge engine following in 1890 for banking on the St Gotthard Railway. The type was taken up enthusiastically in the US, initially by Baldwin in 1904, and developed over the next forty years far beyond any visions of its inventor.

Many other systems of articulation were tried, of which the Fairlie and Kitson-Meyer achieved limited success, the latter mainly on railways in the Andes; two Fairlies survive on the Festiniog Railway in North Wales. But one other system proved highly successful over much of the world from South America to New Zealand. This was the brainchild of **Herbert M. Garratt** who saw the way to adapt the basis of articulated vehicles for heavy artillery to locomotive use, and took out a patent in 1907 envisaging two power bogies carrying coal and water supplies, with boiler and cab on a separate frame mounted on them while leaving them free to rotate. Perhaps more by luck than judgement he managed to interest Beyer Peacock & Co in Manchester in the idea, and in 1908 they built the first, small, Beyer-Garratt locomotive for Tasmania (it is now in the National Railway Museum, York). As with the Mallet, this was built as a compound, but thereafter all Garratts used simple expansion. Many hundreds were built, both by Beyer Peacock and by licensees, with Africa the major scene of operation. They ranged from narrow-gauge locomotives for light axleloads up to enormous 4-8-2+2-8-4s for New South Wales weighing 264 tons, and express passenger machines for Algeria and Spain.

A development which complemented these very large articulated locomotives as well as the larger conventional rigid machines was that of the mechanical stoker, which took over when the limits of the human variety were reached. This was almost entirely an American concept; the pioneer was **Crawford**, who produced the first successful appliance about 1905 and saw it adopted by the Pennsylvania RR. It was an underfeed stoker in which the coal was pushed forward by reciprocating plungers working in longitudinal troughs at grate level. The Crawford stoker held its own for about ten years until displaced by stokers using steam jets to distribute coal over the grate. This arrangement soon

continued
engineman who had worked the *Polar Star* between Euston and Crewe in the locomotive exchange with the LNWR in 1910. In 1925 his son had the 'Star' class 4-6-0 No 4026 *King Richard*, and from Taunton we were all right. With 514 tons tare, 550 tons full, to be reduced by 35 tons at Newbury, we covered the 130.8 miles from Athelney to Acton at an average speed of 58.2mph, and that was before the Frome and Westbury avoiding lines had been built, and a speed restriction of 30mph had to be made through stations. It was a really grand run.

In 1935 when I was making footplate runs on a variety of LNER locomotives I had often looked askance at the abbreviated and spartan-like cabs of the Great Northern 'Atlantics', so different from those of the North British in which I had already ridden, and I wondered how I should fare when I came to ride the engines of the *Queen of Scots* Pullman non-stop between King's Cross and Leeds, 185¾ miles. My eventual remit was for a return trip, footplate both ways, in a single day, a July occasion on a day of sweltering heat. I shall never forget climbing into the cab at King's Cross and finding that the wooden ledge which passed for a seat on the fireman's side was too high, and that I had to steady myself, to write, by bracing one foot against a convenient projecting bolt on the cab-side face of the firebox. Write indeed! The log contained in my notebook shows that I took the passing times at 79 places in the journey of 3¼ hours to Leeds, and all the time my stop watch was working overtime, and incidentally clocked the first instance I ever recorded of a maximum speed of 90mph.

Exhilarated but somewhat parched I had only 1½ hours before starting on the return trip and on such a hot day an engineman's bothy was not an ideal place
continued overleaf

became universal, and later types on these lines were able to deliver over 10 tons of coal an hour.

The final *major* development in the steam locomotive was in the use of superheated steam, which brought with it an economy of fuel consumption of up to 30 per cent in one fell swoop. Various engineers dipped a toe into the water, cautiously at first to obtain modest steam temperature increases. But the broad concept of high-temperature superheating was mainly developed by **Wilhelm Schmidt** in Germany, saturated steam being taken in tubes through enlarged flue tubes to pick up heat from the combustion gases. The first application in Britain was on the Lancashire & Yorkshire Railway on a pair of 0-6-0 goods engines in 1906. Other engineers took up the idea and so beneficial did it prove that the use of superheating became almost universal for mainline engines from about 1910. Many engineers devised preferred methods of

Garratt at Victoria Falls. The Bulawayo 'mail' behind 4-6-4 + 4-6-4 Garratt No 358. These engines still work this service regularly. This photograph was taken in 1971 when it was still Rhodesia Railways.
P. B. WHITEHOUSE

Alfred de Glenn. One of the famous Nord compound Atlantics (1904–1912) using the de Glenn system. Under the driver's control various modes of operation could be adopted in addition to compounding, four cylinder simple and two cylinder simple using either high or low pressure cylinders.
MUSEE FRANCAIS DU CHEMIN DE FER

continued
to relax. Moreover I learned that the King's Cross men who were to work the train were to have a 'spare' 'Atlantic', borrowed from Doncaster, their own engine having developed a defect making it unsuitable for immediate duty. That run is another of the classics of all time in my collection. Spare engine or not, and incredibly rough and uncomfortable in the cab, No 4456 was a grand runner and my speed record of the morning was eclipsed by one of 93mph soon after we passed Stoke summit. There was every reason for haste in this direction because Werrington troughs were out of action and we should have to stop and take water at Peterborough. But in spite of 4½ minutes standing thus we were still a minute early passing Huntingdon, and gaining time continued until we were 3½ minutes ahead at Hatfield. So, after signal checks from Finsbury Park we arrived in King's Cross 3½ minutes early after delays amounting to 13½ minutes en route. Our net time for the journey of 185.8 miles was 176 minutes, a superb average of 63½mph. – O. S. Nock

Churchward's Star. A Great Western four cylinder Star Class 4-6-0 No 4056 Princess Margaret *at Tyseley locomotive shed, Birmingham on 9 September 1956. This pictures gives the lie to the story that in the decline of steam all steam depots were filthy and uncared for.* P. B. WHITEHOUSE

laying out the superheater elements and headers, but all followed the same general principle.

Contemporaneously with superheating, work was being done to improve cylinder performance. Piston valves were essential for high-temperature steam, but these had been known for many years. Lubrication for these conditions was a problem, and much development work was necessary for success. But the valve events themselves, the admission and release of steam, needed further improvement to obtain greater power at speed.

In this field the name of **George Churchward** will forever shine. Taking note of developments in the US, he laid down a range of standard locomotives from 1902 onwards for the Great Western Railway in which the valve travel was increased to about 6½in (the norm at the time was about 4in) which, in conjunction with large-diameter valves, brought about increases in power at the drawbar and further fuel economy. His Star 4-6-0s, when superheated, proved capable of sustaining a drawbar pull of 3 tons at 70mph, a standard well above those of contemporary engines. But his work went largely unnoticed until the mid 1920s, except where his disciples moved to other railways.

Others, mainly on the Continent of Europe, sought to improve cylinder performance by departing from the piston valve in favour of poppet valves. **Lentz** in Austria produced several forms of gear to operate such valves, and despite operational limitations these achieved some acceptance. **Arturo Caprotti** in Italy designed a valve gear which was applied on a limited scale in Britain to improve the performance of engines with indifferent conventional valve gear, before World War II. When re-engineered by a British firm in the 1940s, its virtues in the maintenance field were belatedly recognised and some fifty-three locomotives so equipped were built new for use on British Rail. The name of Reidinger may also be mentioned as the designer of another such valve gear which proved successful in British applications after World War II but arrived too late for widespread adoption.

By now the fundamental features of the modern steam locomotive had been tried and tested in service; further developments were to ice the cake without affecting the basic recipe. The optimisation of boiler proportions, very much based hitherto on experience and rule of thumb, was clarified by two men. Most credit is usually given to the work of **Lawford Fry**, whose 'Study of the Locomotive Boiler' based on US practice was published in 1924, but the man who came nearest to giving specific advice for design purposes was **Dr R. P. Wagner** of the Deutsche Reichsbahn in published material in 1929.

Undoubtedly the most illustrious name to come to prominence in the 1930s was that of **André Chapelon** in France. He applied his analytical mind to the pinch points of steam locomotive development, the production of steam in the boiler and its unrestricted flow thence through the cylinders to the chimney. His work on the rebuilding of indifferent French engines into outstanding machines of high output and unsurpassed efficiency, had a spin-off in many countries, including Britain. The two most noted locomotive engineers there in the 1930s were **Sir Nigel Gresley** and **Sir William Stanier.** The former is perhaps

André Chapelon's masterpiece. One of the later series of Chapelon 4-8-0s minus its tender. On the footplate can be seen the pipe through which coal was propelled by a rotating screw into the jet box of the mechanical stoker.
MILLBROOK HOUSE COLLECTION

Sir William Stanier. Remembered today for his successful locomotives built for the LMS railway in the 1930s, the prime example being the Duchess Pacifics. One of the unstreamlined series No 46240 City of Coventry *is seen here near the south end of Shrewsbury station in the early 1960s.* P. B. WHITEHOUSE

best known for his streamlined A4 Pacifics (including *Mallard*, the holder of the world speed record with steam traction), but in pioneering terms it was his almost universal adoption of the three-cylinder layout, with only two sets of Walschaerts gear and a conjugated gear to operate the valve of the middle cylinder, for which other engineers will remember him. He seemed satisfied with its performance, though history will almost certainly record that it did not serve him particularly well; it died with him.

In the innovatory field Stanier will be remembered for his steam turbine locomotive of 1935, with geared drive, which ran for nearly half a million miles with considerable promise before withdrawal in 1950.

Of recent pioneers it would be difficult to find a more prolific one than **Oliver Bulleid**, chief mechanical engineer of the Southern Railway from 1937 to 1949. His Merchant Navy and West Country Pacifics incorporated innumerable features reflecting his dissatisfaction with contemporary practice. Some proved themselves and gained acceptance elsewhere; others, like his chain-driven valve gear enclosed (with the inside connecting rod) in an oil bath casing were disastrous. But his last major design, the 0-6-6-0 Leader which could be summarised as total innovation with no convention, and of which only one was completed – and went quickly to the scrapheap – still causes active controversy.

Since the 1950s new construction of steam locomotives has shrunk to a trickle (except in India and China) and the breed is approaching extinction in commercial service. Yet in certain parts of the world with abundant fuel and cheap labour, the steam engine can still stand tall economically with its rivals. This has brought another pioneer to the fore, **L. D. Porta**, an Argentine locomotive engineer. His research into methods of burning coal in the conventional locomotive boiler led to his development of the gas producer combustion system, in which a much higher proportion of the air needed to support combustion is supplied to the firebox above the fuel bed to burn the gases produced in it. The result is the ability to burn low-grade coal and bring about a sharp

Porta's memorial. The 750 gauge Rio Turbio Railway, 52 degrees south in Argentina is home to a series of Japanese built 2-10-2s weighing no more than 48 tons but capable of hauling 1700 ton coal trains with a considerable reserve of power. This has been achieved by Porta's development of the gas producer combustion system with an ability to burn low grade coal and bring about a considerable reduction in unburnt fuel loss. (See also further information in chapter Dying But Not Dead)
P. B. WHITEHOUSE

Left. Sir Nigel Gresley. *The ex LNER A4 Pacific No 4498 (now preserved) named after this great engineer. One of the members of the class (No 4468* Mallard) *is the holder of the world speed record with steam traction. The engine is working the return portion of the Shakespeare Limited and is seen leaving Stratford upon Avon for Marylebone station London on 16 February 1985. (See also Great Tourist trains page 77)*
HUGH BALLANTYNE

reduction in unburnt fuel loss caused by the ferocious draught through the firebed in a conventionally draughted boiler. This technique was applied to modern locomotives working on the 750mm-gauge Rio Turbio Railway in the inhospitable far South of Argentina, a coal hauler from the El Turbio mines to the sea at Rio Gallegos. The engines, Japanese-built 2-10-2s built between 1956 and 1964 and weighing no more than 48 tons, were modified to use Porta's new combustion system and a new Kylpor draughting arrangement. The proof of the pudding is the regular haulage by these little engines of 1,700 tonne coal trains with a considerable reserve of power.

These ideas have been ventilated, too, in South Africa, where **David Wardale** applied them to two locomotives, the second a Class 25NC 4-8-4 which was rebuilt in 1981 and turned out in striking livery which promptly earned it the unofficial title of 'Red Devil'. This rebuild of an already highly successful design incorporated Porta's gas producer combustion system and double Lempor exhaust, enlarged superheater, much improved steam flow and other features. These enabled it to produce 43 per cent more power than the standard version with specific

Steam Engine Language

Adhesion Factor. This is obtained by dividing the weight on the coupled wheels by the tractive effort. For average conditions this factor should be not less than 4.3 for a two-cylinder engine and approximately 3.8 for a three- or four-cylinder one. For engines intended for operation at high speeds a lower factor may be allowable.

Articulated Locomotive. One which has two sets of cylinders driving separate sets of bogies or engine units; both units may be free to swivel, as in the Fairlie, Kitson-Meyer or Beyer-Garratt, or one only may swivel, the other being an integral part of the rigid main frame, as in the Mallet. The Shay with its geared drive is another form of articulated engine.

Axle Load. The static loading applied by any pair of wheels on the rails. It is an extremely important factor in relation to the civil engineering aspects of the railway when the permanent way authorities determine the maximum axle loading allowable dependent upon the strength of structures such as bridges, the weight of the rail in use and sleeper spacings. Axle loading naturally varies to a degree according to the amount of water in the boiler or coal in the firebox: it is usually measured in pounds or tons.

Bogie. These sets of wheels carry weight at the same time providing a flexible wheelbase. They are vital in guiding (and through this controlling the riding properties of) the locomotive.

Cylinders. This is where the heat and pressure energy present in the steam is converted into mechanical work. The minimum number used on orthodox locomotives is two and the maximum four. In basic locomotive specifications the number of cylinders is normally given along with their diameter and the piston stroke. The latter remains constant but the former will naturally increase when the cylinder is rebored: this increase is limited by the remaining thickness of the cylinder casting or liner. Compound locomotives have both high-pressure (HP) and low-pressure (LP) cylinders which differ in size and often in number. Measurements are in inches or metric terms.

Cutoff. This is the percentage of the piston stroke in the cylinder at which the further supply of steam is stopped by the valve, leaving that already in the cylinder to expand and do further work until released as exhaust. The higher the percentage cutoff, the more power is developed. Maximum cutoff is normally about 75 per cent, but the normal working range is about 15–40 per cent.

Driving Wheels. The diameter of these wheels, connected to the engine piston rod by crossheads connecting rods and coupling rods varies with the type of locomotive, large wheels for fast running, small ones for heavy freight work. Their diameter is given by the thickness of new wheel tyres but as these are turned

coal consumption spectacularly reduced. But the die had already been cast against steam in South Africa, and no more engines are likely to be so modified. Wardale has moved to China, on a project to modernise the Class QJ 2-10-2s until recently produced there. Under the direction of **Phil Girdlestone** somewhat similar modifications on a smaller scale were made to the 2-4-0 *Linda* on the 2ft gauge Festiniog Railway in North Wales. Re-entering service in 1985 she has demonstrated a fuel economy of about 30 per cent and the ability to burn low-grade coal without being a fire risk in the vulnerable countryside. Girdlestone has also been involved in the rehabilitation of some Sudan Railways 2-8-2 locomotives; use of Porta's Lempor exhaust system without other modifications has provided a 12 per cent fuel economy when the engines are working at maximum power.

Today's steam locomotives, be they in commercial service or preserved, have a noble pedigree, springing from Hackworth, Stephenson, Walschaerts, Markham, Schmidt, Churchward, Wagner and Chapelon. In the case of some USA preserved engines, the name of Mallet can be added. Now in some cases the name of Porta can bring up the rear. What a distinguished family!

---

in lathes from time to time in order to ensure correct profiles, the actual diameter is liable to be reduced by up to three inches before tyre renewal is necessary. Measurements are in feet and inches or corresponding metric terms.

Grate Area. An extremely important dimension representing the size of the fire which is in itself the very source of a steam engine's power. Measured in square feet or square metres.

Heating Surface. An important indicator in the design of locomotive boilers; it is made up of the water-side surface area of the fire tubes, of the firebox itself and of any water tubes in the firebox when applicable. Measurements are square feet or square metres. The steam-side area of superheater elements is also similarly specified.

Regulator. Controls the supply of steam to the cylinders. It is usually at the end of the dry pipe in the dome or in the smokebox. There are three main types of valve, a simple sliding grid type, a rotating butterfly type or a poppet valve. With the ordinary sliding type of regulator it is usual to provide a pilot valve on the main one. In a compound locomotive the position of the regulator may determine whether the engine is working simple or compound. In America this is called the throttle.

Reversing Gear. In earlier times this was usually effected from the driver's cab by means of a lever moving in a sector plate: in more modern ones by a wheel and screw arranged either horizontally or vertically. With lever reverse, cutoff positions are seldom marked, but a cutoff indicator is normal with screw reverse. On some types power reversers (steam or air) have been used from time to time but these have often caused problems due to 'creeping'. The reverser controls the cutoff point of admission of steam to the cylinder via the valve gear.

Steam Pressure. Another standard parameter, the pressure at which the boiler is intended to work as well as the one at which the safety valves should be set to open. Steam pressure is measured in pounds per square inch, kilogrammes per square centimetre and (occasionally) in atmospheres.

Tractive Effort. The nominal figure which provides an indication of the locomotive's drawbar pull or pulling force. It takes into account the number, diameter and stroke of the cylinders, the diameter of the driving wheels and the steam pressure; a figure of 85 per cent of the boiler pressure is usually taken as the mean cylinder pressure. Tractive effort is measured in pounds or kilogrammes.

Water. Carried in tanks on the side of the boiler, or in well tanks or in the tender. The amount of water carried is directly relative to the length of run the locomotive can perform with a given load. Water is measured in gallons (British or US) or cubic metres.

Weight. The total weight of an engine and tender when fully loaded taken in conjunction with its wheelbase is an important factor in assessing its effect on bridges etc.

4
A DAY IN THE LIFE OF AN ENGINE DRIVER

THE 'good old days' when a driver had his own engine have long gone but are still vividly recalled.

They were days of very long working hours, sometimes to the detriment of health and safety. They were the days of highly polished engines, of drivers carrying out minor adjustments or repairs to suit their own fancy. Of booking on duty an hour early to titivate *their* engine. It was not unknown for them to fit a padlock to the regulator handle of *their* engine to prevent anyone else moving it. There were indeed drivers who worked particular trains with the same locomotive for years rather than a cycled link roster. But in Britain the system was finally laid to rest in 1919, when the trade unions negotiated an agreement for an eight-

All Human Life

To some it seemed romantic, to others forbidding. But for engine men around the world the footplate was simply a place of work, kept more or less smart according to the character of the crew, sometimes given a touch of homeliness because of personal belongings brought on board, and the place where one ate (eggs perhaps fried on the shovel), drank tea or coffee (no shortage of hot water) and felt elated or depressed.

Usually two men (driver or engineer and fireman) shared long hours together, enjoying or not each other's songs and jokes, sharing reading matter, often indeed exchanging sandwiches. The driver might read poetry aloud or practise a sermon he was due to deliver on Sunday; the fireman might admit a small crime or even ask permission to marry his mate's daughter.

All human life was on the footplate – and inevitably occasionally also death. In extreme emergency the driver normally suggested the younger man jumped while he himself stayed at the controls.

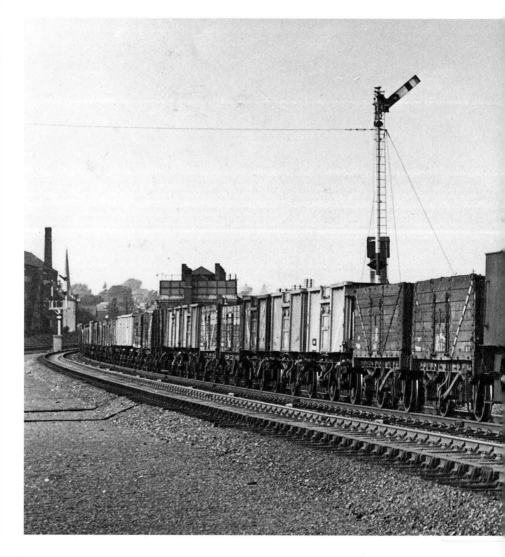

hour basic working day for enginemen. There was no way that management could then accept an engine standing idle for sixteen of the twenty-four hours each day. But with a little ingenuity it was sometimes possible to roster two regular crews to an engine, with beneficial results.

In certain other countries, different systems evolved to suit their own circumstances. The US railroads were generally divided into operating divisions of about one hundred miles span. Enginemen worked between division points and waited for a return working. In parts of Africa, a system of 'caboose' working was used; an engine on long through journeys and manned by two crews, was accompanied by a van containing sleeping accommodation, the crews taking turns to rest on the move. 'Lodging' away from home was commonplace in Britain, either in purpose-built hostels ('barracks' to many drivers) or in private houses. The quality varied enormously. At a few depots there were cases of men being required to lodge on several consecutive nights, sometimes within a score of miles of home! World War II sounded the death knell of widespread lodging turns, though it lingered on the East Coast main line between King's Cross and Newcastle until the early 1970s.

So what constituted a typical driver's day? It covered the whole range

Main line coal train. An ex LMS Stanier 'Black Eight' 2-8-0 as British Railways No 48109 heads a train load of empty coal wagons at St Albans on the line from Toton to Cricklewood in 1956.
P. RANSOME WALLIS/NATIONAL RAILWAY MUSEUM

Patience is a Virtue

'How did I become an engine-driver?' you ask. 'The same way that *your* father became whatever he is, I suppose. It "happened".' My father was a driver, and as we lived near Willesden engine-shed it was natural that when I became old enough I applied there for a job and got it.

That was thirty years or so ago, but I didn't begin on the engines. For a year or two I was doing odd jobs about the shed. If engines were wanted specially, if a man went 'sick' and we had to put someone else in his place, then I, with one or two other lads, had to go and fetch the drivers or the firemen wanted. There were plenty of other things to do, too, such as fetching tools, giving a hand to a repair gang, and so on.

When I was sixteen I was put on as lad cleaner. It was dirty work, especially in bad weather, for the engines often came in filthy. We boys had to clean the big surfaces, the boiler covering, cab sides, tender sheets, wheels, buffers, etc. But we got to know a fair amount about the engines, and before long I was put on to the motion, rods and other parts, with, now and again, a chance to help the fitters on repair jobs.

After another year or two as cleaner I went in for the fireman's examination and passed. That made me a 'passed cleaner,' but it was a good while before I got an engine. I used to help move engines about the shed and yard. – The classic beginning to 'A Chat with the Engine Driver' from the legendary *The Wonder Book of Railways*, read by *all* English-speaking boys in the years between the two World Wars.

from a simple eight-hour shunting turn to a three-hundred-mile overnight sleeping-car train, head down during the day and returning the following night. It also involved booking on duty at literally any hour of the day or night; the term 'unsocial hours' is a recent one, but enginemen have felt its impact for very many years. But perhaps we may look at a Wellingborough driver working mainline coal traffic to Brent Yard (Cricklewood) and bringing empties back, in the 1950s. It was a run of just under sixty miles each way, and the day's mileage was fairly good for such non-vacuum braked mineral working.

Our typical driver (let us refer to him as Charlie) is in a goods link of twenty sets of men working north to Toton Yard and Coalville and south to Brent, with a few odds and ends thrown in to retain route knowledge. One week he books on for am turns – not necessarily the same train, and so the time can vary within limits – and the following week for pm turns, working through a twenty-week cycle. The morning turns are the most popular, provided the starts are not too early, as they do not interfere with Charlie's social life. A few drivers are happy on the back shifts, giving them a morning on their allotments. But this week it is neither fish nor fowl – book on at 11.55am to work the 12.25 from Finedon sidings, the engine prepared and taken to the yard by another crew. He will not be home until turned eight, later still if there is any holdup.

Charlie puts his bike in the rack and goes into the drivers' lobby, announcing his arrival to the timekeeper. While he is casting an eye over the Late Notice case for any advices of additional permanent way restrictions which did not get into the Weekly Notice booklet, or water columns that are 'dry', his mate gives him a 'hello'. A glance at the big Engine Arrangements board tells him the number of the engine for his outward train; he collects a couple of clean sponge cloths from the stores, and they start their walk down the shed yard to Finedon sidings, where their 8F is already attached to the train and simmering. The guard is waiting for them. ' 'lo, Charlie. You've got 48 equal to 55 of coal, no fitteds.' There is a bit of good-natured banter, the guard admonished to stay awake and use his handbrake on the downhill bits, not the upgrades, and the fireman told to keep the engine on the boil. 'You're right away when you get the board' are the guard's final words as he starts walking back to his van (which he will probably board on the run). The Yard Inspector gives Charlie an 'away you go' wave from his office doorway and Charlie cracks the regulator to gradually pick up the slack in the loose-coupled train. As the train emerges onto the Up Goods Line, with all couplings taut he puts the regulator handle up to the stop and sets the cutoff for the climb up to Wymington Tunnel. The 8F is making cheerful, staccato music at the chimney and another of the procession of Toton–Brent coal trains is on its way.

Even with the same train, no two days are alike. They may be put out on the fast line at Bromham or at Kempston Road. There will be random signal checks. They can expect to go back slow line at Elstree, but it could be earlier at Harpenden Junction. A wagon may develop a hot axlebox – these are still the days of the ex-private-owner grease-lubricated wagons – and need to be put off, smoking, at an intermediate station. There may be a duff lot of coal on the tender which will tax the ability of Charlie's mate to keep the 8F's pressure anywhere near the red line. And the silent co-operation between driver and guard in braking the train on the undulating grades, one of the highest skills of trainmanship, can be variable.

But today things go reasonably well, and Charlie pulls into Brent loaded Wagon Sidings within a few minutes of the advertised. Hook off, take the engine on to Cricklewood shed and leave it on the approach to the coaling plant for the disposal men to deal with. Then it is off to the lobby to put in a repair card ('Exhaust injector very stiff to regulate') and into the messroom for food and to refill the mashing can. Charlie's mate grumbles that his wife never puts enough pickle in his cheese sandwiches.

Their return working with empties is booked to leave Brent just after four, before the commuter rush, once again engine prepared. If they can get off the shed a little early so much the better. The Engine Board tells them the road where they will pick up their engine; unusually it is an Austerity 2-8-0. Charlie argues wryly with the Running Foreman about this, but gets no change from him. They look the brute over, noting the general grime, the coal in the tender bunker, and particularly the play between the engine and tender buffing blocks, before taking the engine off the shed. The fireman stirs the fire up with the dart and tests both injectors – these seldom fail, unlike the 8F's – before washing down the footplate and setting the delivery valves of the sightfeed lubricator.

The return trip is uneventful by freight train standards. They know full well what they are in for on the falling grades. The engine's lack of reciprocating balance makes it shuttle in time with the coupled wheels, the train leans on it, and there is a continuous violent bucking reaction

Sophisticated Scrap
In the Western World, which manufactured all in all some 600,000 steam locomotives, (the largest numbers being built in the USA, Germany and Great Britain, respectively) it was an easy job to cut up and recycle. It was so commonplace that no one gave it a second thought. A few lucky engines were placed in museums, the rest recycled. But in some countries, including the USA and Canada, the steam engine was an immediately obvious part of their heritage, which had made possible growth and expansion. So rather more machines escaped the scrapman's torch and were given to townships for display on plinths. It also happened in some parts of South America, where the heritage of mostly American-built locomotives has been appreciated.

In Britain, the only country in the world to make a fetish of naming its steam engines, it has been the nameplates which have *continued overleaf*

Types of Steam Locomotive

Steam locomotives dominated operations on the world's railways for the first 120 years of their existence, that is, until shortly after World War II. In some places, of course, it still does; indeed, new construction continued until 1988 at least. The final product, the *Forward* or QJ class 2-10-2, built by and for the Chinese National Railways, was typical of steam construction in the world for many years. It is fascinating to compare it with Stephenson's *Rocket* for the Liverpool & Manchester Railway which took the road 147 years earlier. What impresses is the sameness rather than the difference, at any rate in fundamentals. The path of evolution from *Rocket* to *March Forward* is remarkable as much for the small number of forward steps as for the large number taken sideways or on branch lines.

Rocket already had a fire-tube boiler with multiple tubes, water space round a firebox and a fire which was drawn up by exhaust steam blasted up the chimney. The more steam was used, the more the fire was drawn. There were two cylinders linked to driving wheels by con-

necting rods, all outside the frames in full view.

Major progress came straight away with some of Rocket's immediate successors of 1830. *Phoenix* had a smokebox and with *Northumbrian* the previously separate water space round the firebox was integrated with that of the rest of the boiler, exactly as in *March Forward*. The coupling of pairs of other wheels to the driving wheels by coupling rods had been applied to previous Stephenson locomotives which worked at Killingworth colliery near Newcastle, as well as, of course, to his *Locomotion* on the Stockton & Darlington.

The *Invicta*, built the same year for the Canterbury & Whitstable Railway in England, had cylinders which, although still inclined, were placed at the front and, in addition, her four wheels were coupled.

With the *Planet*, built later in 1830 for the L & M, Stephenson (and most British locomotives) left the main line of evolution for a branch. The cylinders were placed out of reach under the smokebox, the drive being provided for by an expensive double crank in the driving

69

continued
been kept and sold as souvenirs. In the 1930s those evocative names carried by ex-London & North Western locomotives could be purchased for ten shillings (50p) each delivered to your home wrapped carefully in sacking by a railway dray often horse drawn. *Experiment, Lady of the Lake, Thunderer* or *Phantom* were all on that typed list that you could get from the stores at Crewe for a stamped addressed envelope. Swindon works carried a similar torch for the Great Western Railway: *Queen Boadicea, Red Gauntlet* or *Winnipeg* could be bought for one pound – more expensive because of their great weight. Later as steam's death knell was sounded the prices went up but ex-works they were never beyond double figures. You simply had to get in the queue. Today some Great Western Castle nameplates are sold for more than £5,000 in a sophisticated market. – P.B.W.

as the tender rebounds off the shaking engine. On the short undulations after St Albans, Charlie keeps some steam on even on the downhill bits, to keep the train off the engine even though this puts his speed a bit over the limit. This also gives the guard a snatch-free ride. But on the long fall from Sundon to Bedford he cannot do this, and they just have to suffer the discomfort and din. Coal cascades ankle deep onto the footplate from under the tender coal doors and there are no big enough lumps to jam and stem the flow. It adds to the fireman's work to have to shovel all this coal off the footplate to get working space for the next round of heavy firing.

Now they are onto the sharp pull from Sharnbrook up to Wymington Tunnel. Before the hard work is over the fireman is beginning to run down his fire so that he does not leave a boxful for the disposal men to paddle out. The climb over, they coast down the winding goods lines to Irchester Viaduct, Charlie gathering the train up with just enough steam on so that he can run inside off the down goods north of Wellingborough at the right speed, amble down the reception road and gently buffer up his train to bring it to a stand. The shunter hooks the engine off the train, and Charlie runs it back to the shed, pausing on the way to pick up the guard. 'By God, that was a rough trip,' he says with lugubrious face. 'I'm black and blue all over.' 'Nonsense,' replies Charlie. 'You never woke up till Irchester.' Back in the lobby, he puts in a No Repairs card for the Austerity, which has served them roughly but well. A glance at the Roster Sheet for tomorrow shows no red ink alterations to their next turn of duty; he books off with the timekeeper and starts to cycle home. What, he wonders, will Jean put in front of him for his meal tonight?

---

axle. This branch line was a long one, locomotives of this layout being supplied – some still by Robert Stephenson & Co – 120 years later to an order placed by the Western Region of British Railways. It will be appreciated that not only had the cranks and connecting rods to be accommodated between the frames but also two sets of gears to activate the valves.

The cylinders first reached their final horizontal forward position with the 2-2-0 locomotive *Vauxhall* built for the Irish Dublin and Kingtown Railway in 1834. The designer was a Liverpool engineer called Forrester. The arrangement became standard in the USA from 1835 onwards.

Bogies first appeared under William Hedley's *Puffing Billy* of 1813 during the time (1815 to 1831) it was altered from a four-wheeler to an eight-wheeler. This double-power-bogie arrangement is today – with diesel or electric drive – by far the commonest in the world.

The idea of pivoted wheels for guidance originated in the USA – the great Matthias Baldwin of Philadelphia produced a 4-2-0 with a leading bogie as early as 1834 – but bogies and pony trucks with side movement did not develop until the 1860s. On the other hand, the bogie tender of our Chinese 2-10-2 is an arrangement which appeared in the USA early in the 1830s, as being appropriate to the lightly laid tracks there.

Egide Walschaerts of Belgium in 1846 devised the valve gear that bears his name, but it saw little use for many years. In the early years of the century, Walschaerts' gear came suddenly into fashion. It eventually became virtually universal. The gear that bears Stephenson's honoured name can be arranged to give excellent steam distribution, but is awkward to place outside the wheels, whereas Walschaerts' in that position is convenient, cheap and practical.

In 1859 a Frenchman called Henri Giffard produced his injector – a simple and static arrangement of cones – whereby steam is used directly to force water into the boiler. In this way, the complications and expense of troublesome feed pumps became a thing of the past. Actually in making his invention Giffard had in mind steam aircraft but this early spin-off from the space age has been of great benefit to the cause of steam.

Flat or 'slide' valves were normal last century, but around 1900 began to give place to the less friction-bound piston type. Complexity and the steam locomotive never agreed. For example, the compound principle was tried over a period – short in Britain, long in France – whereby a second set of cylinders was provided which would take in the steam exhausted from the first ones

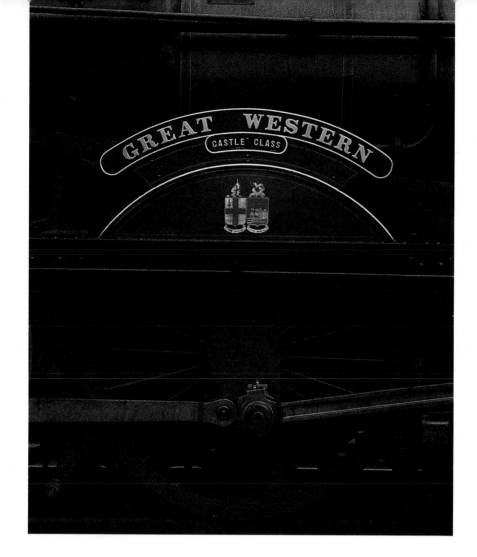

Great Western. Perhaps one of the most sought after British nameplates is seen here attached to its original owner. No 7007 was the last Castle class to be built by the Great Western Railway at Swindon. It emerged from the works in July 1946 and was withdrawn and scrapped as from February 1963.
P. M. ALEXANDER

and extract additional work from it. The process had achieved big savings when applied to steam engines in factories and ships. But, for two reasons, compounding never (not even in France) became a universal practice: first, the gain in efficiency was reduced when, as on a railroad, the demand for power constantly varied. Second, the extra machinery needed extra maintenance and the savings were not enough to justify this. Similar remarks applied to other multiple-cylindered locomotives which did not use the compound principle.

In 1891 it was Germany's turn for a valuable contribution: Wilhelm Schmidt fitted a locomotive with what was called a superheater. By the laws of physics water boils at a temperature precisely dependent on the pressure; hence, since efficiency is improved by working at a higher temperature, and increasing the pressure leads to problems in making the boiler strong enough, Schmidt thought that further heating the steam after it had left the boiler might do the trick. His simple arrangement of tubular elements inside enlarged fire-tubes worked well in improving thermal efficiency without a violent increase in maintenance cost. Accordingly, superheating became a universal feature from the first decade of the century onwards.

Early in the new century the steam locomotive reached its final form. It remained to improve the materials and the details. As an example of what could be done, one could cite an improved axlebox bearing introduced in the 1930s on a British Railway – the London Midland & Scottish – by a locomotive engineer from rival Great Western. Failures due to overheated axleboxes on the 70 principal *Royal Scot* express locomotives fell from 80 per year to 3 in consequence. Such an instance illustrates the kind of improvements in repair and maintenance costs that could be and were achieved by careful study of every detail. In this way enormous reductions were constantly being made in the cost of running the conventional Stephenson steam locomotive throughout the whole period of its existence. In contrast was the continued inability of the most experienced designers and engineers within the space available to vary the basic Stephensonian principles with economic benefit. Put another way, the application to locomotive practice of features well proven in marine and stationary steam engines was never successful.

One very distinctive feature of the steam era was that locomotives were usually designed and built to order for individual railways. Therefore they reflected geographical, climatic and operational conditions and, also, of course appeared in fantastic variety.

71

5
GREAT TOURIST TRAINS

TIME was when the sophisticated globe trotter could board a variation of the *Orient Express* to arrive smoothly and in considerable comfort at Vienna or Budapest, Bucharest or Istanbul, all as a matter of course. Transatlantic liners swept slowly and majestically up the St Lawrence river to Montreal, disembarking their passengers to cross the plains and mountains of Canada hauled by huge Canadian Pacific or Canadian National steam locomotives. Even better, one could take a ship to Portuguese West Africa and train (a through train at that), from the coast over the magnificent 3ft 6in-gauge Benguela Railway with its eucalyptus-burning Garratts across the Congo and down the twin Rhodesias to a peaceful South Africa. For all these services comfort was the watchword and to be pampered a delight.

Today as the 125 HSTs of Britain, the TGVs of France, the Bullet trains of Japan or the New York–Washington Metro Liners glide like imitation aeroplanes from city to city, in an increasingly standardised way, one has to turn from the national railway systems of the world to private enterprise and charter for individual attention and character. It is true of course that what is left of the old *Orient Express* still plies out of Paris but this is a run-down relic of a once romantic train, full of Yugoslavs, Bulgarians and Greeks on their way home with cash earned in northern Europe all cramped in smoky compartments playing cards and talking incessantly through the night. In those conditions the old stager might well consider a new version of the Agatha Christie thriller. To the man in the street flying Concorde is now the epitome of luxury.

Yet luxury train travel – and steam haulage – is still available for those who take the trouble to seek it out. Railways and particularly steam railways have halted at the brink and made a spectacular comeback with more tourist routes springing up than sheep counted before sleep. Special tourist operations chartered at high cost over state-owned systems now wend their expensive ways over scenic routes using trains put together by entrepreneurial operators who have seen financial reward from such revivals, have found and renovated stock and returned it to use for pleasure purposes.

The new, some would say replica, *Venice Simplon Orient Express* slips out of London's Victoria station en route for Paris, Zurich, Innsbruck and Venice; this, like South Africa's famous Blue Train, never sees a steam locomotive. But others like Mr Glatt's ex-Wagon Lits coaches making up the luxurious *Nostalgic Orient Express* to Istanbul most certainly do. Both of the *Orient Express* variations run other excursions and are available from time to time for private hire including steam possibilities. Each of these Pullman and sleeping car trains is made up of vehicles once used in regular service on luxury trains; they have been

Steam Impulse

The *Simplon Orient Express* stock pulled into Ravenglass Station and a gentleman rushed off the platform and into the Ratty Arms asking in the most agitated manner for 10p coins for the phone. He returned a few moments later to explain. He lived at Ulverston and he and his wife had been preparing to go out for the afternoon when he had been sent to get a shovelful of coal for the fire. As he was getting this, he heard the loco whistle, so he put down his shovelful of coal and went down to the station. The train pulled in. A lady on the platform turned to him and asked if he as a railway enthusiast would like to make use of her complimentary ticket as she was unable to go on the train. He took the ticket and boarded the train . . . One thing that has eluded us is what his wife thought of the matter as she stood waiting with her hat on for him to return with a shovelful of coal and what she said when he returned some four hours later. – *The Ravenglass & Eskdale Railway Magazine*'s Tail lamp column by D. Gard, 1988.

72

sought out and not only carefully but also beautifully restored. The *Simplon Orient Express* uses wooden-framed Pullmans once found on such trains as the *Golden Arrow* or the *Yorkshire Pullman* on its British sector, whilst both have ex-Wagon Lits vehicles again restored to pristine condition for their European ventures. Their owners began by buying one carriage here, another there and restoring them down to the last ornamental brass lamp. The *Nostalgic Orient Express* (which sometimes becomes the *Midnight Sun Pullman Express* running from Zurich up to Copenhagen, Oslo, Stockholm, Oestersud and the Arctic Circle at Narvik) uses coaches from the old *Sud Express*, the *Côte d'Azur Pullman* and the *Train Bleu*. It carries one hundred passengers with thirty staff. The food is excellent (though that standard can, as always, depend on which crew is on duty on which trip) as it is on the *Simplon Orient*. It was hard not to drool over a brunch of scrambled eggs with salmon, lobster and baked potatoes. But these are very plush operations for those whose pockets are deep. Some of the *Nostalgic Orient Express* vehicles also take in long, fascinating and very well-organised steam trips typified by the *Csârdâs Express* which covered 2,200km between 10 and 18 September 1988 starting at Nurnberg and journeying through southern Germany, Austria and Hungary using numerous classes of

Nostalgic Orient Express. Alfred Glatt's superbly restored coaches running behind steam when visiting the Albtalbahn (Ettlingen – Bad Herrenalb in West Germany) on 8 April 1984. This Intraflug special is being hauled by ex DB 01 class Pacific No 01 1066 (Swartzkopff 1940) now owned by the Ulmer Eisenbahnfreunde.
WOLFGANG STEPHAN

Palace on Wheels. Metre gauge YG class 2-8-2 aptly named Desert Queen *at the head of this very Indian institution at Delhi Cantonment station March 1988. It has just brought the Palace on Wheels back to the Indian capital after a week of touring the north-western desert area.*
P. B. WHITEHOUSE

steam engine, often three in a day. An example of just how well it *can* be done.

On Sunday mornings from October to March a metre-gauge train headed by one of India's YG class 2-8-2s, and banked by another, climbs up through the Aravalli hills deep into the Thar desert of Rajasthan and crawls westwards towards the old city of Jaisalmer where time has stood almost still for nigh on eight hundred years. It is topped by a rich honey-coloured fort standing proudly on a triangular mound, its walls flowing smoothly into the surrounding contours. This is India's westernmost city, and the far terminus of the *Palace on Wheels*, four days out from Delhi. At 9pm on the previous Wednesday evening the train slid out of Delhi's Cantonment station into the clear but dusty Indian night, made up of some thirteen ex-Maharajahs' saloons (suitably adapted and running on steel underframes with modern bogies), two dining cars also from private stock, a lounge car and service vehicles. It has called at Jaipur with its Amber Fort, Chittorgarh, and Udaipur, where the city of Jahr and its palaces rise from the limpid blue waters of three lakes. Before returning to New Delhi there will be Jodhpur, the bird sanctuary at Bharatpur, and the fabulous Taj Mahal glistening in white marble. Just now it is hot, very hot indeed, and a solitary camel stands gazing into nowhere as the two engines lay down a pall of black oil smoke across the sand dunes. Notwithstanding the brochure

74

publicity, apart from departures from Delhi on the first Wednesday evening and the return in the early morning of the next, this is the only day that steam is used. Certainly the *Palace on Wheels* is one of today's great tourist trains, but perhaps luxurious would be a misnomer even if courteous car stewards *are* given the American name of 'captain'. The experience is a very Indian one.

South in Sri Lanka steam has come out of retirement to run the tourist train, the *Viceroy Special*, from Colombo. Little seems to have been heard of it in recent times and it tends to run only on specific charter. Locomotive workings on this unique train have included three classes of rehabilitated 4-6-0s. BIA No 257, B8 No 240 and one of Sri Lanka's fascinating B2s No 213, a tender tank engine.

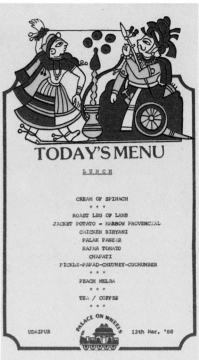

A lunch menu on the Palace on Wheels.

Maharaja's coach. Panel and crest of the Bombay Baroda & Central India Railway as carried on one of the tourist vehicles on the Palace on Wheels. P. B. WHITEHOUSE

Back in Britain, the most expensive train of all is the *Royal Scotsman*, running out of Edinburgh's Waverley station on a week-long tour of the Western Highlands and the whisky country, returning via Aberdeen and the Forth Bridge. This trip does include steam on the West Highland leg from Fort William to Mallaig (using either an ex-LMS class 5 4-6-0 or maybe an LNER design K1 2-6-0) where there is a regular programme of steam through breathtaking mountain scenery. The *Royal Scotsman* carries only twenty-eight passengers in its eight coaches (saloon car, observation car, dining car, service car and four sleepers) which accounts for a very high tour price. All but one of these superbly restored coaches are painted in the plum and spilt milk of the old LNWR/Caledonian Railway companies; the saloon is an ex-Great Northern Railway vehicle.

Other British luxury trains include the *Shakespeare Limited* from London's Marylebone station to Stratford-upon-Avon. This Sunday Pullman, offering a standard roast beef lunch and a cream tea, is hauled by privately owned locomotives on hire to British Rail, performers including examples from all four of the major pre-war companies including an LMS Stanier Pacific, an LNER A4, a Western Castle (actually built post-nationalisation) and a Southern King Arthur. Steam-hauled wine-and-dine trains are also a regular feature on several preserved or tourist railways, luxurious examples including the *Wealden Pullman* on the Kent & East Sussex and the Pullman plus ex-Royal Train vehicles based at the Birmingham Railway Museum.

The Golden Age of American railroading died when the population took to the air, and though you can still cross the continent comfortably by train in the USA or Canada, the haulage will never be steam or the aura anything like it was in 1929 when 77 per cent of intercity travel in the US was by rail. But North America is far from bereft of steam tourist trains, and Great Steam Tourist Trains at that. The star performer in Canada is the Royal Hudson, an ex-CPR 4-6-4, whose class origins go back to 1930 and the Montreal Locomotive Works – though the construction of the fleet of sixty-five engines continued until 1940. Some of the later members of the class, including No 2850 which worked the Royal Train for their majesties King George VI and Queen Elizabeth in 1939, were streamlined. By dint of good fortune a sister engine No 2860 avoided the scrapheap, ending up in Vancouver BC as a last working member of the class, largely because the then premier Dave Barrett was a steam enthusiast. The engine (together with another ex-CP veteran, Consolidation No 3716 also of Montreal Locomotive Works but an old timer from 1912) is now a star tourist attraction heading the Royal Hudson steam train over the British Columbia Railway to Squamish, one of the more scenic sections of main line anywhere in North America, taking in the spectacular views overlooking Vancouver Harbour and Howe Sound. Like the two steam locomotives, many of the coaches were also rescued from the scrapman and rebuilt to their original condition, some dating back to 1872. The normal tour train, (you still need to book ahead) runs to fourteen vehicles including baggage car, and is an excellent example of a complete passenger set from the late steam era using coaches built in Canada for transcontinental services by the Canadian Pacific. Probably they were all hauled at one time in regular service between Revelstoke and Vancouver by No 2860.

Palace on Wheels

What sets the final seal of authenticity is that the Palace is powered, for some of its journey, by steam locomotives. This is not just an indulgent concession to the whimsicalities of tourists, for well over half the passenger trains of India are steam-driven anyway. One can see them, blowing or simmering quietly, at every turn in the more rural districts, adding a note of splendour to the scenery. But the Palace locomotives are special. To fit the image of the golden coaches, they are giant monsters of shining brass-work, with glistening pistons and proud coats-of-arms at the head of the boiler. They bear names like *Desert Queen* and *Fort of Jodhpur*, and their crews are hand-picked from the cream of engine drivers for this most prestigious train in all India. – Christopher Portway

---

Opposite above. 1985 saw the return to main line running of Tyseley's No 7029 Clun Castle. *During the second week-end in June a number of runs were made to Stratford-upon-Avon and here No 7029 is passing Wilmcote with* The Shakespeare Express, *12.48 from Hall Green to Stratford-upon-Avon. HUGH BALLANTYNE*

Opposite below. A real treat for all Gresley fans with two of the magnificent A4's standing together ready for the off at Stratford-upon-Avon prior to both working trains back to Marylebone. 12 October 1986. On the right is the record breaking No 4468 Mallard *whilst No 4498* Sir Nigel Gresley *heads the return* Shakespeare Ltd. *HUGH BALLANTYNE*

Lord Mountbatten. *One of the ex Ceylon Government Railway 5ft 6in gauge unique tender tank locomotives built by Vulcan Foundry, Newton-le-Willows in 1922, and now used on the Viceroy Special. These engines (Class B2) were latterly based on Kandy.*
C&V JONES TRAVEL

Royal Scotsman. *Britain's most expensive tourist train, marketed by Abercrombie & Kent, high-quality travel agents. This one week four figure sum per passenger train does have steam for part of its journey – over the BR steam route from Fort William to Mallaig. Motive power is either an ex LMR class 5 4-6-0 or a BR (E) class K1 2-6-0.*
KEITH SANDERS

The whole operation runs over what is now termed BC Rail (originating as the Pacific Great Eastern Railway) and is managed by the Royal Hudson Steam Train Society. To quote some of the earlier publicity material: 'You are about to take the train that left forty years ago.' In fact despite its buildup as a major British Columbia tourist attraction, the Royal Hudson Steam Train is BC Rail's Train No 3 (with its return working Train No 4 southbound) and the only regularly scheduled steam operation to appear in the working timetable of a major North American railway. As BC Rail emphasise the Royal Hudson Steam Train is not a museum or a theme park but a very real scheduled daily passenger train operating on Canada's third largest railway. One interesting development arising from the rebuilding of the section of railway through West Vancouver is its co-existence under today's street noise abatement regulations with heavy freights as well as Budd Railcars regularly passing through residential areas. Soon after the Royal Hudson returned to service the municipality amended its byelaws to require every steam locomotive to sound its whistle at all crossings. Diesels must still remain silent.

In the United States there are numerous steam revivals covered elsewhere in the book, but two stand out as something special. Worked

Royal Hudson. Canadian Pacific 4-6-4 No 2860 after turning on the wye at the far terminus, Squamish, on 17 June 1983. This is a regular tourist train operated out of Vancouver by the British Columbia Railway. P. J. HOWARD

Viceroy Special. Sri Lanka Railway 4–6–0 Sir Thomas Maitland, *built by Robert Stephenson Hawthorns at Darlington in 1928. It was rescued from an engine shed where it was rusting away with a banana tree sprouting from its chimney being saved by the efforts of Cliff Jones a Lancashire railway enthusiast and travel agent whose ingenuity gave birth to the Viceroy Special.*
C & V JONES TRAVEL

Viceroy Special

A plume of smoke put the *Viceroy Special* on the rails. If Cliff Jones, tour operator extraordinary of Lancashire's Eccles, had not seen it issuing from a Colombo siding he would never have discovered the treasure-trove of Garratts and other steam locomotives rotting away outside the Dematogoda running sheds. His far-sightedness and enthusiasm was contagious and Sri Lanka Railways went to work with a will producing a train that it hoped might invigorate the country's sagging tourist input.

You don't have to be a railway buff to ride and enjoy the *Viceroy Special* – though a penchant for train travel helps. The *Viceroy Special*, I should explain, is a lovingly restored train that trundles happily and evocatively over much of the rail network of Sri Lanka carrying a maximum of some 40 souls around this lush and very lovely island of friendly welcoming people. It offers a superb platform for observing the mountains, tea plantations, rubber forests, rice paddies and general life and environment of the Ireland-sized country and, since it keeps well away from the northern areas of Tamil unrest, a visitor is entirely safe.

Currently three old steam locos have been brought back into service, two of which, at different
continued opposite

today by private operators these are truly Great Tourist Trains. They can be found in Colorado and New Mexico running over the narrow-gauge tracks of the one time 3ft-gauge network belonging to the Denver & Rio Grande Western Railroad. They take in the Durango to Silverton route and the mountainous line over the Cumbres Pass between Antonito (on the Denver–Santa Fe and Albuquerque line) and Chama, a junction for the one-time continuation of the narrow gauge (now converted to standard) to Farmington. Each takes the traveller in adequate comfort close to the awesome peaks of the North American Rockies through tunnels, along the very edges of precipitous gorges and over breathtaking trestles. The former was once a branch built to collect silver from the lode now worked out and later defied the attempts of its parent company to close it (state permission was refused because of its tourist value) whilst the latter remains a truncated version of a once vast network which connected commercial outposts in the Rocky Mountain region. Originally known as the San Juan Extension of the Denver & Rio Grande Western, this line was also built to service rich mining camps, this time in the San Juan Mountains. The Colorado and New Mexico narrow-gauge systems were among the favourites of that classic writer of American railroad folklore and short-line historian, Lucius Beebe, who called the San Juan route the most spectacular example of mountain railroading in North America. Today it is owned by the States of Colorado and New Mexico and is a registered National Historic Site. The railway is operated as a tourist attraction on a leasing basis by Kyle Railways Incorporated.

The Durango to Silverton train, so long a bête noir of the D&RW (who tried to accelerate closure of both this and the San Juan route by cutting back services and pretending that neither line existed) is now a regular operation tracing the Animas river up through mountain scenery normally only accessible by horseback or on foot with the ninety-mile round trip taking four hours behind 3ft-gauge Baldwin and Alco 2-8-2s of 1920s and 30s vintage – all formerly D&RGW machines. It is a long haul with passengers carried in open-sided observation cars and replicas of the stock once in general use. The experience is close to the thrill of old time narrow-gauge railroading. But railfans should note that access to the locomotive depot and yards at Durango, the main terminus, has in the recent past been very much forbidden, in contrast to the more relaxed view taken by the Cumbres and Toltec authorities who welcome the enthusiast and produce a separate leaflet explaining the functions of the various artefacts and equipment.

The Cumbres and Toltec must rate as one of the Great Tourist Trains of the World with its sixty-four-mile-long tracks climbing up to a height of 10,015ft as the locomotives (sometimes double headed) heave their train, snakelike up to Cumbres. Trains start from either Antonito or Chama, passing at Osia where there is a lunch stop and engines are changed, each to return to its home base after turning on a wye. Passengers are carried in converted boxcars though some new replica coaches are now to hand. Unlike the Silverton train, this is a June to October season only; it gets very rough up in those mountains in bad weather. Occasionally there are winter time snow plough spectaculars on charter to railroad enthusiasts who get an opportunity to see and photograph old time freight trains charging their way through the drifts. As with the Silverton line the locomotives are ex-D&RGW 2-8-2s, though this time Baldwins of 1925.

Tourist trains and railways are now a part of modern railway folklore and essentially the raison d'être of steam's eleventh-hour renaissance. Begun back in 1950 when enthusiasts rescued the little Talyllyn Railway in North Wales from oblivion their numbers have increased year by year, country by country, even spreading into such unlikely areas as communist Czechoslovakia whose guardians of the people's liberty look more than twice at visiting rail enthusiasts especially if they are equipped with a camera. The Great Tourist Train is not always luxurious and most make comparatively short journeys only but all provide that extra tang to the otherwise staid and utilitarian transportation on offer by the great

continued
times, haul the three refurbished coaches – two observation and one restaurant car – at speeds rarely in excess of 40 mph giving ample opportunity for photography – even when the train doesn't stop at requested points along the line for just this purpose. A heavier, more powerful Garratt engine will soon be operational again as well as more coaches to augment those already in use with the Darlington-built B1A 4-6-0 *Sir Thomas Maitland* and J1 Class 4-6-4 *Lord Mountbatten* locos of circa 1915 or thereabouts – this last the only one of its kind in the world. Those so inclined can be happily accommodated 'up front' in the cab where they may become schoolboys (and girls) once more, being jarred to the bone and subjected to doses of soot, steam, coaldust and mugs of hot, sweet, oil-laced tea from an ever-tolerant engine and crew.

Unlike the *Viceroy's* contemporaries, the *Venice-Simplon Orient Express* or India's *Palace on Wheels*, the little Sri Lankan train is neither expensively luxurious or carries a sleeping car. A number of tasty lunches are served in the bar-equipped restaurant car in addition to mid-morning snacks and afternoon tea in the comfortable air-conditioned observation coaches. The train crew become one's friends so heartwarmingly anxious are they to please.
– Christopher Portway

Cumbres & Toltec

Scenic Railroad

Daily Excursion Trips

through the Scenic Rockies of
Colorado & New Mexico
on North America's longest and highest

NARROW-GAUGE
STEAM RAILROAD

Leaflet

*Narrow Gauge in Snowdonia. A
modern-day picture of the historic
1ft 11⅝in gauge Festiniog Railway
which runs from the Cambrian
Coast at Porthmadog up into the
mountains at Blaenau Festiniog
using ex Penrhyn Quarry engines
(rebuilt at the FR's Boston Lodge
works) and two fascinating 0-4-4-0
double Fairlie locomotives actually
constructed at Boston Lodge. Here,
in the rocky hills close to Blaenau
double Fairlie* Merddin Emrys *in
smart red livery and her train of red
and white stock are almost dwarfed
by the magnificent scenery. No
wonder this was called the Toy
Train in Faerieland in the
company's old publicity.* PETER
JOHNSON

systems of state. One such line, very much a pioneer both as a steam-hauled narrow-gauge railway per se and as a revitalised railway with high tourism stars is the Ffestiniog in North Wales based on Porthmadog.

The very word Porthmadog has a Welsh ring about it and it is impossible to get there without passing through some of the best or a little of the worst scenery in Wales. But whichever route is taken, Beddgelert and the old Welsh Highland way, past the dismal (but now a tourist attraction in themselves) slatetips below the Crimea Pass or the high Bala road or the coastal and rail routes past Harlech Castle and the wonders of Portmeirion, the country can scarcely fail to impress. And for those with an eye and ear for history it is also an exciting place. The Harbour station of the Ffestiniog Railway exudes atmosphere; though

Left. Toltec engine. Denver & Rio Grande Western 3ft 0in gauge 2-8-2 No 487 at Alamosa, Colorado in 1961. MILLBROOK HOUSE COLLECTION

During World War II there was a very large number of British servicemen in Egypt but their total was small compared with the teeming populations of Egyptian cities, particularly Cairo. The country had an efficient railway system, Egyptian State Railways. The largest station, Cairo Main, had nine platforms and was equipped with modern Westinghouse electro-pneumatic signalling which included point detection, track circuiting and illuminated signal-box diagrams, all indications of British influence.

The express train service of Lower Egypt included seven daily trains each way between Cairo and Alexandria, worked by magnificently handsome green painted Atlantics. Some of the ESR's equipment was before its time, steam rail-cars were in use before the war, and some Ganz diesel rail-cars, built in Budapest in 1935 were also in regular use; they were the first in the world to be air-conditioned.

There was a heavy suburban traffic round Cairo. The most important line was that from Bab-el-Luk station in Cairo to Heluan-les-Bains, serving some intensely populated areas close to the city and some high-class suburbs further out. Heluan itself was a very important town with a large cement works. The trains consisted of saloon coaches hauled by some very smart 2-6-2 tank engines. The track was in good condition, and the vehicles rode well. The locomotives had good acceleration, necessary on a line with many intermediate stations. Passenger traffic was very heavy, most of the passengers, of course, wearing Arab dress. The stations were very picturesque, although they were perhaps not appreciated so much at the time. Many young Arabs earned their livings on the stations, selling food and drink to passengers, or cleaning their shoes. – Frank Harrison

today it is hemmed by modern holiday flatlets it is generous in its portals – certainly by the prevalent standards for small railways, and one is reminded of the times when people booked for Blaenau Ffestiniog as they did for the *Flying Scotsman* or the *Orient Express*, secure in the knowledge that they would be met at the other end by a coach and four.

It is high summer and the crowds throng the booking hall and platform whilst alongside stands a rake of 2ft-gauge red and cream coaches, some dating back from the days of the old railway (the Festiniog Railway introduced the first British bogie coaches in 1873) some new but still built in the company's works across the great embankment known as the Cob, which holds back the sea and lies round the curve at the station's exit. At the head end waiting for time is a unique and remarkable locomotive, the brass plates on its tank sides proclaiming that it is Fairlie's Patent and that its name is *Merddin Emrys*; it is painted a deep and glorious red. This is one of the line's two double Fairlies whose lineage dates back to 1871 and though rebuilt is very much original in outline. It is a double bogie machine with twin boilers and a central cab, generations ahead of its time and the forerunner of the arrangement which is now standard for diesel and electric locomotives. The train is composed of compartment stock first and third class, a buffet car and an observation saloon. As the moment of departure looms a whistle echoes over the now quiet platform, twin regulators are pushed open and the double engine moves its train round the curve and onto the Cob – the hour-long journey to Blaenau Ffestiniog has begun. The old Festiniog Railway once labelled this as a trip into Faerieland and they were not far wrong.

Up in the hills to the east Moelwyn Mountain looks down on the Vale of Festiniog and in the far distance the shape of the nuclear power station reminds us that nearly a century and a half has passed since steam's whistle was first heard among the woods across Llyn Mair. Cars begin to make their way up to the small yard adjacent to the new island platform station at Tan-y-Bwlch with its wrought iron footbridge giving character to the now more modern scene. Car doors slam and the stillness is shattered by the excited voices of children demanding to know when the train will arrive. Soon, coming from across the lake the distant sound of a double Fairlie climbing with a heavy train attracts the crowd's attention and they look towards the moving plume of steam threading above the tree tops. As the sound gets louder it is joined by a long and melodious chime from the whistle of *Merddin Emrys* and this is soon joined by the clack and rattle of wheels over rail joints. Slowly this sound moves round, now seemingly coming from the crowd until with a final echo from the last rock cutting *Merddin Emrys* comes rattling and hissing into the platform and draws up alongside the water tower.

The journey is now half way over but the climb continues as the train crawls up towards Dduallt and the great new spiral (built as part of the new works necessitated by the construction of a new lake for a pumped hydro-electric scheme) and the only one of its kind in Great Britain. What is more it was built entirely by volunteer labour. *Merddin Emrys* skirts this man made lake, its waters almost lapping the carriage steps and regains the old track formation as the slatetips become reality. The new terminus at Blaenau Ffestiniog is now only minutes away but here

Ready for the Yukon trail. A White Pass and Yukon 3ft 0in gauge GEC diesel alongside No 72 an Alco 2-8-2 at Skagway British Columbia in the late 1960s. The railway was then in full operation albeit with diesel workings on the main line except for snow clearing and the occasional special.
MILLBROOK HOUSE COLLECTION

too a new scene has been set, for in the recognition of success a joint station has been built with the upper terminus of BR's Conwy Valley branch enabling tourists to continue on to the North Wales coast by dmu. It is all part of a true adventure story and the journey has been on one of the Great Little Trains of Wales.

What of the future? Old steam engines, at least those properly restored and cared for, never die and we can confidently expect new tourist opportunities. A particularly exciting one might be a restored White Pass & Yukon at Skagway. When cruising up the Alaskan coast took off in popularity in the 1970s, the liners were met by a narrow-gauge express on the quayside for the fierce climb from the Panhandle of the Alaskan coast to the Yukon territory of Canada. The mines which gave the system its basic traffic alas closed and when reopened the ore was taken down to Skagway by trucks with trailers. The great railway installations of the Canadian-owned railroad at its Alaskan headquarters are however already a major tourist attraction and restoration of part of the route of fierce gradients (stops were necessary to allow brakes to cool) is becoming a practical reality. What a thrill it will be to see a narrow-gauge steamer beside the cruise ships! But trains will never again fight those cruel gradients in blizzards. You can attend a film show and buy many souvenirs of the days the gold miners and others went into the unknown white wilderness by the daily passenger train whose passage had been as dramatically and expensively cleared by the locomotive with steam turbine snow blower fighting through the drifts a foot at a time.

Photo Call

In 1977 I had a fascinating trip on a magnificently restored steam engine in the USA. This was the enterprise of Chessie Systems Inc, a working alliance of the Baltimore & Ohio, the Chesapeake & Ohio, and the Western Maryland railroads, in conjunction with Ross Rowland, a New York commodities broker, who had purchased and at his own expense had restored to full working order No 2101, a fast mixed traffic 4-8-4 of the former Reading RR. Chessie Systems Inc, used her on a number of steam specials. I travelled from Baltimore to Cumberland with an enormous train of 18 cars, representing a load of some 1250 tons. And we had several spells at 65 to 70mph on favourable stretches of the line.

continued overleaf

Chessie steam. Chesapeake & Ohio 4-8-4 No 614 restarting the Safety Express from Prince, West Virginia on its run from Charleston down the New River Valley to Hinton with twenty two coaches including a dome car, 31 October 1981.
P. J. HOWARD

Silverton train. The 3ft 0in gauge Silverton train on its way from Durango in Denver & Rio Grande Western days. The scene is Los Animas River Canyon.
BOB PETLEY

continued
The really big thrill came towards the end, when we stopped, and all passengers who wished were invited to detrain. The line was quadruple tracked at that location, and a triangular plot had been cordoned off into which the spectators were ushered. Meantime the train itself was propelled backwards down the line until it was completely out of sight, and the many photographers in our party were able to position themselves ready for the reappearance of engine No 2101 and the train. Ross Rowland certainly did us proud, for he came up in a terrific acceleration at fully 70mph, with exhaust going sky-high, and a tremendously satisfying beat. – O. S. Nock

Country Steam

Circumstances conspired that of all developed countries Britain had the greatest continuity in the character and operation of its country railway byways. Such was their diversity and character – many continued as living museums decade by decade – that it is not surprising they attracted international interest. This was always especially strong in the Great Western, the only one to retain its identity when in 1923 Britain's main railways were formed into four Groups.

Very much a country railway, its main line went to Devon and Cornwall through sleeping Wiltshire and the apple orchards of Somerset; even when it *did* go north to Birmingham and the Black Country this was but a smudgey square on the map, its tracks leading north-westwards out of London through Bucks, Oxfordshire and Warwickshire emerging into Shropshire and Cheshire before ending not at mighty Liverpool but among the docks at Birkenhead. There were long sleepy branches too, one from Oxford which might have reached Cirencester but, as though lulled by the soft landscape of the upper Thames came to rest at Fairford – or to be more accurate in a meadow near to Fairford, where the American Air Force man who arrived by the Victorian all stations train stood enraptured by the rural calm before realising his mistake in choice of route. On the western marches too there were delightful rural branches, the Golden Valley, or those winding lines through the country of Teme and Wye, Worcester and Leominster and Bewdley, the junction for Tenbury or Bridgnorth. And with the Grouping the GWR took much of Wales where the Cambrian was met, and absorbed; the branch from Dolgelly to Barmouth Junction with its great bridge across the Mawddach estuary and sunsets so beloved of George Borrow seen from the footpath alongside the single track.

These were the essence of gentle, sunny lines remembered from journeys to grandparents or the sea but there were others too, the Isle of Wight systems later belonging to the Southern but once consisting of no less than 10 separate undertakings now telescoped into just one short section worked by ex-London Underground electric trains; the Cinderella before and after being the Freshwater Yarmouth and Newport. The great North Western and the Midland railways had their country lines too, harder in landscape maybe, but who could resist the Settle–Carlisle route or the erstwhile Cockermouth, Keswick & Penrith beginning alongside the North Eastern's route to Barnard Castle and Darlington on the down side of the main line platforms at Penrith. The LNER in East Anglia (the Great Eastern section were known as the Swedies) could boast as pretty a piece of track as any: Dereham to Swaffham, Cromer Beach to Sheringham, Cambridge to Mildenhall, whilst Scotland, once out of the smoke and grime of Glasgow was nothing but a joy: the Caledonian route to Oban, the North British to Fort William and Mallaig to say nothing of the Highland's rails which were almost totally countrified. Not least in interest if small in stature, the Great North of Scotland had its Speyside branch from Craigellachie to Boat of Garten, every station serving one or more distilleries.

And what finds there were for the steam enthusiast even as late as the 1950s, old engines out to grass working out their days on peaceful single lines. The Great Western by dint of its ability to absorb and not be absorbed was, of course, more standardised but who could resist a Dean goods or Cambrian 0-6-0 taking four chocolate-and-cream coaches (even if they were a trifle grubby) out of Barmouth and down the coast through Aberdovey to Dovey Junction and Machynlleth. Or a small-wheeled 45XX class tank en route from Kingsbridge to the tiny village of Brent, the junction with Brunel's GWR main line to Plymouth and Penzance. Even as late as 1959 the Kingsbridge branch had through trains to London on summer Saturdays often needing to be double headed.

On the LMS and its constituents old stagers were only in the autumn of their lives with ancient Webb engines of LNWR Crewe vintage chaff-chaffing their way with push and pull trains or Francis Webb's 'Cauliflower' 0-6-0s on the Keswick line, panting up the hills and running like the wind down the banks – sometimes at the head of the *Lakes Express*. The Midland engines tended to snort rather than chaff or wheeze, and they too could be found well into the nationalisation period on such diverse lines as the Hereford, Hay and Brecon or the Keighley & Worth Valley, climbing the steep grades to Oxenhope. In East Anglia, the Swedies ran Holden's E4 2-4-0s and J15 class 0-6-0s whilst Norwich shed held onto its rebuilt Claud Hamiltons which shedmaster Bill Harvey ran on the Londons if ever he had the chance. Scottish motive power was 'rationalised' to a greater degree for the LMS (with Caledonian influence predominating) soon slaughtered the Glasgow & South Western's engines and made headlong inroads into the Highlands; but it all took time and Highland 0-4-4 tanks, for instance, lasted on the Dornoch branch until they literally died of old age. The LNER lines were abundant with pre-grouping classes ex-Great Northern K2s on the West Highland – and some North British Glens; Great Eastern B12s were brought in to run the Great North of Scotland's main lines and GN of S 4-4-0s proliferated on its branches. They were great days indeed. In some places you could see locomotives performing the very same duties they had at the identical hour of day two generations earlier, two World Wars merely causing a temporary deterioration in the quality of coal and the variety of traffic!

Country junction. One of the great joys of the railways of yesteryear was to be able to spend an hour at a country junction where the busy (if temporarily rural) main line met the feeder tracks coming in from the small towns or villages nearby, feeders which provided much needed if spasmodic passengers. One such station was Abergavenny Junction where Hall class 4-6-0 No 6943 Farnley Hall pauses with the 4.10pm Hereford to Cardiff semi fast whilst ex LMS 2-6-2 tank No 40145 waits on the left with the connection to Brynmawr, Merthyr Tydfil and Tredegar.
P. M. ALEXANDER

Southern push-pull. An ex LSWR 0-4-4T No 30328 propels a two coach set over this single line to Petersfield with the 11.02am train from Midhurst on 12 May 1951.
P. M. ALEXANDER

In Europe things were somewhat different. For one thing, secondary systems were often narrow gauge. This came about because of the generally more rural nature of the mainland continent and the need to open up the countryside cheaply with local authority interest. Great was the range of self-contained systems in rural enclaves – yet somehow everything connected to everything else.

For example, the story of how the effects of a speed restriction in Kent spread out beyond the English Channel to rural France, the ripples causing the evening railcar of the Société Général des Chemins de Fer-Economiques – a metre-gauge line in Normandy to run 10 minutes late and nearly hit a cow! It went like this. On that day, the 11am boat train from Victoria was held up because of a delay near Tonbridge and reached Dover 11 minutes down. Summer's crowds gave little opportunity for reducing customs and embarkation time; in fact the *SS Invicta* was 16 minutes late into Calais and thus upset the rhythm of the French railway system for the rest of the afternoon. So train No 34, a semi-fast to Paris, arrived at the country junction of Noyelles about half an hour late.

Across the tracks in the yard adjacent to the station, two diminutive metre-gauge tanks, painted a dull green and heading ancient wooden-bodied stock bound for the coast, blew off impatiently, the passengers from Paris (who had made their connection in time) sitting on the slatted seats cursing No 34 for holding them up. Before the late-comers from Calais had time to settle down, there was a shriek from the whistle of the Cayeux engine, an almighty jerk, and with a rolling motion on the mixed-gauge track they were away, the conductor swinging from coach to coach collecting the fares. By St Valéry Canal they had made up a whole minute, and further brisk running took them past the sad locomotive graveyard to Lanchères-Pendé where the driver rushed to a telephone – the method of operating on these French narrow-gauge lines was nearly always based on God and the telephone.

When the ripples of a delay spread along a single-track line, they start a backwash in the other direction and this is what happened at Lanchères-Pendé, the last passing loop before the Cayeux terminus. The telephone conversation was a debate on whether the much-delayed train would prevent the 6.10pm railcar still waiting at Cayeux from making its booked connection with the main line at Noyelles. It was decided that this could still be done.

As the steam train neared the seaside terminus they were shutting the railcar's doors ready to move off. As soon as the offender was in, the railcar accelerated down the lightly laid track just like a country bus, leather seats, luggage racks, a bereted driver with a ticket rack and windows which would not open: all very French. The working was *très économique*; a passenger would flag the Michelin to a halt, climb on board, shut the door after him, take a seat, and the car would set off again. As soon as he regained top gear and was clear of the points the driver turned round, opened the little glass panel and issued the newcomer's ticket, glancing over his shoulder now and again to see that there was nothing on the line.

By St Valéry Canal they had made up five whole minutes, and if this kept up all would be well. Ahead lay the silted-up estuary with its long embankment, replacing the trestle bridge of bygone years, but as they rolled across the countryside a solemn file of contented cows wended their way homeward from the river meadows to the byre, crossing the line one after the other at intervals of five metres or so on a little pathway. To be on time there could be no question of slowing down or waiting, or the Paris train would be gone; the driver put his foot down, played a tune on the horn and judged that, if all went well, he would just get across between the ninth and tenth cow. The railcar rattled and shook and leapt forward, the tenth cow picked up slightly and things began to look awkward, but the driver kept his nerve and his hand on the horn, playing an even louder fanfare. In the nick of time the bewildered cow turned aside into the bushes and the railcar scuttled past to make Noyelles with a comfortable three minutes to spare. What British Railways had lost the rickety and dying Reseau de la Somme had triumphantly regained.

The minor nature of such small lines (narrow or standard gauge) always invested them with a fascinating charm. The rolling stock nearly always heterogeneous, seldom as many as a dozen engines of any one class and the coaches if possible even more non-standard. Few such systems were ever prosperous though in countries such as Switzerland there were (and still are) some honest to goodness lines once using steam which have been so well supported that they are now electrified – and if they do not swell their operator's coffers they provide invaluable social service in knitting their area's economy together.

In recent years a great deal has been written on the merits and demerits (mostly the demerits) of the Irish narrow-gauge lines, but it would be unjust to ignore the broad-gauge operation, also full of character. Even the choice of this unusual gauge of 5ft 3in is very Irish. In the beginning Irish railway promoters cared little about uniformity and the question of gauge seemed to be a matter of arbitrary and personal choice; if this had been allowed to continue the ensuing chaos would have been beyond belief. Intervention by Sir Charles Pasley, the inspector of railways, averted the situation in a way that was not only Irish but a triumph of diplomacy. Realising that to favour any existing gauge would but heap fresh fuel on the fire, he looked for a compromise, finding one by adding all the various gauges together and dividing the total by their number. The result: Ireland's standard or broad gauge of 5ft 3in.

Today Ireland has few rural branch lines but vast lengths of the main and cross country routes are single and to the eyes of those from more populated countries are very countrified indeed. Until the end of steam, (which came more quickly than it did in the United Kingdom), Irish locomotives still consisted almost entirely of representatives of the old companies existing before amalgamation into the Great Southern in 1925, though the more modern power was used on the main line south from Dublin to Cork. It was quite normal to

Island steam. An ex LSWR 02 class 0-4-4 tank No W29 arrives at Ventnor, Isle of Wight. These are British Railways days but although the engine is painted black it still carries its Southern Railway name, Alverstone. The coaches as well as the locomotives go back to pre-grouping days. P. M. ALEXANDER

French metre gauge to the Channel coast. A Reseau de la Somme train bound for Cayeux via St Valery Canal waits impatiently for the SNCF connection from Calais in the early 1950s. D. TREVOR ROWE

North Devon narrow gauge. The last days of the 1ft 11½in gauge Lynton & Barnstaple Railway *(closed by the Southern Railway on 29 September 1935) with a Lynton bound train headed by* Manning Wardle *built 2–6–2 tank* Exe.
MILLBROOK HOUSE COLLECTION

Furthest west in Ireland. Fair day cattle trains pass at Annascaul in the summer of 1951 headed by Hunslet *built 2-6-0 tanks. On the left is a double headed train of empties whilst on the right the first loaded train of the day runs in from Dingle. Both men and machines pause here for refreshment.*
IVO PETERS

Far right. Irish branch line. The 5ft 3in gauge tracks of the Old Great Southern Railway make the diminutive F6 class 2-4-2T and its 'sax whaler' seem even smaller as they stand at Skibbereen (junction with the notorious 3ft 0in gauge line to Schull) in 1950.
P. B. WHITEHOUSE

find a 4-4-0 at the head of a train comprising steel coaches with elliptical roofs and electric lights mixed with a few elderly eight-wheeled clerestories with gas-lit period interiors, and on branch lines ancient six-wheelers without sprung seats and the old pot lamp holders still *in situ* in the roof.

Even into the 1950s there were oddities on the broad gauge. One of these was the Dundalk, Newry & Greenore, almost completely Anglicised in appearance with a stud of six saddle tank 0-6-0s built by Ramsbottom at Crewe in the 1870s and six-wheeled coaches still painted in the colour of the original owning company, the London & North Western. In its last days this LNWR museum piece was worked by the Great Northern Railway of Ireland using small 2-4-2 tanks, but even these failed to destroy the old 'Premier Line' atmosphere. One of the joys of a trip to Ireland's railways at that time was being able to stay at the huge rambling Greenore hotel, a relic of the once hoped for prosperous cross-channel service. In a bathroom overlooking the station platform, one could wallow in the warm water with genuine North Western smoke wafting over the great brass taps as shunting took place down below.

Then there was the ailing and exceedingly decrepit Sligo, Leitrim & Northern Counties Railway, linking the Great Southern (later CIE) at Sligo in the Republic with Enniskillen in the North. Though the sparsity of traffic rendered it an economic nightmare, its days were extended because it crossed the border and thus (like the Dundalk, Newry & Greenore) could not be incorporated into the national system on either side. Trains trundled over the hilly, grass-grown tracks well into the 1950s, using the line's 0-6-4 tanks (all named) built by Beyer Peacock, two as late as 1951. These latter were bought on the 'never-never' and bore unobtrusive plates recording the fact that for the time being at least they remained the property of their builders.

Trains were always mixed, the one coach being a tricomposite which continued to provide second-class accommodation long after the bigger mainline companies had dropped it. There was a single first-class compartment in the middle divided amidships by a central partition into smoking and non-smoking sections – one advantage of the extra width available on the broad

gauge. L. T. C. Rolt, writing in *Lines of Character*, tells of a journey on the SL&NCR when travelling on one of the more modern railcars he found his gaze wandering to the driver who sat motionless and with shoulders hunched gazing with an abstracted and somewhat melancholy expression at the road ahead. A man of sixty odd with a straggling grey moustache whom he would have judged to be a locomotive man even if he had not been wearing overalls and a grease cap. The fact that he had refused to discard the uniform of the footplate for the cleaner but less distinguished apparel of a bus driver made Rolt's heart warm in sympathy towards him, making him think of some old coachmen forced to give up his proud place on the box for the driving seat of a horseless carriage.

The SL&NCR met the GNR (I) at Enniskillen and here the nature of the broad gauge changed, for the Great Northern was one of Ireland's finest railways, its coaches finished with varnished teak like its English contemporary, and its more prestigious engines (including some small 4-4-0s for cross-country work) in glorious sky blue and scarlet. It even offered the anachronism of a timetabled and fully operative horse tram from Fintona Junction to Fintona Town. The five small-wheeled U class 4-4-0s all carried names of small towns served by the railway, and came out of Beyer Peacock's works as late as 1948. They could be found at work at the head of the summer *Bundoran Express*, criss-crossing today's troubled border country to the Atlantic Coast, or out of Enniskillen to Omagh.

One cannot leave Ireland without some reference to the 3ft gauge. Three quarters of a century ago, it was instrumental in opening up remote country areas. Oft told tales relate their trials and tribulations, but with roads in rural areas unpaved until comparatively recently they played a vital part in the nation's transport system. And what variation of motive power there was to be sure: 2-4-2 tanks on Cork's suburban service out to Blackrock, 2-6-0 and 2-6-2 tanks with the faculties of Kerry goats crossing the Slieve Mish mountains from Tralee to Dingle, geranium red 2-6-4 tanks on the County Donegal, and olive green 4-8-0 tender engines on the Burtonport Extension of the long Lough Swilly line. All these have now been dead for nigh on a generation.

Down Under

It is dawn at Tarcoola in South Australia and the long, straight rails across the Nullabor plain seem to merge together to the dusty horizon. The month is September 1949, so the cold winter begins to move into feeble spring, making the footplate of a modified C36 Class 4-6-0 (based on a successful New South Wales Government Railways design) with its huge six-wheel, bogie tender a welcome place to be! The sounds that break the dawn's silence are those heard by railwaymen over most parts of the world: the thud of the coal-pick on a large lump; a sliding crunch and then the musical ring of shovel on the fire-hole door; the singing, indrawn note of an injector; and the low hum of the lighting turbo-generator. And the smell – the characteristic smell of a warm steam locomotive – the same north, south, east and west. The rosy light from the open fire hole sends beams at an angle into the still, dark world; smoke curls lazily from the squat chimney and the scrape of the driver's boots on the ballast tells of last-minute conscientious checking with a flaming smoking torch. Ahead the track is dead straight with the distance across the Nullabor roughly equal to that from London's Euston station to Glasgow. Not a suggestion of a curve for hour after hour. In England on a busy main line the train will be headed by a Royal Scot 4-6-0 whose crews will pass some five hundred or so signals; here, although the single-line sections are approximately forty-five miles apart any semaphore signals erected when the line was built are long gone. In England the driver will be a man of sixty: here he is but thirty-two! So much is the same the world over; so much is different.

Forty years on, the scene has changed with modern practice, and the Indian Pacific Express from Sydney to Perth is a through-service headed by a throbbing diesel, involving joint-ownership of rolling stock. First-class travel includes a cocktail-lounge bar with writing-tables and, maintaining old trans-Australian tradition, a piano.

Few would feel that Australia has a similarity to Ireland but from the railway point of view each began with unique and epoch-making problems over gauges. Ireland solved hers very quickly by government decree resulting in the now standard gauge of 5ft 3in, but Australia's five states (and one territory) that form the

Below. No 707 at rest. Victoria Railways' R class consisted of some 70 locomotives built by the North British Locomotive Company, Glasgow in 1951 – No 707 was the company's 27,000th engine. These 5ft 3in 4-6-4s came late in the day and were handicapped by a simultaneous delivery of diesels. No 707 was restored in the 1980s by a team led by a pair of Victoria Railways drivers and now runs regularly at the head of tourist trains. It is aptly named City of Melbourne. ALAN WILD

Above. Tasmanian streamliner. Over the water from Melbourne Tasmania's 3ft 6in gauge Emu Bay system in the north west of the island enjoyed a short passenger revival in the late 1950s/early 1960s using a new train called the West Coaster. *No 6* Murchison, *a Dubs 4-8-0 (there was a sister engine named* Heemskirk) *stands awaiting her turn of duty at Burnie in November 1960.* SIR PETER ALLEN

Right. The glory of Puffing Billy. A reproduction from one of the evocative posters of this magnificent 2ft 6in gauge line which once belonged to Victoria Railways, but now runs as a preserved tourist operation from Belgrave at the end of the electrified suburban line from Melbourne to Lakeside. This was Australia's pioneer preserved/tourist railway. PUFFING BILLY RAILWAY

federation settled on three 'standard' gauges between them, so that only two neighbouring states had compatible trackage. Victoria and South Australia shared Ireland's 5ft 3in (1600mm) gauge, whilst South Australia then got into a muddle on its own by having subsidiary 3ft 6in (1067mm) lines; this latter gauge is also used in Western Australia and in Queensland. The inconsistencies in gauges are slowly being ironed out by extending the tentacles of the New South Wales 4ft 8½in (1435mm) gauge to major cities, and since the 1960s there has been a through transcontinental route to replace the previous one which had three break-of-gauge points.

So, with the railway systems operated mainly by the states, steam power varied to a large degree, despite the fact that few Australians in the days before cheap and regular air-services saw much beyond their own back yards. The typical Australian railway scene has always been busy urban commuter routes, multiple tracked or a straggling single-line running from here to the remote horizon and beyond. Of all Australian railways the New South Wales system followed English precedents and practice most closely up until the 1920s, when the resemblance became less marked particularly when it came to heavy 4-8-2s and Garratts. Some of the older engines had truly classical lines. The Victoria locomotive fleet was a modern and up-to-date one with handsome machines reflecting individual character in a unified style which was perhaps somewhat reminiscent of Indian practice, whilst South Australia tended towards a more marked and severe American appearance in its locomotives, even if most of them were actually built in Great Britain. Queensland's 3ft 6in gauge railway had some thirty Garratts and other modern classes after the early 1950s. Western Australia tended to follow suit, though

this railway modernised its stock in the 1950s, including the V Class heavy freight engine of 1955. One could almost say that the last new steamers (ordered after a sad experience with the first batch of diesels) could be mistaken for branch line locomotives in South Africa. Not to be forgotten, but on a miniscule scale, is the 3ft 6in gauge system in Tasmania, a trackage which once had some semi-streamlined 4-8-0s and Garratts, now gone to their last rest.

Steam is long gone from regular service but, thanks to the determined enthusiasm of a large number of railway enthusiasts, both professional and amateur, not only are there regular main line steam operations using preserved historic and modern power, but also a number of very successful tourist lines. This has to be seen as a tremendous credit to a huge and comparatively unpopulated country where distances between centres are enormous making it difficult to keep up with day-to-day matters, and limiting operations to the city areas.

Right. New South Wales steam on shed. Two of the New South Wales Government Railway 4ft 8½in gauge class C38 Pacifics on the ready track at Enfield depot, Sydney. It is an autumn morning in 1967. No 3828 has brought in the Southern Highlands Express whilst No 3808 is booked for a freight to Moss Vale. R. K. EVANS

Below. Narrow gauge in the north. When Queensland built its railways, the authorities, (probably bearing in mind the sparse population), elected to build their railway system to the Cape gauge of 3ft 6in. In the later days of steam 4-8-0 No 862 is fired up at the Maiyne Road shed, Brisbane. The Queensland engines were always nicely kept, the express engines having green-painted boilers while the suburban engines were light blue. SIR PETER ALLEN

6
BYGONE BYWAYS

THEY called her the Slim Princess, the little narrow-gauge train which travelled the parched lands of the Owens Valley north of Los Angeles and in the foothills of the Very High Sierras. One hundred per cent steam until the autumn of 1954, ten-wheeled Baldwins worked the service day in day out – but then the diesel came. It was, as so often the case elsewhere, the beginning of the end. In any case the 3ft gauge, at least for common-carrier purposes, was well past the sunset of its days. The fact that this was the last such line in the whole of the USA became just a statistic and the little 4-6-0, with its circular tender tank and its silvered smokebox, kept as reserve power, a memory.

Like many a country line before it, the Baldwin-powered Slim Princess gave rise to folklore and anecdotes as the engines plied their smoky ways over the semi-desert land between Keeler and Laws (almost in the evening shadows of Mount Whitney, the highest point in the USA and with a station carrying its name).

The station at Laws, an 1880 structure worthy of becoming the setting for a TV thriller, had no electricity, kerosene lamps providing the light for any night work. Most of the rolling stock was of 1890s vintage: even the last surviving ten-wheeler, No 9 dating from 1909. Neither the old Carson and Colorado nor later the SP's management interfered with this distant outpost, and tales are told of how the passenger trains as well as freights would stand idle in the middle of nowhere whilst the crew including the engineer and firemen – and maybe a passenger or two if there were any – did a little hunting. Even in later times train crews were not averse to carrying a rifle in the caboose and taking a shot at a deer. Herds of elk (now preserved) roam the valley near the Tinemaha reservoir south of Laws and could often be seen from the train. One prize story tells of a bull elk taking a dislike to the conductor whilst the train was shunting at Aberdeen. The animal chased him for several car lengths before he climbed the ladder to the boxcar roof in record time. The railway was totally incorporated into local life. Indians were permitted to ride free in the freight cars (though forbidden to enter the passenger stock). Water barrels left along the tracks were refilled by the train crews without charge. Locomotive tenders were fitted with a spout and hand valve and the train's arrival at a station or halt was the signal for both Indians and the rest of the populace to help themselves. Looking at the deserted scene today it is almost impossible to imagine those halcyon days of the late 1920s.

The United States, so well known to Europeans as home to the great transcontinental trains, retained a great diversity of small railways over the years, most of them independent, using a very apt Americanism – they were 'short lines'. Many of these went into their decline in the

---

Delivering London Papers

The little carriages seemed to warm, and even to swell, as the London newspapers were loaded aboard them, and when *Yeo* backed on, the train was truly alive. Just now, there had simply been empty carriages, of ancient and diminutive sort. Now there was – *The Newspaper Train!* Yeo's crowned chimney soared proudly above her squat front end; her big round dome shone with polish lovingly bestowed. In the leading coach the first-class smoker, all magnificent with buttoned-in-leather, seemed to be awaiting a nabob or at least a magnate.

Alas, it went on waiting; we were still the only passengers as that strange little train leapt into motion, abruptly as a buck rabbit, and scuttled round the curve to the riverside. *Lew*, the new engine built for the Southern Railway in 1925, was outside the shed at Pilton. This, and the *Yeo* which had hauled the first train on May 10, 1898, were fated to haul the last one together, a few days hence (September 29, 1935).

Now we bucketed up the valley as normally and as noisily as if the train had another half-century ahead of it, the engine shouting her *aubade* to the rising sun, the

continued overleaf

The Slim Princess. Southern Pacific Baldwin ten wheeler No 18 takes a freight over Owens River Bridge on the 3ft 0in gauge Keeler-Laws branch near the end of its days in 1954. SOUTHERN PACIFIC RR

continued

carriages rolling merrily on their 1 ft. 11½in. gauge.

At each station, the London papers were dumped out. Who would carry them next week, and how much later would they be for some people? Who knew? At Bratton Fleming, where the station building crouched under a rock, we crossed the 7.3 out of Lynton, with *Exe* going bunker-first, immediately followed by a first-class observation car, likewise back-to-front. On we went, through the rock cutting and over the shoulder of Exmoor, with *Yeo* spurning her nine miles at 1 in 50 as if she would cross the Andes, given time.

All the engines were out except *Lyn*, the Baldwin 2-4-2 tank which was the last survivor of the American engines sent to the British Isles during the great locomotive shortage of the late 'nineties. We found her in the tiny erecting shop where she had first been assembled from her crated components, long ago in 1898. She was never in service again; they were to take her out and break her up with *Exe*, *Taw* and *Yeo*, the three Manning Wardle 2-6-2 tank engines of 1898. Only *Lew* survived, to go to a coffee plantation in Brazil, after working the Lynton & Barnstaple's demolition train. The planter said he would have bought the others had he known of them. – C. Hamilton Ellis

Brittany Survivor. No 31, one of the red Corpet Louvet built 0-6-0 tanks of the C de F des Cotes du Nord heads a mixed train over a very typical viaduct in the early 1950s. A short section of this once extensive metre gauge railway continued to operate out of St Brieuc after World War II. YVES BRONCARD

1930s but their lives were prolonged after the Japanese attack on Pearl Harbor and the ensuing demand for gasoline and rubber allowing steam to live on in a never-never land. Mixed trains continued to run behind wood burners and high-stepping ten-wheelers of considerable vintage whilst the narrow-gauge systems, especially those in Colorado, appeared with a new lease of life, though then these were more byways than the 3ft-gauge trunk routes selected by General William Jackson Palmer and his hard-headed pioneering engineers as being ideally suited to the limited finances at their disposal in the 1870s. Sadly, these one time rip roaring Colorado lines are now part of history though fortunately some sections are preserved as tourist attractions. As their night was falling during the 1950s we should be grateful that those wonderful days of steam were chronicled and recorded by such men as Lucius Beebe, Charles Clegg, Jim Shaugnessy and William D. Middleton among many others.

Europe was criss-crossed by narrow-gauge tracks though World War II took a great toll of those in France. Nevertheless many survived to await the onslaught of the road, some well into the 1960s. The French were always at their best with minor railways using Michelin railcars to stop the rot from becoming deadly and, like the County Donegal in Ireland, providing literally a railbus service, though steam in diverse forms – usually ancient tank engines – worked the freights. The French lines were on the whole better laid and much faster. So much so that a ride in a 'Michelin' often seemed like one in a stockcar race which the driver had in his pocket.

A few like the Côtes du Nord in Brittany crept back into temporary life after the fighting, even running weekend passenger excursions behind some delightful Corpet-Louvet 0-6-0 tanks in dark red livery. Others, exampled by the metre-gauge network of the Reseau Breton radiating from Carhaix like a five-pointed star, either became partly standard gauge or retired from the fray a decade and more later. This truly magnificent piece of railway used 4-6-0 tanks and 0-6-6-0 Mallet tanks for freight right to the end.

Spain had a remarkable series of lines using beautifully kept engines, impeccable Krauss 2-6-2 tanks on the Asturian Railways, ex-Algerian Pacifics on the La Robla Railway and Beyer Peacock 2-6-2 tanks on the Alcoy-Gandia. There was even something to be seen on the now tourist-trodden Ibiza (officially railwayless) where there were two lovely old 750mm-gauge German engines serving the saltpans. Portugal fared even better with some steam often in the form of 0-4-4-0 and 2-4-6-0 Mallet tanks or antediluvian 2-6-0 tanks from several builders, all with beautifully polished copper-capped chimneys, hard at work on the little railways running up the valleys off the Douro river. Italy too was alive with byways, the Val Gardina in the north twisting up into the foothills of the Alps from Chiusa to Plan – an almost perfect steam Kleinbahn using 0-6-0 tanks, the Calabrian lines and the almost decrepit Bari–Barletta tram which crossed the edge of the runway at the old airport much to the consternation of incoming aircrew who were not party to 'local rules'. The steam train was supposed to be halted by an Italian sentry specially stationed for the job but sometimes things went awry.

Yugoslavia (and indeed most of the Balkan countries) had its railways

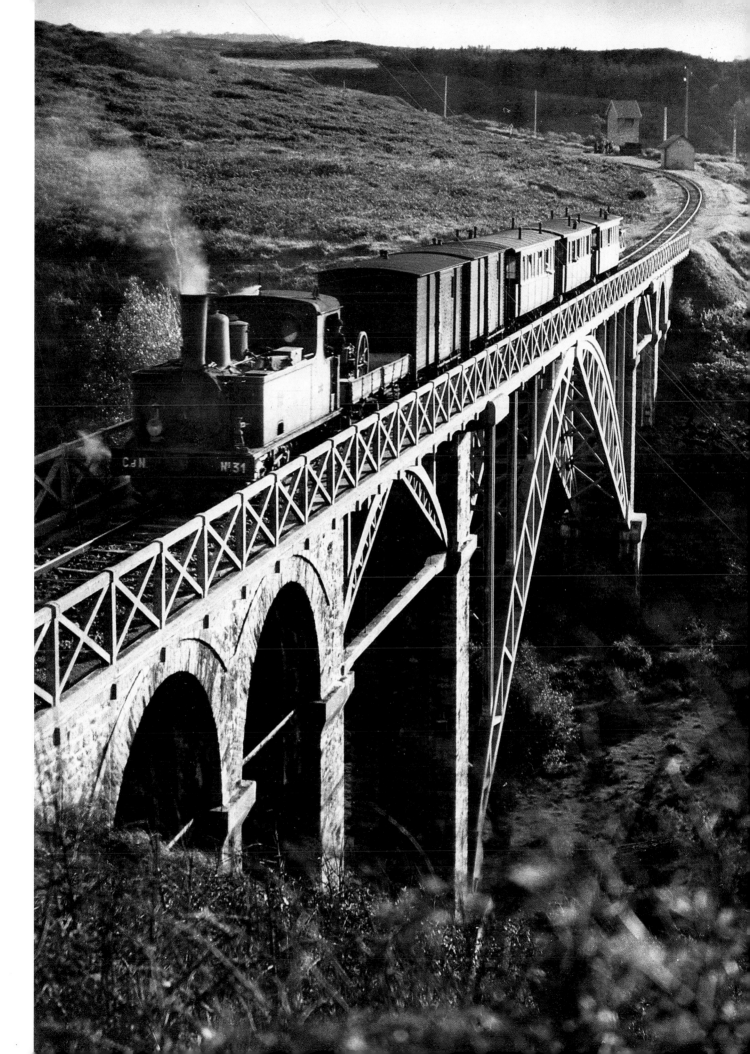

Paraguay

When the writer visited the Paraguayan capital of Asunción in 1980 the location of the railway was obvious. The loco shed had a cloud of smoke hanging over it, so he made for the hand-gate giving access to it. He was met, at navel height, by a sub-machine-gun, and was told that there was no entry to the shed for strangers. It is difficult to argue with a sub-machine-gun, but a visit to the 'Jefe de Ralaciones Publicos' transformed the situation, resulting in a conducted tour of the depot.

In steam was No 151, a 2-6-0 built by the Yorkshire Engine Co at Sheffield in 1953. It had a highly decorated smokebox door commemorating nationalisation of the railway in 1961. There was also a 2-6-0, No 81, which had been purchased from the Urquiza line of the Argentine Railways. No 226, a fine old 4-6-0 built by the North British Loco Co in 1912 was moving some wagons of timber. It still bore 'Ferrocarriles Argentinas' on its tender. The PRO said that, when they heard that the FA were withdrawing these 4-6-0s, they sent some wagons of timber to Argentina in exchange for them. – Frank Harrison

of character though the state railway's narrow-gauge system from Belgrade to Dubrovnik was very much a trunk line. Even so up near the Macedonian border at Lake Ochrid the prize length of all Balkan railways was surely the 2ft-gauge line from Gostavar using ex-German military railway 0-8-0 tanks, trains taking no less than sixteen hours to cover the hundred miles or so to Ochrid. The accommodation was in little dark coffin-like coaches with ventilators only in the end doors – a rather sick-making experience when packed in with the locals all smoking a particularly pungent brand of tobacco – and their livestock at the same time. But at least there were balconies, with open-ended platforms where on warm summer nights you could sit and watch the stars go by, and look towards the little engine as it threaded its winding way up into the steep Macedonian hills.

Not that Europe had a monopoly of such railways, they could be found on all five continents. Egypt for example had a busy network of 2ft 6in-gauge lines, almost a steam tramway system, which linked the small townships of the Nile delta using Sentinels and sturdy little Krauss 2-4-0 tanks. At the southern end of the continent South Africa, until recent times supported a network of 2ft-gauge railways in Natal, most of them using baby Garratts for their motive power. The Congo, Mozambique and Madagascar were also threaded with local railways built to open up the countryside for trade and commerce.

Even so one comes back to the United Kingdom and Ireland for some of the more delightful byways of comparatively recent times where but less than forty years ago Hunslet 2-6-0 tanks built in Victorian Leeds were needing the faculties of Kerry goats to haul their trains of decrepit cattle wagons over the legendary tracks of the dreadful Tralee & Dingle. This, almost the most westerly line in the whole of Europe, hung onto life until the summer of 1953 by just a single thread: the once-monthly cattle train running out of Dingle on the last Saturday of the month taking the animals from the sparse and rocky lands to the sweeter pastures further east for fattening. It was on one of these occasions that they lost a chimney on the double-headed empty stock train shortly before reaching the western terminus. Anxious, the men rang the foreman at Tralee for instructions.

Steam on the Pampas. Encarnation shed in Paraguay in November 1988 with a North British Locomotive Co 2-6-0 built in 1910 as Ferrocarril Presidente Carlos Antonio Lopez (ex Central del Paraguay) No 104. It has recently arrived with the weekly international train from the country's capital Ascuncion (one through coach) to Argentina. All the FPCAL locomotives are woodburners. P. B. WHITEHOUSE

Beyer Peacock in Spain. One of the
beautiful little 2-6-2 tanks belonging
to the British owned 34 mile long
Alcoy-Gandia Railway on the
east coast of Spain. No 2 (built in
1890) heads an up mixed train at
Beniares in May 1967.
J. M. JARVIS

Lake Ochrid train. An 0-8-0
Feldbahn tank engine No 99.4.032
built in Germany during World
War I climbs the grade near
Michova on the 600mm line from
Gostivar on 26 August 1959.
A. LUFT

'Go back and find it,' he said. So gingerly they set off over the grass-grown tracks and a mile or so on there it was; they threw it onto the bunker and set off back but it was now dark and in any case Dingle was home to one of the crew so that was that for the day.

Saturday proved to be a typical 'soft' Irish day with a mist coming in from the sea so they needed the two engines and in spite of No 2T having no chimney they set out; she seemed to steam remarkably well under the circumstances. Rumour has it that Tralee had to send out a lorry of sand for the slippery grades up in the Slieve Mish mountains but they made it back to base in good time for early morning mass on Sunday.

Perhaps though the epitaph for any lover of railway byways should come from words written by that great traveller of these fascinating lines – Bryan Morgan: 'As a man grows older his commitments grow greater: his time for sitting in hotel bars at midnight and working out all the permutations of map, timetable and the faith which suggests that there will be a bus service from the next remote railhead grows less. All the time too the Light railways of the world are closing: I was born too late.'

Enthusiasm For Steam

There is no single answer to the question 'What causes an enthusiasm for steam locomotives?' because it occurs in all walks of life. An apparently disproportionate number of clergymen have been affected, but also men in many other occupations and professions unconnected with the railway. Last but not least are the hordes of railwaymen who spend hours of their own time studying what is effectively an aspect of their work.

The writer's first recollection of the subject was at about the age of five when he wondered why, every time his father and uncle met, they seemed to get involved in an argument. By the age of six he had realised that it was caused by the fact that father was an ex-Great Central driver and uncle an ex-Great Northern. From father he learnt that GN 'W' 4-4-0s were weak-kneed things, and that GN Atlantics could never start a train out of the curved Platform 7 at Lincoln without slipping all over the place. From uncle he gathered that GC engines, in general, were 'firemen-killers', and that they easily set fields of corn on fire. There was also a lot of argument about partly open regulators and 40 per cent cutoff as opposed to wide open regulators and 15 per cent, although this did not convey much at the age of six. Father did, however, have a low opinion of King's Cross driver Sparshatt, who was always in the news for high-speed or long-distance runs, because he was 'GN'.

At a very early age came the first footplate ride. Home was near the ex-Great Central Lincoln–Grimsby line, and banking engines were frequently sent to Monks Abbey signalbox to bank High Dyke–Frodingham iron-ore trains up to Reepham. On occasions father was on this work, and the writer can recall being lifted over the sleeper fence to ride up the bank on ex-GE J69 0-6-0T No 7377. A few years later came the opportunity, on Saturdays when school was closed, to ride on the C12 4-4-2T working the little branch train between Woodhall Junction and Horncastle. Father's instructions were that it was OK at the Junction and Horncastle, because the stationmasters there were 'all right', but to hide behind the cab side-sheets at Woodhall Spa because he did not trust the b----- there. 'What the eyes don't see the heart can't grieve over.' The Woodhall Junction SM's uniform was a bit confusing to a youngster, as it often included plus-fours. All became clear when he was seen disappearing towards Woodhall Spa with a golf bag over his shoulder.

Eventually the question come: What was one going to do with life. A silly question because the answer was obviously 'Same as you'. Without hesitation came the retort 'You're b----- well not. You're going to be a b---- clurk.' And so it came to pass! In due course came employment as a junior clerk on the LNER at Bardney, on the Lincoln–Boston line. Once every sixteen weeks came the great opportunity, when father worked the train which fitted late shift at Bardney, to ride on the engine from Lincoln. What a shame that line has gone. All the way from Lincoln to the bridge over the River Witham at Bardney it wound along on a bank above the river on one side and a canal on the other. Between Five Mile House and Bardney was the very sharp Longwood

Curve. One of the porters at the former station used to delight in announcing, on the arrival of a train, 'Five Mile No House'. All now gone the way of many lines. And once part of the East Coast main line at that.

Then came the War and five years away from the LNER but, before going overseas came several opportunities to ride with father. On one occasion he was on the 'Control Dido', an engine and one coach used, at shift change times, to take the Control staff from Lincoln to the wartime emergency Control Office at Blankney. It was expedient to keep out of sight at Blankney, so that the chief controller would not start asking questions why the engine needed an RAF guard. It was easy to be unobtrusive at night because the engine was blacked-out and had a tarpaulin on top between the engine and tender, to avoid the attentions of the Luftwaffe. It was the last ride with his father who died while the writer was serving in Italy.

After the war came the LNE traffic apprentices examination, followed by a three year course in all the traffic departments. Included in this was a period of three months in the district motive power superintendent's office at Doncaster. One month was spent on the footplate. This was not work but a pleasure worth paying for.

The first trip was on B1 4-6-0 61124 on a triangular trip Doncaster–York–Hull–Doncaster. Approaching Kipling Cotes the vacuum gauge started to drop. On went the large ejector without effect, and we started coming to a halt. With a painted look on his face the driver said 'Well b----- me. Thirty years without the cord being pulled and it happens on your first day.'

No particular trips were laid down by the powers-that-be. The laws which applied to drivers were ignored. There was no question of the eight-hour day, or twelve

hours rest between jobs and, if he had been paid mileage, he could have retired at the end of the period. It was a question of sampling as many LNER classes as possible, on everything from slow freights to fast expresses. One trip, on K2 2-6-0 61777 from Doncaster Decoy to Ardsley gave a jaundiced view of the class. The engine was so rough it was tiring to stand on it. It was a relief to have a minute or two on the front of the tender. And the noise! Put a guitar to it and it could have been top-of-the-pops!

All the classes of Pacific were sampled. A4 60028 Walter K. Whigham was like a Pullman Car compared with the K2, even when the former was going at twice the speed of the latter. Many impressions remain of this period. For example looking out of the side of A1 60125 Scottish Union at high speed, on a winter evening between King's Cross and Grantham, with the rain and smoke beating down, trying to see the oil lamp in a semaphore. The hard graft of firing Austerity 2-8-0 90270 on a train of coal from Doncaster to New England via Boston and stopping for water at, of all places, Bardney, and going through the three-mile long Wood-head Tunnel, full of smoke, on B1 61365.

After many different posts on the railway the writer found himself in industrial relations. On many occasions the men's representatives would try to pull the wool over management's eyes. Thus a Scottish union official had a party piece about the Lickey Incline being nothing. On the Glasgow & South-Western they had to put bankers on light engines. Argue seriously and your respect was instantly lost. Yet one recalls all the hours spent in mutual improvement classes when firemen and drivers discussed, in their own time and without pay, the complications of steam engine working and of Rules and Regulations. In what other industry could that be found?

Man against the Elements

In the struggle to keep boiler tubes clean in service, the super-heater flues always presented the worst problems, due to the obstruction of the element tubes and their clamping bands. If steam or compressed air lancing would not shift the fused ash buildup ('birdsnesting') the elements had to come out.

Some would pull out with no great difficulty. If not, the next method to try – if the smokebox was accessible – was to pull them with a wire rope attached to another engine. If *that* did not work (and some were so blocked that the vertical downcomer pipes would pull out straight before the element itself would budge) then you were in for a rough time, belting them out from the fire-box end.

Squatting on top of the brick arch, with whatever light was available, you inserted a long steel bar ('dolly') down the flue to the spear end of the element and spent an hour or more with a four pound lump hammer or a short-handled seven pound sledge trying to move it. There was no other option; it *had* to come. If you still had a passion for steam after a day of that, you could really say you were hooked! – A. J. Powell

ATHI river lies east of Nairobi (5,600ft high on a plateau) and is the last water stop on the three-hundred-and-fifty-mile climb from the coast at Mombasa, the ocean terminus of the legendary *Uganda Mail.* In the loop is a long freight headed by the finest Garratt design ever built, an East African Railways 59 class 4-8-2+2-8-4 glorious in its deep red livery but somewhat disfigured in appearance by a recently fitted Giesl ejector. The cab fittings are glittering, the footplate spotless and the driver a turbanned Sikh sporting a clean white shirt.

The 59 class engines date back from the later days of British colonial rule, 1954 and were designed for both passenger and freight work; they are the railway's most prestigious motive power and carry the name of East African mountains, this one is No 5904 *Mount Elgon*; she is not only the biggest Garratt on the metre gauge but also one of the most up-to-date members of her type. All the latest and best features of steam practice have been incorporated, four sets of Walschaerts valve gear, oil firing, air brakes and a big fat boiler allowing continuous hard steaming for fourteen or fifteen hours at a stretch, all uphill on a ruling gradient of 1 in 65 (1.5 per cent). For nearly twenty years the 59s have been queens of the system but by 1973 the advent of the diesel has begun to make an impact and their work is now restricted to the heavy freights.

After ten minutes at the column water begins to overspill the great front tank on the articulated locomotive and the fireman, a native Kenyan, pulls hard at the control valve to stem the flood. No 5904 simmers in the afternoon sun and waits for the eastbound train to come down over the single line headed by a member of the earlier 57 class 4-8-2+2-8-4 Garratts, one of the few left in service. Another ten minutes and tablets are exchanged, the stationmaster gives the Sikh driver the

East African giant. In June 1969 metre gauge Garratt No 5904 Mount Elgon *pauses to take water at Athi River on the then East African Railways system now Kenya Railways. This is the last water stop prior to the long climb up to Nairobi partly alongside the game park.*
P. B. WHITEHOUSE

'right away' and he takes off the brakes. With the regulator opened the observer on the footplate feels a shudder as the great Garratt steels herself for the climb ahead and then they are on the move taking the grade as easily as a duck to water, the beats from front and back engines coming in and out of synchronisation as the train gets underway. Round the curve and up along the edge of the escarpment they go with glimpses of the paved road running parallel on the right and the eastern border of the Nairobi Game Park on the left; giraffe and gazelle ignore the sound of the hard-working engine as the long snake of a train climbs up towards the Kenya capital.

In those early years after the close of World War II steam was barely challenged in Africa, and the Garratts were riding high not only in Kenya but also in South Africa, Mozambique, the Rhodesias (now Zambia and Zimbabwe) and Angola where they burnt not only oil but also eucalyptus logs from plantations economically grown alongside the tracks. To ride on an Angolan woodburner on a clear star-twinkling West African night with the wood ash sparks drifting in a great firework display over the train only to die out before they reached the ground was something never to be forgotten. Other powerful Garratts included the South African Railways class GMAM and the Rhodesian 20th class 4-8-2+2-8-4s. Beyer Peacock's works in Manchester, England, excelled themselves with the deliveries of the GMAMs, for the contract stipulated that the engines should be delivered in seven months, this was done with a month to spare. Garratts were (and still are) ideal for African railways

South African Garratt. A GMAM class 4-8-2+2-8-4 takes its train up over the Montagu Pass between George and Outshoorn in June 1971. This section of the 'Garden Route' from Capetown to Port Elizabeth was then steam operated from Worcester onwards.
P. B. WHITEHOUSE

with their relatively small construction budgets, tight curves twisting round the contours of the hills, comparatively light track and often steep gradients. At first glance one would have thought that the same would apply to South America but the mountainous Andean railways never really took to them or to any other flexible engines.

Over the years various types of articulated locomotives have been constructed to allow the number of coupled axles to be increased without too long a wheelbase and the Garratt has proved to be one of the most acceptable. Its system allows for two sets of cylinders and motion mounted in power bogies and supplied with steam from a single large boiler resting on cradles supported by them. Fuel supplies are carried over the bogie at the cab end and water in tanks over both. The Garratt's great asset is its availability on lines where a high tractive effort is required over routes laid with light rail and tight curvature. They are still in use in some numbers in Zimbabwe both as 4-6-4+4-6-4s for passenger work and 4-8-2s+4-8-2s or 2-8-2s+2-8-2s for main- and branch-line freight.

A class of thirty-three Garratts with the 2-6-0+0-6-2 wheel arrangement was built for the LMS in Great Britain for working heavy coal trains between the marshalling yards at Toton in Nottinghamshire and Brent on the north-eastern outskirts of London. The motive here was to eliminate the use of two engines and crews on loads up to 1,400 tons. Unfortunately the LMS authorities insisted that the axleboxes should be similar to those on the ubiquitous class 4 0-6-0s, opposing the more liberal bearings which Beyer Peacock wished to offer with a result that these tended to overheat: not a popular occurrence with the operating people on a heavily trafficked piece of railway.

Even in the 1920s and 1930s eight coupled wheels sufficed for the heaviest freight duties in British operating conditions. A unique specimen of this wheel arrangement was the 2-8-0+0-8-2 Garratt No 2395 built for the LNER in 1924 for banking trains on the Worsborough incline between the marshalling yard at Wath-on-Dearne and the Sheffield–Manchester main line of the former Great Central Railway at Penistone. This was the most powerful locomotive ever built for British use. It consisted of two three-cylinder 2-8-0 steam engines supplied from a single boiler of 7ft diameter. The coupled wheels were 4ft 8in in diameter and the weight in working order 174 tons. Worsborough Bank was seven miles long, with two miles at 1 in 40. Before the Garratt came on the scene two banking locomotives had been necessary with a train of over 1,000 tons.

An earlier system of articulation was patented by the French engineer Anatole Mallet in 1885. The patent described a locomotive with one pair of cylinders acting on fixed axles at the rear, and the other pair driving the axles of a leading swivelling truck pivoted at the front of the fixed frame. Mallet had been a pioneer of compounding and his first locomotive combining this with articulation was an 0-4-4-0 using high-pressure cylinders on the main frame and low-pressure on the swivelling truck. Purists have maintained that the true Mallet is always a compound and that the giants built in later years with his articulation system but simple propulsion should not be so described, but they have been overwhelmed by popular usage. Several classes of pure Mallet still exist

Steam on the Express
Until the mid 1960s there were two nightly steam trains from Auckland to Wellington and vice-versa along the North Island Main Trunk line of New Zealand. The *Night Limited* was faster, left later and had better carriages and more sleeping cars. Its shabbier *alter ego* the *Express* had mostly second-class sitting cars with worn, shiny red leather seats. It also stopped much more frequently.

Late autumn, 1965, the diminutive red carriages stretch along Auckland's main platform towards a long, low Class Ja 4-8-2 that is to haul the *Express* to Hamilton's Frankton Junction. Steam gently oozes from under the carriages, a reminder that train-heating problems are still preventing the use of diesels on long-distance services – and low night temperatures make heating essential in all seasons.

The all-black Ja pulls away smartly at 3.40pm, and rattles past docks and sidings, the steam shed housing more long, low eight-coupled steam engines. The last suburbs are marked by a brief stop at Papakura and then (with only three more stops on to Frankton) the sudden steep climbs make the engine breathless. But there are exhilarating downhill swoops at up to 60mph – seeming much faster because of the low centre of gravity.

Evening descends. Time to reflect on fellow passengers on the shiny red leather seats. In this car-owning democracy with frequent air services the railway relies on an odd selection: a handful of students returning to Wellington and South Island universities, casual workers, a few elderly, genteel poor unable to afford a car and a
continued opposite

in preservation and possibly one or two are still at work occasionally on the metre-gauge lines running up from the Douro Valley in Portugal.

The first US Mallet was not an ordinary service locomotive but an 0-6-6-0 built for banking and heavy shunting work on the Baltimore & Ohio Railroad by Alco and put into use in 1904. It was a compound, and many of this type of Mallet were built in the following years but converted to simple working later. From 1924, when the Chesapeake & Ohio ordered twenty four-cylinder simple 2-8-8-2 Mallets this type of propulsion increased in popularity. On its appearance, the B&O 0-6-6-0 Mallet was 'the world's largest locomotive', but was soon outstripped. From then onwards, however, a Mallet of some type always held this distinction.

A few Mallets were built specifically for passenger work. The Atchison Topeka & Santa Fe put two 4-4-6-2 compounds with 6ft 1in driving wheels into service in 1909 but they proved unstable at speed and were converted into 4-6-2s. In 1932 the Baltimore & Ohio experimented with two simple propulsion 2-6-6-2s with 5ft 10in wheels in express passenger service. A more significant step in Mallet development occurred in 1936 with the advent of the Union Pacific's 4-6-6-4 simple expansion type. These engines were appropriately called 'Challengers'. The mid 1930s were the age of the versatile steam locomotive. Except for the specialist high-speed passenger work, mixed-traffic designs clearly had economic advantages and did excellent work. The leading four-wheel bogie of the UP 'Challengers' gave good stability at up to 80mph and while the class

New Zealand's glory. Double headed Ka class 4-8-4s Nos 933 and 958 take a Wellington to Auckland express over the coastal plain near Waikanae, thirty miles north of Wellington on 13 September 1955.
DEREK CROSS

continued
Maori prisoner handcuffed to a slightly embarrassed young constable. As the carriages whip around the curves they slide from side to side, but (the lights too dim to make reading enjoyable) doze off until the rattle of side chains and the shuddering snatch of the centre coupling tells that Frankton Junction is near. Through the misted windows, the blur of lights, drifting steam and the throb of diesel engines are New Zealand's largest marshalling yards. - Richard Joby

East German Mallet. One of the few genuine Mallets still at work in the world. No 99.502.4 is an 0-4-4-0 compound tank used on the metre gauge line out of Gernrode in the Harz Mountains of Saxony.
P. B. WHITEHOUSE

Beyond the Khyber Pass

I had reached Quetta by way of the Khyber Pass and its fabled Landi Kotal/Peshawar line and, there being no space within the train, had ensconced myself a-stride the front left-hand buffer of a Sheffield-built steam locomotive of the same vintage as myself. With me on my buffer was a grinning Pakistani and another couple of them rode the opposite one; the resulting journey down the pass being, for me, a high spot of my train-travelling life. The subsequent Nushki Extension progression might be described as a low-spot but not by me.

Between Dalbandin and Nok Kundi, a distance of 104 miles, the region is wholly without habit-ation, virtually devoid of veget-ation and is a positive hell upon earth. The line crosses long stret-ches of *dasht* covered with sharp black stones broken only by pat-ches of coarse sand. For eight months of the year the heat is intense and the '120-day wind', lashes the sand so that it flies up to lacerate the skin. The whole desert is coated with sulphur dust, and water, when it is obtainable, is a concentrated mixture of com-mon and Epsom salts. When there is any rain the year's fall may occur within an hour. The river beds, bone dry for ninety-nine out of a hundred days, then hurl this water, laced with quantities of stone, at the exposed railway. To overcome this obstacle the engineers built Irish bridges or 'dips' and the driver of trains using them was expected to utilise his discretion as to whether he could get through without the water putting out his boiler fire.

At Nushki I had taken to the
continued overleaf

as a whole was intended for fast freight work the last six engines of the forty built were ordered specifically for passenger service. On the main line between Salt Lake City, Las Vegas and Los Angeles they ran regularly at 70mph on heavy passenger trains, often of twenty coaches.

The coupled wheel diameter of the 'Challengers' was 5ft 9in. A redesigned pivot between the main frame and the leading engine unit transmitted a load of several tons from the rear unit to the front, reducing the tendency to slip and helping the locomotive to exert usefully the high tractive effort of 97,400lb. To give some idea of its size the overall length of the locomotive and the fourteen-wheeled tender of the later builds was 121ft 11in. Some other lines used Mallets for passenger work but the Union Pacific was the most consistent operator on passenger trains.

The demands of mounting traffic in World War II led to the building of 'Challengers' being resumed in 1942 but by that time an even larger locomotive was on Union Pacific rails. Between Cheyenne and Ogden on the transcontinental line the railway climbed with a ruling grade of 1 in 65 for thirty-one miles to Sherman summit at an altitude of 8,013ft in the Laramie Mountains. Eastbound trains leaving Ogden faced some sixty miles of adverse gradients, much of it at 1 in 88, and heavy going through the mountains for all the 176 miles to Green River. The Union Pacific planned to work trains of 3,600 tons over these sections and in 1940 approached Alco for a still more powerful locomotive. The outcome was the 4000 class 4-8-8-4 better known as the 'Big Boys', supposedly from an inscription chalked on the smokebox of one of the first locomotives before it left the works. Every kind of dimensional and statistical record has been claimed for the 'Big Boys' although in fact some North American Mallets exceeded them in grate area, tractive effort and adhesive weight. No other locomotive, however, challenged their overall length (engine and tender) of 132ft 10in and total weight of 539.7 tons. The first of the class was delivered to Omaha in early September 1941, only a year after the order was placed.

Basically the 'Big Boys' were an enlargement of the 'Challengers' but there was much refinement of engineering detail. A distinction from other Mallets which exceeded them statistically in some respects were that these were built for heavy, slow freight trains whereas the 'Big Boys' were express locomotives designed for speeds up to 80mph. At 5ft 8in, the diameter of the coupled wheels was only 1in less than in the 'Challengers'. An admirer has written: 'It is no exaggeration to say that the "Big Boys" occupied the same place in the world of steam locomotives as does Beethoven's Ninth Symphony in the world of music: a supreme concept whose awesome size was skilfully blended with beauty in a manner never likely to be equalled or surpassed in today's plastic age.'*

Sadly the 'Big Boys' were built against the background of advancing diesel power in North America. Mass production of diesel electric locomotives which could be ordered 'off the shelf' had been begun by the Electro-Motive Division of General Motors in the USA in 1939.

Although in the USA by the late 1930s the Pennsylvania's electrifi-cation had reached Washington and as far west on the main line to Chicago as Harrisburg, the darkening international scene was likely to

*Durrant, A. E. *The Mallet Locomotive*, David & Charles 1974.

continued
locomotive, an American oil-burner of 1930 vintage, as a possibly more comfortable situation than the over-crowded coaches. The crew had no objection to my presence and, though the roaring boiler added to the heat, I could, by sticking my head out of the cab, catch the pitiful remnants of a breeze while a continous supply of oily sweet tea served to lubricate my shrivelled frame.

The train crawled at near walking pace which was just as well for the track was badly worn. It was I who saw the bent rail ahead and, following my shout, we slammed on the brakes to drift gently up to it. The offending rail had expanded with heat and, for reasons known only to railwaymen, failed to contract.–Christopher Portway

defer extensions for some time. The Pennsylvania had long been faithful to Pacifics, but in seeking more power for its top-rank passenger trains it consulted with the locomotive builders and finally accepted the recommendation of the Baldwin Locomotive Works of a 'Duplex' type. The Duplex was a rigid frame locomotive with two sets of driving wheels, each with its own pair of cylinders. The first Pennsylvania Duplex was a 6-4-4-6 and was the largest rigid frame locomotive ever built. Overall length of the engine and its sixteen-wheel double-bogie tender was 140ft 2½in. The combined length of the firebox, boiler barrel and smokebox was 62ft 4in which was the reason for the three axle bogies at front and rear. This monster went on show at the New York World Fair in 1939 and later worked passenger trains between Chicago and Crestline (286 miles) being debarred by its weight of 473.2 tons and long rigid wheelbase of 26ft 6in from the main line east of that point. Later Pennsylvania Duplex locomotives for passenger work were 4-4-4-4s weighing 432.7 tons and measuring 122ft 10in overall. These could work over the whole 713 miles between Chicago and Harrisburg and often achieved 100mph with trains weighing 910 tons. They were difficult to maintain, however, and the lower piston thrusts and other advantages claimed for the Duplex construction were outweighed by the drawbacks. These locomotives and a 4-4-6-4 freight Duplex proved a costly and unrewarding experiment in the last years of Pennsylvania steam.

Reference has been made elsewhere to the Texas Pacific's 2-10-4 locomotive waking the echoes in the Lone Star State as early as 1926. Matters were quite different in Great Britain, with its much tighter loading gauge inherited from the world's very first railway development. In the 1920s Britain had only one representative of the ten-coupled wheel arrangement, the 0-10-0 built by the Midland Railway in 1919 for banking trains over the two miles of 1 in 37 where the main line from Bristol to Birmingham attacked the Lickey Hills. An earlier experiment with the ten-coupled engine had been built by the Great Eastern Railway in 1902 – an 80 ton 0-10-0 nicknamed the *Decapod*. It had been designed in response to pressure to electrify the suburban services out of Liverpool Street, the intention being to show that steam could equal the performance of electric units. During its trials the locomotive is reported to have accelerated a train of about 250 tons from standstill to 30mph in slightly better than the 30sec claimed for the electrics. This was apparently convincing, for a Bill for electrification of the suburban lines was defeated in Parliament much to everyone's surprise. The *Decapod*, however, was too heavy for general use and ended its days converted into an eight-coupled freight locomotive.

At this period six-coupled locomotives seemed unchallenged for the fastest and heaviest passenger trains on the British main lines but in 1934 H. N. (later Sir Nigel) Gresley sprang a surprise with the 2-8-2 wheel arrangement in his locomotive No 2001 *Cock O' The North*. More power was needed for hauling heavier trains between Edinburgh and Aberdeen on the East Coast Main Line. Gresley's famous Pacifics were restricted to 480 tons northbound and 420 southbound, but the night trains now included third-class as well as first-class sleeping cars and could weigh

Left. Power personified. One of the famous Allegheny 2-6-6-4 four cylinder simple locomotives en route from Limeville, Kentucky to the Great Lakes port of Toledo, Ohio on the Chesapeake and Ohio Railway. No 1627 has 160 70ft coal wagons behind her tender – a tonnage equal to that hauled by the TI 2-10-4s, 42,000. A heavy train indeed. MILLBROOK HOUSE COLLECTION

Cock O' The North. One of Britain's largest passenger locomotives. Built for the LNER and designed by Gresley this 2-8-2 No 2001 was put into use on the Edinburgh to Aberdeen services in 1934. A three cylinder engine, it was capable of taking well over 500 tons with ease over the hilly and twisting road. No 2001 is seen in the late 1930s, leaving the Mound Tunnel, Edinburgh with an express for Aberdeen.
P. RANSOME WALLIS/NRM

A mighty American. Union Pacific 4-6-6-4 Challenger No 3985 restored to working order once again and in steam at Sacramento May 1981. This engine is regularly in use for steam railtours out of Cheyenne.
K. P. LAWRENCE

well over 500 tons. No 2001 was a three-cylinder engine, and as Gresley was satisfied from his experience with the K3 class 2-6-0s and as the use of a bogie would have made the locomotive too long for the 70ft turntables it was given a single leading axle. The trailing axle was carried in Cartazzi axleboxes as standard on the Pacifics.

The dimensions of *Cock O' The North* were impressive. Overall length of engine and tender was 73ft 8½in. Coupled wheel diameter was 6ft 2in and the coupled wheelbase 19ft 6in. A tendency in the British popular press to hail this locomotive as a world beater in every respect and the only express passenger 2-8-2 was frowned upon by a respected technical journal of the day which scoured its archives to discover some four-cylinder compound express locomotives of the Saxon State Railways built about 1910, and more recently, in 1924, an Italian State Railways 2-8-2 class used on heavy, fast passenger trains between Rome and Florence. (It forgot what might be happening in the USA and Canada!)

Not long after *Cock O' The North* appeared, a 4-8-0 locomotive of the PO-Midi Railway in France embodying André Chapelon's principles impressed British observers by making 'an epic journey' from Calais to Paris with a load of 646 tons on the *Golden Arrow* Pullman boat train. The 103.1 miles from Calais Maritime to Amiens were run in 85 minutes 32 seconds and the further 80.2 miles to La Chapelle in 70 minutes 25 seconds. A well known writer on locomotive practice wrote at the time: 'The exceptionally free exhaust passages from the cylinders to the atmosphere are responsible largely for the free running of this eight-coupled design, which makes for a close approach to the ideal of an express engine, capable of the highest speed in conjunction with extraordinarily rapid acceleration.' On this occasion the usual speed limit on the French railways was waived and the train reached 90.7mph on the descent at 1 in 200 from Survilliers.

Chapelon was a man of analytical mind. After World War I he joined the PLM Railway as a probationer, but did not hesitate to criticise some of the driving methods he observed and had the satisfaction of being told by his instructor that all his criticisms were well founded. He was later appointed to the research and development department of the Paris–Orleans Railway and it was here that his rebuilding of an unsatisfactory Pacific locomotive produced the improvements that established his reputation. Later rebuilds of PO Pacifics as 4-8-0s attracted widespread interest in France, and after the formation of the French National Railways in 1938 locomotives built to Chapelon designs were widely used on the system. The 4-8-0s were Chapelon's favourites and have been described as probably the most brilliant steam locomotives ever built.

The climax of Chapelon's work on passenger locomotives came in 1946 with the three-cylinder compound 4-8-4 No 242.A1, a characteristic Chapelon transformation of an unsatisfactory original. There is an echo of the *Decapod* here, for when the locomotive was demonstrated to a South American delegation in 1952 it was scheduled to equal the times of the fastest electric trains between Paris and Le Mans (131.1 miles). In fact the time was cut by 6 minutes in spite of a 10 minute stop at Chartres to take water and a load of 810 tons compared with the limit

Classic Chapelon. SNCF 4-8-2 No 241 AI on display after withdrawal outside the French Railway Museum at Mulhouse.
MILLBROOK HOUSE COLLECTION

of 640 tons for the section.

Most enthusiasts today however remember the magnificent class 241P 4-8-2 evolving from the PLM design of 1930. This was really a stopgap construction in 1946 arising from the decision of the SNCF to pursue a policy of mainline electrification but a strong case was made for a limited number of large express passenger engines particularly for the old PLM route to Marseilles. Even though the design was a compromise, the 241P was a fine engine and by 1949 thirty-five of the class were built. They enjoyed an almost normal lifespan for this type of twenty years. To ride behind one out of Nevers to Clermont Ferrand in the Central Massif was a tremendous thrill. The engines were often driven to their limits, as they were also on the Brittany route from Le Mans where train loadings could reach 950 tons in high season. Four of these fine machines have been preserved including 241P16, which is one of the principal exhibits in the French National Railway Museum at Mulhouse.

One of the last steam engine classes to be built in any numbers and a true giant for the 3ft 6in 'Cape Gauge' used throughout Southern Africa is the South African Railways class 25. Some members of the class were originally constructed as condensing engines for use over the parched section of the Cape Town to Johannesburg route through the Karoo Desert, these massive machines were turned out by both Henschel in Germany and North British in Scotland. The last big non-articulated power to be built for the area and after conversion to non-condensers (25NC), they are still at work today albeit recently only on heavy freights or relief passenger trains. In their condensing days the tender wheelbase was actually 7ft 10in longer than the engine. Their final base for operation has been Beaconsfield shed, Kimberley, for work on the main line south to De Aar and east to Bloemfontein. Most have been allocated to regular crews who lovingly care for them. The cab's brasswork is so clean that it almost dazzles. In some cases the class 25 NCs carry names individually bestowed by their crews.

Last and today by no means least are the simple QJ class 2-10-2s built

Not Believed

When on 14 September 1891, engineer Charles Hogan of the New York Central & Hudson River Railroad drove a special, carrying road executives and newspaper-men from New York to East Buffalo at an average speed of 61.44 miles an hour, allowing for stops, frock-coated business men stopped their hansoms in Fifth Avenue to buy the extras telling of the fastest long-distance haul ever made on a railroad. *The Sun* devoted three front page columns to the event and Mr Hogan never expected to get so much flattering attention again. In May 1893, however, at the throttle of Engine 999, he drove the *Empire State Express* between Syracuse and Buffalo over a measured mile at a speed of 112.5 miles an hour and the whole world gasped and there were those who wouldn't believe a word of it. Gentlemen in the Holland House bar shook their heads, incredulous, when the ticker brought the news and when next year, No 999 was placed on view at the Columbian Exposition, a guide-book to the fair remarked that 'for this locomotive such impossible rates of speed have been claimed as a mile in 32 seconds'. Since that time faster runs have become commonplace but the luster of the fame of engineer Hogan and No 999 is secure forever as part of the American legend. – Lucius Beebe in High Iron, 1938.

[The locomotive is preserved at the Chicago Museum of Science and Industry.]

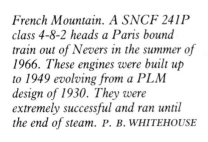

French Mountain. A SNCF 241P class 4-8-2 heads a Paris bound train out of Nevers in the summer of 1966. These engines were built up to 1949 evolving from a PLM design of 1930. They were extremely successful and ran until the end of steam. P. B. WHITEHOUSE

in the Datong works of the People's Republic of China and still under construction at the end of 1988 though this is said to be the final year. These are one of the last three steam engine classes to be built in the world, all of them Chinese. Well over four-thousand QJs are at work, most of them in the north but found all over the whole of the country. The design dates from the early days of 'Liberation' when Sino-Russian friendship was still in evidence and a decision was made to set up the works at Datong on the Mongolian border. This led to the construction of the class with the aim of replacing many of the ageing locomotives once belonging to the railway companies of the 1930s and to assist with the huge expansion of the Chinese railway system then being planned. Construction began in earnest in 1962. Because of the huge deposits of coal readily available, this is the standard Chinese fuel for all steam engines and the QJ is no exception. Because the grate area is 73sq ft,

American record breaker. In May 1893 engine No 999 headed the Empire State Express and allegedly attained 112.5mph over a measured mile between Syracuse and Buffalo. This record run is not regarded as 'official' world wide.
MILLBROOK HOUSE COLLECTION

117

A South African triumph. One of the Cape Gauge (3ft 6in) class 25 4-8-4s of South Africa Railways (built by Henschel in Germany and North British in Scotland) at the head of a heavy freight at Modder River en route to Kimberley in March 1977. Some of these engines carried unofficial names probably presented by their regular crews.
P. B. WHITEHOUSE

China's last mainline steam design. The QJ class 2-10-2 can be found at work over most of the country on both passenger and freight duties. Built at Datong works up to the end of 1988 (the final year of Chinese steam manufacture for mainline duties) these ubiquitous engines must be among the few classes likely to see service in the twenty-first century. New QJs are seen here outside Bautouxi depot near to Bautou West station.
CHINA RAILWAY PUBLISHING HOUSE

the class is fitted with an automatic stoker; this is not always used if a fuel saving bonus earning crew has charge. The QJ has an overall length of 86ft 2in with a 20 ton axle load enabling it to travel over virtually any main or cross-country route. They are modern engines in the extreme even providing cooking facilities and a toilet for the crew of three men, driver, assistant driver and fireman. China is dieselising and electrifying fast, especially in the hilly west but ongoing steam is far from out of keeping with any modernisation programme; vast supplies of cheap fuel and equally cheap labour see to that. So the QJ is almost certainly one of the few steam engine classes destined for use in the twenty-first century.

In Pre-Grouping Days

York was a place where passengers changed trains and trains changed engines. The North Eastern Railway, the Great Northern and the Great Central ran green locomotives into York. The Midland engines were red, the Great Eastern blue and the Lancashire & Yorkshire black. North Eastern and Great Eastern trains had Westinghouse air-brakes, the other companies used the vacuum brake. Some vehicles, eg those working from King's Cross to Newcastle, had both types of brake; they were 'dual fitted'. There was thus plenty of variety at York before the railway 'grouping' of 1923 began to reduce it.

Here comes a train from London to Edinburgh with a Great Northern 'large Atlantic' (No 251 of this class is in the National Railway Museum at York) rolling slowly to a stand at the north end of No 9 platform. The fireman drops off, brings from the front of the engine one of the headlamps, places it on the rear of the tender, and slides down between the edge of the platform and the buffers to reach the coupling.

In the meantime the driver has had a mighty struggle to pull the reversing lever from 'forward gear' to 'backward gear'. He has to hold the lever with both hands and get it back a few inches at a time with heaves of his body.

When the fireman has disconnected the pipes between the tender and the train and has placed the exposed ends of the brake pipes on their dummies he shouts 'Ease up!' whereupon the driver opens the regulator and the engine moves backwards compressing the buffer springs against the train which is held fast by its fully applied vacuum brakes. The driver snaps on the brakes on engine and tender to hold them with the coupling slack so that the fireman can lift it off unless he has been quick enough to do so while the tender was coming back at him.

He returns to the cab, noting that the starting signal is 'off', calls 'right away' to the driver who struggles to push the reversing lever into forward gear, takes off the

Pacifics at York.
Right. The great curve and the magnificent arched roof show off A4 No 4498 Sir Nigel Gresley *at its best.* HUGH BALLANTYNE

Far Right. Sir Nigel Gresley's A3 Pacific No 60087 Blenheim *alongside a water column.* ERIC TREACY

brakes, opens the regulator fairly wide and the engine runs smartly ahead clear of the points through which the relieving engine will come in order to back onto the train. Here she is, a resplendent Class Z 3-cylinder North Eastern 'Atlantic' with brass-rimmed chimney, brass-edged driving wheel splashers and plenty of brass fittings in the side-windowed cab. She rolls slowly up to the train, the driver leaning out of the cab to see where to stop and just before the buffers touch, he snaps on the engine's Westinghouse brake with a fierce hiss of air from the valve in the cab.

The engine may have stopped with the buffer springs so compressed that the fireman can lift the coupling onto its hook, but this does not always happen. If not this fireman too calls 'Ease up!' whereupon the driver takes off the brake, opens the regulator to give another squeeze and the fireman lifts the coupling on.

A Class Z can work either vacuum brakes or Westinghouse brakes on the train and the fireman connects the right pipes for what they are going to do. He shouts 'Blow up' and the driver turns on the ejector for vacuum brakes or moves his Westinghouse brake-valve to the 'release' position whereupon the steam-worked pump begins pumping air with a 'snort snort snort' about 200 times a minute. The driver sets the engine in full forward

gear by turning a small handle whereupon steam pressure does the hard work. Sumptuous engines these! A gauge in the cab tells the driver when the appropriate vacuum or pressure has been created in the train-pipe. At the far end of the train the guard checks the brake situation by a gauge in the brake-van. The fireman has moved a lamp from the back of the tender to the front of the engine.

Presently the starting bell rings (a York speciality), the fireman looks at the starting signal and calls 'right away'. The driver opens the regulator gently, ready to shut it again quick, if the driving wheels should slip, and the engine moves slowly forward. He does not hurry her, for if impatience causes a slip, it loses more time than it could possibly have gained.

In World War II when engines had got into bad condition and regulators could be very stiff and jerky, the LNER 'Pacifics' gave daily displays of frightful slipping in trying to get away from York. The wheel rims would fly round with sparks coming from the rails, and a roaring column of steam, smoke and white-hot cinders would erupt from the chimney. It was magnificent for the beholder but it was hell for everything else and when better times came after the war it became once more a rare spectacle. Compared with pre-grouping conditions, the engines themselves were grim rather than gorgeous.

8
DELIVERING THE GOODS

IMAGINE the heyday of world steam in the 1920s and in particular the tremendous loads hauled over the tracks of the North American railroads. Let us go back to 1926: the traffic is really rolling with little or no competition from the roads and both locomotives and trains are huge.

Texas is a part of the world where we have been conditioned to expect action on a heroic scale and the railway is living up to it. Train No 67 on the Texas and Pacific Railroad is a long freight made up of sixty-eight cars weighing 2,490 tons and is being remarshalled at Baird to increase the load to ninety-nine and, with a 1 in 57 gradient ahead, even the giant 2-10-4 needs a banker to get away; with a wide open throttle it takes a full minute for the train to move at all.

At Abeline another car is added and the weight behind the engine's drawbar is 3,600 tons; the train is so long that the observer who has left his bag in the rear caboose takes three-quarters of an hour to collect it and return to the locomotive.

They move off again with the exhaust reaching 50ft up into the night sky as the 2-10-4 demolishes the next twenty-eight miles in 56 minutes reaching a speed of 47mph on level stretches. Though the engine is coal burning the cab is spotless, for there is an automatic stoker in use. Driver and fireman are wearing immaculate white gloves. The gradient steepens again for the last five miles before the summit at Sweetwater and the speed is now down to 5½mph; on the last 1 in 90, the engine begins to slip. Time for immediate action: the fireman, armed with a shovel, deftly swings himself down onto the trackside, runs a few paces forward and shovels ballast under the main drivers. The engine gets its footing and they triumphantly pass the summit.

The pattern of long trains for North American freight continues to this day, albeit using containers on flat wagons headed by a series of intercoupled throbbing diesels. As of old it is the freight which keeps the railroads alive; today the long-distance passenger train is a rare animal, almost an anachronism (certainly often an operating nuisance over heavily used sections) in the New World.

In Europe it has always been different. The shorter distances between big towns encourage fast regular intercity trains as well as heavy commuter services which compete well with road or air. The image projected by today's operators concentrates the mind on pre-packed sandwiches and drinks in buffet cars, aeroplane-type food and services in restaurant cars (where they exist at all). Freight is not everything, and on many routes – especially in Britain – is now often limited to container trains and block coal trains running at relatively high speeds – well averaging, say, 45mph on a good day. No more country sidings, few

Gruesome Steam
When a steam brake failed and the loose-coupled British mineral train behind ran out of control into another freight, the steam crane came to the rescue – and that often meant gruesome work.

After such a crash at Chapel-en-le-Frith in 1957, because the guard of the standing freight was missing, every wagon was lifted off an horrendous pile in case he might be trapped below. Gingerly they went until they rerailed the tender of the offending engine. Still nobody underneath, but with a few more puffs the crane lifted the engine – and there was the unfortunate guard, trapped against the platform wall. He must have died instantly, swept there when the runaway slammed into his van.

marshalling yards; in some countries even the newspaper proprietors rely totally on road and air for their deliveries.

In a sense this is full circle, for though the earliest of all lines were specifically for the carriage of coal, the proprietors of some of the old trunk routes thought mainly in terms of passengers. When the great London & North Western Railway of England was first asked to carry coal from the Midland Railway, it was only approved on the condition that the wagons were sheeted over to hide their loads. One high ranking manager declared: 'Coal, coal! They will be asking us to carry dung next!' But in most of the world during most of railway history, it is freight that has brought in most of the revenue: freight from the mines, the factories and the countryside, freight for exports, and imports, and freight for the military. And in steam days the amount of coal that the railways carried for themselves was prodigious. In 1937 Great Britain alone used over a million wagons (roughly one for every forty-five people) to carry 286,617,000 tons of goods and 9,103,000 head of live-stock in trains varying from 100 tons in weight to 1,000 tons capacity and journeying 140,109,000 miles. The railways in those days could not pick

Overleaf. Junction between railways. A Great Western Railway Hall class 4-6-0 approaches Banbury with an express parcels train in 1946, two years before Nationalisation. To the right is the LNER line (ex Great Central) from Banbury to Woodford and north to Nottingham and Sheffield. This was an important traffic exchange yard. It is now closed.
P. B. WHITEHOUSE

European freight. A West German class 50 2-10-0 heads a northbound goods at Troisdorf on 29 September 1954. The pattern here is closer to that in Great Britain than North America, shorter, lighter and more frequent trains. G. JEFFERSON

and choose for by an 1854 Act of Parliament they were 'common carriers', having to accept any load offered to them at set published rates – anything from a packet of pins to a ship's rudder. Nothing could have been a better incentive to the setting up of rival road concerns.

To try to equal the competition and for mundane freight work the railways needed two vital things; quick overnight transits plus simple, strong and reliable engines. The engines came in large numbers: shunters, trip-working classes, long-distance small-wheeled types to move the coal and larger-wheeled ones to take the 'next day' delivery services. The express freights were the first to drop the ancient usage of grease-filled axleboxes, their higher speeds demanding vehicles running with oil lubrication, screw couplings and passenger-standard brakes, ran at average speeds approaching 45mph. By 1937 Britain had nearly seven hundred of them running round the clock, handled by big mixed-class traffic or even express passenger engines.

There was an atmosphere of romance about these fast freights, such as the 7.45pm from London's Camden to Liverpool's Edge Hill which covered the 191 miles at an average speed of 38.97mph. Watching one of the night flyers, as they were called, dash through a wayside station was quite something. First came the thrill of identifying the engine class: was it one of Stanier's new three-cylinder Jubilees, or perhaps a Black 5 mixed traffic 4-6-0, or even maybe a reboilered North Western Claughton still painted red and carrying a nameplate, *Vindictive* perhaps or *Sir Charles Cust*, two headlamps winking from the smokebox front and buffer beam. The bulky shape of the engine and the glare of the

Fast freight. An unusual picture of an express passenger locomotive in use on freight duties. To combat road competition in the 1930s the British 'Big Four' railway companies introduced city to city express freight services running at average speeds of up to 40mph. This example of a Birmingham to London fitted freight is headed by a composite 4-4-0 No 1099 – a class regularly used at the period on the two hour express services.
MILLBROOK HOUSE COLLECTION

firebox door were followed quickly by the long line of vans and sheeted wagons, mysterious in themselves, clattering over the 60ft rail lengths, to be brought up in the rear by a swinging goods brake van with its side and tail lamps. As the dust settled and the clatter grew less the final sight was that of an inverted triangle formed by these flickering lights, the signalman's assurance that the passing train was complete.

Some freights began their journeys at busy junctions where once competing railways exchanged their traffic and where there was nearly always a locomotive shed of special interest to the enthusiast with 'foreign' engines being serviced for their return trips alongside those of the host railway. Take Banbury. Here the Great Western accepted trains from the LNER's old Great Central line, long-distance passengers and freights. The freight traffic was very heavy necessitating large exchange marshalling yards to the north of the station. Days watching the trains being made up and dispatched were a joy to be savoured. The variety of power was not that great for the GWR was a very standardised railway but even so it was there, 28XX class 2-8-0s for the long hauls, some mixed in with the ex-ROD 2-8-0s surplus from the War Department and similar to their sisters coming in off the GC section, large 72XX 2-8-2 tanks worked the ironstone trains and for the faster fitted freights a Hall class 4-6-0 which, if its load was within limits, would not need to

Mixed traffic and freight engines. Shrewsbury locomotive shed in 1964 with three classes of locomotives available for freight duties. Left to right are BR standard Britannia class 4-6-0 No 70005 John Milton *(with its name removed), ex Great Western Railway Hall class 4-6-0 No 4959* Purley Hall *and World War II Austerity 2-8-0 No 90010.*
P. B. WHITEHOUSE

127

*Opposite. Southern fast freight.
H.15 class 4-6-0 No 30522 (one of
the King Arthur boiler batch) on an
up express fitted freight on 15
September 1951. The engine carries
the headcode for Southampton to
Andover via Eastleigh.*
P. M. ALEXANDER

*Soft fruit special en route to Covent
Garden Market. Ex Great Western
Railway Hall class mixed traffic 4-
6-0 No 5998* Trevor Hall *coupled
to a new straight sided tender nears
the summit of Hemerdon bank east
of Plymouth with a load of cattle
wagons full of strawberries on a
summer's day during the early
1950s.* M. W. EARLEY/NATIONAL
RAILWAY MUSEUM

stop at Warwick for a banker up the 1 in 100 to Hatton.

Look at a late evening scene as a Hall backs onto its train, already made up by the yard shunter. The guard has put his equipment in his long-wheelbase van with its home yard 'Banbury' painted in smart white letters on the exterior wood boarding, and checked that his stove is drawing well. He climbs down onto the ballast, walking slowly towards the head end of the train noting which vehicles have to come off at Birmingham's Bordesley Junction for the LMS and which go on through Snow Hill station to Hockley yard by a 'trip' freight. At the same time he checks that all the handbrake levers are in the 'off' position, all loads secure and that the fastenings of the wagon sheets and doors are properly made. It is a cold night so the goods guard accepts a cheery invitation from the loco crew to 'come up and have a warm' as he exchanges notes with the driver on their load and running times. They have twenty-nine on for 334 tons and it should be first stop Leamington Spa. After a few words of banter the guard gets down to the opposite side of the track and makes his way back to the van glancing at the wagons as he goes; he climbs up, and looks at his watch. Half a minute to go and the yard signal is at green; as the minute hand of the guard's company watch

comes up to departure time he keeps his eyes on the yard inspector who gives a wave of his hand.

Looking back from the engine, the fireman sees a green light showing from the swinging lamp at the rear of the train; they are ready to go. He calls 'right away mate' to the driver, takes off the tender handbrake and picks up his shovel. The driver's hand comes off the ejector handle and moves to the whistle chain and a poop tells the signalman he can send 'train entering section' to the box ahead. A steady hand grips the polished regulator handle moving it to the first valve and the wheels begin to turn, cylinder cocks open; they close as the Hall moves slowly past the observer, the staccato blast making flickers of light through the firehole door casting weird shadows over the footplate and onto the billowing steam beginning to pennant overhead. The wagons pass by slowly, creaking and bumping as they cross the points, each pair of axles beating more rapidly over the rail joints as the train gathers speed. Last comes the brake van with its little stove chimney smoking cheerily, the guard leaning out and watching progress as they move onto the main line. He gives a wave to the 'bobby' and flashes a light to the driver to indicate all is well. In a few moments all that is left is a low rumble, disappearing twinkling red lights and overhead steam, flushed pink and orange from the firelight flickering out of the engine's cab.

Fast freights were mainly the perishables, fish from Mallaig, Aberdeen and Grimsby, frozen meat from Liverpool, milk from the West, Cheshire and Midland counties, fruit, vegetables and other farming produce from the West including the famous broccoli specials from

British Garratt. One of the ex LMS 2-6-0 + 0-6-2 Garratts built for the Toton to Brent coal trains on one of these duties. Note the ex Midland Railway signals still in use and the train almost wholly comprised of privately owned colliery wagons.
MILLBROOK HOUSE COLLECTION

Last days of steam. Ex LMS railway Stanier design 2-8-0 class 8F No 48077 takes a freight through Garstang, Lancashire in June 1977 the year prior to the abolition of steam on BR's standard gauge tracks. COLOUR RAIL/B. MAGILTON

Cornwall to London. Some idea of the importance of these trains is evidenced by the regular use of express passenger locomotives. Aberdeen to London, on both the LMS and the LNER, could produce Pacifics on their thirteen-hour runs. The 9.45am Scottish meat special from Aberdeen to Broad Street carried its cargo in a then new form: containers, their contents on sale at Smithfield market early next morning. It was far from unusual to see Jubilees or Patriots on the 4.55pm from Alexandra Docks, Liverpool, engines stationed at Edge Hill shed coming onto the train once it had climbed up the heavy gradients through the choking tunnels behind a brace of ex-LNWR 0-6-2 coal tanks. Wagons of frozen meat from the Argentine came separately from Canada Dock. With stops at Rugby and Willesden the journey was completed in just over seven hours.

Once most of the fruit went to town in 'chips' or baskets in specially ventilated fruit vans. Strawberries were carried in vans chilled by ice in bunkers under the roof. All this was profitable traffic needing to be kept on the move and careful handling. The GWR even named an engine (No 3353, one of the double-framed Bulldog class 4-4-0s) *Pershore Plum*. The Southern Railway too had fast freight traffic in abundance especially over its rails from the south and west; one of these was the 9.38pm from Exeter to Nine Elms known unofficially as the *Market* or the *Flyer*.

Although this traffic was the highlight of the freight scene the great coal-carrying routes from South Wales or the Yorkshire and Nottinghamshire coalfields were the real money spinners. So heavy did this

131

Rustic corner. A country freight scene at West Meon, Sussex on 17 September 1951. This general view shows the station layout and surroundings with ex LSWR L12 class 4-4-0 No 30434 on the daily pick up goods from Alton to Fareham via the Meon Valley branch. P. M. ALEXANDER

War Time

World War II, when Britain was in the front line, evokes many memories of heroic acts by enginemen driving through air raids and handling emergencies, risking their lives splitting trains partly on fire, often working with rundown machines fed bad fuel. But for many who were in their teens one item broadcast by the BBC stands out especially: the German plane that was brought down by the force of the explosion of the boilers of the locomotive it was bombing.

Mechanical Splendour

Few who have ever watched the valve gear and side rods of a steam locomotive in action could seriously argue that the Industrial Revolution created any more fascinating machine. The engine room of a steam ship is quite interesting, as is a dynamo or a highspeed printing press; but what action compares to the opposed motions of main rod and eccentric crank, or the combination lever chasing the crosshead back and forth along the crosshead guide?

Here is power one can see. Deceptively the locomotive bellows and complains as the throttle is eased out. It seems that those slender rods and slim spoked wheels could never move so ponderous a weight as the engine alone, to say nothing of the thousands of tons of passenger or freight cars behind. Slowly the wheels turn. They may slip a little, but presently traction grips the rails. Surely the frail main rod will snap under the great stress of more than 200 pounds per square inch of boiler pressure going to work. As usual, however, the engine operates perfectly, and within minutes she is playfully obeying the law of physics as she gathers mileage on the main. She may have baulked and been annoyed at starting, but now it may take two miles to stop her with the brakes on full emergency!

As the engine overcomes momentum and settles into her stride, little smoke is visible, for she is running at her designed efficiency speed. Now one can ponder the 'monkey motion' as the aggregation of links, levers, bars and rods dance everywhere across the huge drivers in orderly fashion. Now the incongruity of equating hundreds of tons of steel with scores of miles per hour slowly resolves itself, and one can only marvel at such a machine, beguilingly female in her prim delicacy, yet overwhelmingly powerful and rugged. – Zon Ziel

Metre gauge Mallet. The daily freight between St Agreve and Le Cheylard on the Reseau du Vivarais in July 1961. The engine is one of the line's SLM built 0-6-6-0 compound Mallet tanks based on St Agreve. When the snow was deep in winter these engines were used to haul the passenger services normally worked by railcars.
P. B. WHITEHOUSE

A Knight to the Rescue

In 1965, merry-go-round coal trains were a very new idea. Everybody accepted the principle, but the practical details still had to be worked out. In Scotland, for reasons which we need not go into here, it was necessary to carry out stopping tests from ½mph to simulate conditions under the loading bunker at Monktonhall colliery. These were done on the up through line at Dunbar, using a slow-speed-fitted Class 26 diesel and a train of 28 45-ton gross weight hopper wagons, the last three being empty to reproduce the worst situation in positioning the train for loading.

Of course the inevitable happened one afternoon. The Class 26 lost all traction power, dead. There was the train, stuck and blocking the main line. But over in the goods yard was a well-worn St Margarets V2 2-6-2, chimney towards Edinburgh, so it was commandeered to take diesel and train back to Millerhill Yard, 25 miles away.

continued overleaf

traffic become that special motive power was built to deal with it, first 0-6-0s then 2-8-0s and, on the LMS, 2-6-0+0-6-2 Garratts which plied the Midland route between Toton near Nottingham and Brent sorting sidings just north of London, raising the average speed from 18 to 21mph! Trains of ninety wagons weighing up to 1,400 tons were common, following each other closely like a giant conveyor belt bringing the coal to London and the South that would heat buildings, make electricity and gas and drive much other industrial steam power. By the mid 1930s, the LMS, LNER and GWR all made use of 2-8-0s as their main workhorses. The LNER introduced a couple of Gresley-designed Mikado 2-8-2s for its South Yorkshire traffic working southbound out of New England shed, Peterborough.

Branch lines too had their regular freights mostly in the form of 'pick up goods', a van load for here, two for there and a shunt at every station. For many years most stations on main line or branch had their goods shed or siding which were visited by the daily freight train which collected or detached wagons. The final destination of the 'pick up' goods was a large mainline yard where the wagons were sorted into long-distance freight trains. Many wagons in the old days were 'private owners', open 10 or 12 tonners which were the largest that could be handled under the majority of colliery screens. Most of this local traffic was worked by engines in the autumn of their years, many of them 0-6-0s once belonging to the old pre-grouping companies, Dean Goods for the Great Western, LNWR Cauliflowers and Midland 3Fs for the LMS, similarly ancient 0-6-0s came from the GN, GC and GE classes on the LNER with their equivalents on the Southern. In Scotland the LNER employed old D40 and D41 4-4-0s on the whisky trains on the Speyside branch. After World War II passenger trains were withdrawn on an increasing number of branch lines which stayed open often in a slowly decaying form for just the occasional freight. These services usually provided the last work for elderly engines. In the 1950s when attempts were made to introduce a modicum of standard steam classes on British Rail a light-axle-load 2-6-0 was built for use over the various branch lines; they were based on a similar type developed by the LMS Railway in its final years. This 'modernisation' came rather late in the day for by then the branch line was becoming an endangered species.

It was much the same over most of Europe and indeed most of the world – and on all gauges. France, however, followed a differing pattern from the 1930s, making extensive use of railcars for cross-country and branch-line passenger services. These could (and still do) rattle along at a brisk pace leaving steam and (later diesel) to deal with the daily freight. A glance at the *Indicateur Chaix*, that French timetable of all timetables, would give the impression that some of those branch trains ran as frequently as city buses, but that was only until one read the notes at the foot of the tables. For example the huge Vivarais network in the Massif would show footnotes numbering as many as A to R and little drawings of buses told the uninitiated when they would unexpectedly go by road. But they still kept the 0-6-6-0 Mallet compounds for the freight *and* where the winter service indicated a letter 'M' which read '*circule en cas d'Intempéries à la place du service*'. This meant to those in the know that when the snow lay more than half a metre deep the railcar

was taken off and a Mallet would come to the rescue; a not infrequent happening along the hilltops by Tence and Le Chambon where the line ran at an altitude of over 3,000ft.

Again, the North American story is different: with open countryside and few bridges, the loading gauge always far more generous than elsewhere, the trains with their central drawbar always heavier and less frequent than those of more populated Europe. Yet even in the US the short lines and narrow-gauge railways are remembered for their rugged individuality and folklore, their one or two locomotives achieving greater fame (and indeed rendering greater service to the community) than any human kind.

The last impact of the steam locomotive on freight working must, of course, be in China where the huge QJ 2-10-2s, sometimes double-headed, take 2-3,000 ton trains out of the busy hump yards laden with the same merchandise as those of Britain and America half a century ago: coal, livestock, minerals, timber, everything. It remains a rewarding sight.

The big steam sheds are commonplace in China while steam locomotive works still maintain and repair the engines and to be a mainline driver is still a privilege. Here is a last bastion and it is something to be seen and savoured before it is too late.

135

The climb to Shap Fell. The crack train on the LMR route from London (Euston) to Glasgow, the Royal Scot passes Strickland, between Penrith and Shap, headed by Stanier's Duchess class Pacific No 46240 City of Coventry *in British Railway's green, though somewhat grimy. The coaches are early BR red and cream.*
ERIC TREACY

continued

The steam engine could not work the air brake on the train, but the diesel still could, so the two drivers agreed between them a system of whistles and waves for brake control. The steam man asked what the load was, but the guard had only just arrived to relieve and did not know. So the officer in charge of the tests, tongue in cheek, was (to coin a phrase) economical with the truth and told him that he had 25 of coal and three empties, plus the engine In normal freight working this would have been a bit under 600 tons, so the driver accepted it without demur and prepared to depart.

He had quite a job getting the train on the move, and made terribly heavy weather of it. Even in the dips he did not manage to get up to 30, and on the hills . . . that V2 was being hammered unmercifully. The caravan finally reached Monktonhall Junction and turned off the main line, but on the rising, curving goods line to Millerhill Yard the V2 got steadily slower and finally expired. A Clayton diesel had to come to assist – and made nearly as much smoke doing it as the steam engine.

While they waited, the driver let it be known that *he'd* never had 28 wagons pull so hard. Had the air brakes been dragging? Only then was he told that he had just shifted about 1260 tons of train single-handed. – A. J. Powell

Steam In The Hills

As the traveller hands his ticket to the blue-uniformed attendant standing on the platform at Lanzhou (in north west China) and climbs up into the only soft class coach on the whole fourteen coach train, he reflects on recent sights and sounds reminiscent of Europe and North America forty years ago. Lanzhou is a city at the eastern end of the one time Silk Road, the route of Marco Polo and other western explorers and the road for caravans the centuries over. Now it is the railhead for the railway reaching out into the far western outposts of the Gobi Desert, beyond the Great Wall's end on to Urumqi and perhaps the Russian border.

What joy! You can hardly turn round without seeing or hearing a steam engine. Lanzhou is home to QJ class 2-10-2s, which take their trains over the mountains east to Zongwei, west to Xining en route perhaps to Lhasa and over that long desert line over the summit at Wu Wei and then on to Jiuquan, Jiayuguan and Yumen. Today the QJ holds the fort for steam and may well do so for another decade. The large steam locomotive repair factory, a huge steam depot and a turn round fuelling point just off the platform's end, bear witness to steam's currency. An almost unbelievable sight well into the closing years of the twentieth century.

It takes just over an hour for train No 171 (which has spent two days coming all the way from Shanghai) to reach Hekounan. This is the first water stop and here the pilot engine, another QJ, comes on for the steep climb over the mountains to Wu Wei three hours further on. This section is one of the last remaining double-headed turns for steam on express workings in China and therefore the world. It is certainly the last such working over mountainous terrain. As the traveller lies on the top bunk in his four-berth cabin, the sound of the two exhausts from the hard-working engine filters through the double glazed windows and he is tempted to get up (trying not to wake his snoring companions) and go out into the corridor to listen and look. Even though it is a bitterly cold early autumn night, the view is rewarding. The moon is out and looking ahead his eyes latch onto two glowing firebox doors lighting the cabs, the leading engine's headlamp and the cottonwool white smoke from

the chimneys as the train twists its way up the single line into the green mountains. Pure nostalgia, but tinged with sadness at the passing of an era.

Somehow there is little which can excite a steam enthusiast more than the spectacle of a steam engine tackling a steep gradient. Its exhaust shoots high into the air, the sound reverberates from the surrounding hillsides: here is the very essence of primeval power.

All over the world enthusiasts have flocked to watch the great trains climbing great grades: the *Royal Scot* climbing Shap Fell in Westmorland, the *Cornish Riviera Express* breasting the summit at Dainton among Devon's green Dartmoor foothills, the workings up the grades around Hof in West Germany at the end of steam on the West German State Railways.

In Britain perhaps the greatest fascination was watching trains crawling up that hill of hills, the 1 in 37.7 Lickey Incline, on the south western outskirts of Birmingham. The Lickey was always a problem for steam. It needed not only one but sometimes two or three bankers to ensure a safe arrival over the top at Blackwell summit. Summer Saturdays were the special days. The trains – heavily loaded, lengthy ones, were almost continuous. The observer could look down the slope – dead straight for nigh on three miles – watching for the puffs of white telling of the next toiling train about to set out from Bromsgrove. Steam could literally be seen a good five minutes before any sound could be heard,

En route to Lanzhou. Late in an October afternoon a QJ class 2-10-2 skirts the edge of the Gobi desert as it climbs up towards Lanzhou in the far west of China. The train has left Beijing at 1101 the previous day and has many miles of steam haulage yet. Engines will be changed at Lanzhou for the great climb up to Wu Wei. P. B. WHITEHOUSE

Opposite. East to west express. A Shanghai to Urumqi train leaves Lanzhou behind a QJ 2-10-2 in October 1987. A three-day journey each way it gives little respite for the train crews who virtually live on the job shift on shift. The engine will have come on at Lanzhou. P. B. WHITEHOUSE

139

though once you caught the sound it became steadily louder rising to a crescendo as the train engine went past, followed by a double crescendo as the banker came by.

You did not have to be a railway enthusiast to be moved by such a spectacle and sound, though for many tourists steam spelt access to the world's most dramatic mountain scenery rather than being an object in itself – and it has to be admitted the soot and the grit occasionally got in the way.

Take, for example, the Garden Route of South African Railways. The train climbed (and still does behind a throbbing diesel) the Montague Pass en route from Cape Town to Port Elizabeth, hauled by a Garratt which came on overnight at Worcester. Or again those great Canadian and American transcontinentals over the Rocky Mountains. Or, quite different, the last steam-worked rack railways in Switzerland. And never forget how narrow-gauge steam (with frequent reversals) conquered the Himalayan foothills in India. The diesel's throb and the electric's swish now mostly do the job, though in the Andes of South America the Guayaquil & Quito still uses steam on its 'Mixto' out of Bucay to Alausi. The clean electric train climbing up through the St Gottard or over the route of the *Glacier Express* still provides its moments of memory for tourists, but for steam enthusiasts the excitement has gone. It is like looking at a stage with a magnificent set but without the actors.

Steam on the rack rail was always special, with an often familiar snorting steam engine, its boiler slanted to keep the water level parallel to the mountain slope, and its low pressure cylinders used for regenerative braking on the steep descents. Even the Swiss Brienz-Rothorn Railway for a generation and more a solid bastion of steam has at last, if only in part, succumbed to dieselisation. Fortunately, a number of concerns have restored once-stuffed survivors to working order as part of the rising tide of steam tourism. (The Rigi, Pilatus and Monte Generoso in Switzerland are examples) but the everyday steam spectacle has largely gone. No longer do the Furka Oberalp's elegant 2-6-0 rack tanks raise echoes in the mountains or the wedge ploughs clear the snow at the foot of the Rhône Glacier. This latter steam spectacular was superseded as a deviation route was built allowing all-the-year-round operations.

Nor does the jungle of Sumatra echo to the regular sound of 3ft 6in-gauge Swiss, German and even 1960s-built Japanese rack tanks, some so modern as to be fitted with the flat ugly chimney of the Giesl ejector. Every now and again when the summit shed at Padang Panjang is stuck for parts, a survivor from the silent rows of dead engines comes to life, but you have to be very lucky to be there at the right time. Further south, in the Antipodes, another mountain line has also been silenced by the construction of a tunnelled bypass. New Zealand's north island hills no longer echo to the sound of H class 0-4-2 tanks climbing the 1 in 16 to 1 in 13 incline on the route from Wellington to the Wairarapa Plains, a bottleneck which caused terrible delays. These were Fell system locomotives with additional horizontal driving wheels bearing on a central third rail.

A few, very few hill lines, have remained totally faithful to steam. They include the world's first rack railway, the Mount Washington Cog in New Hampshire USA, the Nilgiri in South India and, until very recently, Great Britain's only example, the Snowdon Mountain Tramroad taking 4½ miles to climb the highest mountain in Wales and dating from 1896. All the Snowdon's steam locomotives were built in Switzerland, four dating back to its opening, the others in 1922–3. Originally there were five of these engines but No 2 *Ladas* had a very nasty run-away accident. This happened on 6 April 1896 when the train comprising the engine and two coaches were returning from the summit. *Ladas* suddenly mounted the rack rail, left the track and dived into a deep ravine. Fortunately the locomotive crew jumped to safety. Equally fortunately the coaches were not coupled to the engine (in accordance with Snowdon Mountain Railway Rules) and kept to the rails. The true reason for the accident was never resolved, though additional safeguards were introduced and since that time the railway has worked accident free. Stark and steep, this is a spectacular journey albeit a seasonal one – and then only when weather permits. In high summer several daily trains are still steam hauled since the new diesels are not numerous enough to work the whole service.

Opened as early as 1869, Sylvester Marsh's centenarian Mount Washington Cog climbs the wind-swept mountain at an average gradient of 1 in 4 and a maximum of 1 in 2½: a tremendous achievement for those early days. Its current fleet comprises eight 0-2-2-0s, all geared of course, similar in design to the first of the type which came from the Manchester Locomotive Works (later Alco) around 1875. The most recent was actually built locally under the auspices of the railway's own master mechanic as late as 1972, making it the first full sized steam locomotive to enter service in the USA new for almost twenty years. One of this railway's more remarkable achievements is that three out of the line's 3½ miles are built on low timber trestles.

The Brienz-Rothorn Railway, between Lucerne and Interlaken, is twenty-three years younger, not opening until 1892. Even then it was the first purely mountain rack railway in the Bernese Oberland, a vivid illustration of Sylvester Marsh's pioneering work. Four and a half miles long, the Rothorn line climbs 5,515ft with stretches at 1 in 4 (25 per cent). Steam has kept its place because the railway is partly shielded from the harsh reality of economics forcing electrification elsewhere due to Canton

Fell line. One of New Zealand's most notorious sections of railway lay on the route from Wellington, North Island, to the Wairarapa Plains. It is now bypassed by a tunnel thus avoiding the time consuming break up of trains which were laboriously heaved up the hillside by the H class 0-4-2 tanks specially built to grip the Fell third rail seen on the bottom left of the photograph. DEREK CROSS

and Federal Government sponsorship – though once it was a near thing with a move to replace the whole lot by a cable suspension line. Public outcry at this possible desecration went a long way to maintain the status quo. Offering some awe-inspiring views, the train slowly pushes its noisy way towards the summit where the panorama is even more breathtaking. The traveller who has the time for an overnight stop at the hotel Rothorn Kulm has the added privilege of a sunset and sunrise

Opposite. Patagonian steam in the hills. The 2ft 6in gauge General Roca section of Argentine railways still works regularly out of Esquel taking some fourteen hours to reach the junction with the main line from San Carlos de Bariloche to Buenos Aires at Ing Jacobacci. A Henschel 2–8–2 heads a morning train over the hills out of Esquel in December 1988. P. B. WHITEHOUSE

Swiss steam special. One of the Rhaetian Railways metre gauge 2-8-0s No 107, kept in reserve for the occasional excursion, heading into the mountains in October 1970. P. B. WHITEHOUSE

rarely equalled – and the glorious bonus of the sight of the little trains, smoke billowing from pushing engines making their way up the green mountainside as they come to collect him for his onward journey to Lucerne or Interlaken the next day.

It may sound strange that steam lasted so long in many mountainous regions of the world, particularly in such remote places as the Andes of South America, but careful thought will show that there are two distinct reasons: one economic, the other technical. On the economic front, electrification, which on the face of things seems a simple answer, cannot be justified unless the formidable capital investment in power distribution and traction requirements. This can only be covered by intensive use of the route, which is impossible in sparsely populated districts just being opened up. Apart from the initial high capital cost of diesels, they are not well suited to great heights. But the higher you go, the lower the boiling point of water and thus the lower the steam operating cost. The early unsupercharged diesel could hardly drag itself along, let alone heave a heavy train at altitudes reached by such lines as the Central of Peru where 12,000ft is far from being a summit. Today this technical difficulty has been overcome but the sight of black smoke pouring out of a General Motors diesel as it climbs up to the Galera tunnel (the summit of the line at 15,583ft and the watershed between Pacific and Atlantic Oceans) on the line from Lima to Huancayo shows that even today

The Midland route to Scotland. Ex LMS rebuilt Royal Scot class 4-6-0 No 46109 Royal Engineer *passing Ribblehead on the famous Settle-Carlisle route in the late 1950s.* ERIC TREACY

efficiency is not as high as could be hoped. But the lack of availability of spare parts and the need for costly boiler overhauls, coupled with improvements in diesel technology, have eventually turned the scales against steam.

Mention has already been made of the Guayaquil & Quito, and the narrow-gauge line out of Huancayo to Huancavilica. Various other South American operations were still on the boil a decade and less ago. Chile ran a superb country branch line up towards the Andean foothills at Lonquimay. The Argentines still keep their Baldwin and Henschel 2-8-2s alive in the 2ft 6in-gauge shed at El Maiten. And the tram engines (although this is now purely a tourist operation) are regularly in steam on the old inclines at Santos near São Paulo in Brazil.

serve the Hartz mountains in East Germany where the 99 class 0-4-4-0 Mallet tanks, over seventy years old, run out of Gernrode and over a 1980s-opened link of the metre-gauge Harzquerbahn-Selketalbahn. These ancients are not the only steam power on the East German narrow gauge; the most modern and numerous occupants are heavy squat boilered 2-10-2 tanks which work both passenger and freight trains. Sadly replacement diesels are now being built.

On the tourist routes steam has made a comeback over several hilly sections. Scotland has a regular service in summer in the BR-sponsored trains on the West Highland to Mallaig line. Another British mountain line, part of an old trunk route, has hung by a thread for many years: the Settle & Carlisle, built at great cost by the erstwhile Midland Railway to get its trains into Scotland. Like many other hilly lines, it has been expensive to maintain and although it does provide an alternative route if severe problems occur over the West Coast mainline, ordinary traffic is thin. So maintenance has been minimal and BR are seeking closure or a sale to a private buyer. Meantime it has provided a spectacular setting for many steam services, both BR's own and charter trains. *Flying Scotsman, Sir Nigel Gresley, City of Wells, Kolhapur, Green Arrow*, and countless others have given pleasure not only to thousands of enthusiasts, youngsters experiencing steam for the first time, and of course the locomotives' owners. If all the photographers lining the trackside, cars leapfrogging from point to point, had each given a quarter of the train fares to help keep the line open things would be different. It is one of the curiosities of the passion for steam that, enjoyable though being a passenger may be, you see and hear more watching from the trackside or in the case of this line even a distant Pennine vantage point.

As has been mentioned elsewhere in this book steam has also come back to the Rocky Mountains of Colorado, New Mexico, and to other USA short lines including one in West Virginia – the Cass Scenic Railroad which operates over a reconstructed logging line using Shay type geared locomotives and climbing 11 per cent grades including two switchbacks through the forests up to a summit appropriately named Bald Knob at an elevation of almost 5,000ft. An important tourist attraction, the Cass Scenic Railroad is run by the State of West Virginia.

One last memory of China where the bark of steam was heard as far south as the metre-gauge line built by the French out from Indo-China (Vietnam) to Kunming, the trains crossing trestle bridges, tropical jungles and steep ravines. Today modern diesels do the job ably (though even they need to be double headed on the steeper bits), but until 1987 two trains left Beijing (Peking) daily, bound for the Great Wall each carrying local tourists and each with a QJ 2-10-2 at the head end. After Nankou and up through the steeply graded pass to Qinlongqiao, where there is a reverse, another QJ was attached as banker and what a sight *that* was passing under the tunnel beyond the station with the Wall itself straddling the mountains, the landscape green in spring, brown in autumn and stark rock in winter.

Add to these the once daily journeys of the South African Railway's Garratts up through George, and over the Montague Pass down to Outshoorn, then with 19B and 19D 4-8-2s on to Port Elizabeth or over the Lootsberg Pass, and within recent years the world-travelling steam enthusiast has been kept more than busy.

Europe still has a little steam left in the mountains, with Crosti-boilered 2-8-0s at front and rear of ski trains into the lower Alpine ranges, and the Swiss Rätishe Bahn's metre-gauge 2-8-0s on regular excursions to and from Landquart, Davos and Chur. So keen are the commercially minded Swiss that a regular booklet entitled *Steam in Switzerland* is available from the Swiss tourist offices such as in London. Small dinosaurs still

Settle-Carlisle today. The National Railway Museum's restored Stanier Pacific No 46229 Duchess of Hamilton *takes the Cumbrian Mountain Express southbound over Ais Gill on 9 January 1984.*
HUGH BALLANTYNE

Wheel Arrangement Shorthand
In British and North American terminology, 4-6-2: first the leading wheels, 4 or a bogie, then the main driving wheels, 6 coupled together, finally the trailing pair or pony truck. So a simple 0-6-0 has no leading or after wheels, just the drivers, 3 on either side. Certain wheel arrangements including 4-6-2 'Pacific' have attracted names.

English language	European	Commonly – used name
0-2-2	A1	–
2-2-0	1A	–
2-2-2	1A1	–
4-2-0	2A	–
4-2-2	2A1	–
4-2-4	2A2	–
0-4-2	B1	–
2-4-0	1B	–
2-4-2	1B1	–
4-4-0	2B	American
4-4-2	2B1	Atlantic
4-4-4	2B2	
2-6-0	1C	Mogul
2-6-2	1C1	Prairie
2-6-4	1C2	
4-6-0	2C	
4-6-2	2C1	Pacific
46-4	2C2	Baltic
2-8-0	ID	Consolidation
2-8-2	1D1	Mikado
4-8-0	2D	
4-8-2	2D1	Mountain
4-8-4	2D2	
4-6-6-4	2CC2	Challenger
4-6-2 + 2-6-4	2C1 + 2C1	Garratt
4-8-2 + 2-8-4	2D1 + 1D2	Garratt Berkshire

9
DYING BUT NOT DEAD

Engine Driver's Life
The locomotive engine is the most beautiful mechanical construction of this or any other time. We watch it under steam from a distance, from meadows where in the sun the cattle graze, and it seems to fly as the swallows fly – skimming above the horizon, and presently we see its colossal form crossing the mighty arches which span the valley of the river. Hence it is that there are never wanting among us volunteers for the wild-like life of the rail. The boy intended by fond parents for quite a different career, dreams of the speed and the adventures of the road, and in his wakeful hours he strolls as far as the crossing-gate to talk with the the railway men.

The passion grows with his growth, strengthens with his strength. He leaves all thoughts of sea behind; he will neither be a sailor, nor a miller, nor a butcher. He has resolved to be a locomotive driver, and at last he finds his way, either by permission or by ruse, to the engine-shed doors, looking wonderingly at the big engines as they come in off the track, with their steely limbs covered with the dust of many a county. There he sees the steeds that make his eyes glisten again; engines that have struggled in the embraces of a gale; that have, on the iron highway, in thunder and in lightning, defied the elements and ridden through the storm safely home. Others there are, now over the pits, gentle as lambs, with limbs of burnished iron and cleating smoothly finished; these will soon be hitched on to their
continued opposite

LIKE the vanishing elephant of Africa the steam locomotive lives in a hostile habitat. Predators are everywhere, fed by the oil barons and appearing in various guises, highly organised truck operators, wildcat truck operators in the less developed regions like the Andes of South America and above all the diesel giants epitomised by General Motors and General Electric.

All this may well be progress for there is no doubt that the instantaneous availability of the diesel locomotive is a boon to any railway's operating department – if the machine is kept in good order. And thereby lies the rub, for to ensure reliability requires both skill and a ready access to hard currency for spare parts. Both are not always available in the Third World, so it is here that the dinosaurs of steam still lurk in dark corners on call to replace their handy but complicated successors stuck with maintenance problems. Yet these very steam engines have themselves been kept going largely by cannibalisation of their less fortunate brothers and sisters. The situation obviously worsens year by year. Add to this spasmodic injections of aid and the diesel salesman's patter and the result is obvious: those once proud steamers, now old crocks lying in ill-kept and semi-derelict sheds or repair works, cannot be relied upon to keep the traffic moving forever. Remember, too, that passenger services the world over have always been supported by revenue provided out of freight which today is increasingly grabbed by road operators. The slither towards the red makes any kind of survival tenuous in those countries whose rail systems have worked on a shoe string and where the greatest individualism survives.

Yet, surprisingly, the steam engine does survive not just in its hundreds but in its tens of thousands. There are three main centres, each in decline in its own way: Southern Africa, India (only recently this could be said of Pakistan but the diesel salesmen from General Electric, Henschel and Hitachi have been busy here of late) and China. Elsewhere there are pockets with one working engine here, a couple there, and, small sections of railway where steam is actually still supreme. Most of these pockets lie south of the Equator, though Europe has a few, most behind the Iron Curtain. Poland is still a relative (and the word is chosen carefully) stronghold as was East Germany until very recently; even now its fascinating narrow-gauge lines are very much alive – and really flourishing – with steam. To the west, Italy keeps a few steam engines in reserve, mostly 2-8-0s and 2-6-0s, some with modern Crosti boilers, and on the edge of Asia Turkey has for years been a steam enthusiasts' Mecca though today little can be guaranteed on a regular basis (indeed officially steam is dead). Of course, as with the world's wildlife, some steam engines have been saved to inhabit forms of industrial archaeological safari parks or run on special trains to earn tourist money, but that is another story which can come later.

The major subcontinent which uses steam on an occasional basis or in isolated areas is South America; this applies to almost every country except Venezuela and the Guayanas, though Chile has little if anything which is active regularly.

Though strictly Central America, Guatemala also possesses two or three live steamers but these are little used except in emergencies or for shunting purposes. This 3ft-gauge state-owned railway links the Atlantic and Pacific coasts, the division point being Guatemala City 5,000ft above sea level and a natural divide. Here outside the shed on radiating turntable roads lie a number of Baldwin 2-8-0s, officially stored, though 2-8-2 No 205 (BLW 73097/1947) is maintained in working order as are two others at Puerto Barrios (Nos 200 and 204 BLW 74130 and 74134 respectively, both Mikados of 1948) kept for the occasional shunting turn if no Canadian-built diesels are available. There is likely to be no improvement here for although spare water tenders are kept at strategic points the basic facilities are in poor order. Yet Guatemala is a fascinating country to visit with its heavily graded lines, spindly viaducts and volcanoes dominating the landscape. The last known regular steam workings were over the Zacapa to El Salvador and Zacapa to Puerto Barrios sections. Two 2-8-2s are in store at Zacapa and three dumped. But in the fashion of South American practice, one never knows: indeed only in 1987 a number of steam specials were chartered by a Britain-based group.

Quito, once home to the Incas and now the capital of Ecuador, lying exactly on the Equator, attracts the steam enthusiast's attention. Here is a 3ft 6in-gauge line (most of the slimmer railroads in the Andes are 3ft 0in or metre), the Ferrocarriles Equatorianos or the Guayaquil and Quito once but certainly not now nicknamed 'the good and the quick'. Today this is the sole Andean railroad regularly using steam, though now the ageing Baldwins rarely appear beyond the lower coastal section lying between Guayaquil and Bucay. Here there is a large shed containing mostly stored and dumped engines kept for possible use on the dieselised hill section to Sibambe and Riobamba. Unfortunately the tracks into the mountains are liable to severe washouts which often cut the line into isolated sectors and, with new adequate roads which are crowded with truck and bus traffic the future can scarcely be secure; and that is looking at things at their best. Nevertheless, steam often heads the daily Mixto out of Guayaquil and ventures into the Andes – a truly thrilling sight.

No 53 is a red-painted Baldwin-Lima-Hamilton Consolidation of 1953 and a Bucay engine. She stands at the head of three boxcars and a couple of red-painted wooden-bodied coaches packed to the rooftops with locals en route for the market at Alausi some 6,000ft up and thirty-five miles on. Conductor and train men wearing standard American-type railroad hats, but otherwise in casual wear, watch as a pig is hoisted up to a box-car roof. The driver is smart in a white shirt, for No 53 and her sisters are all oil burners. As the sun starts to show above the forest, and the equatorial mist begins to part, the cavalcade moves off, climbing all the way, 5,925ft in twenty-seven miles, towards the notorious Devil's Nose switchback at Sibambe. Huigra, seventy-two miles from Guayaquil, is

continued
cars, and in the darkness of the night will be rushing on in direct line, swiftly and heedlessly ahead, with the glare of the head-lamp reflecting on either side towards their destination.

The lad's heart feels that the shed is blissful Eden – the garden of Paradise. It is his *first* heaven.

The driver of an engine has dropped a handful of waste; he runs to pick it up, and hand it to the driver. He has for the first time spoken to one of *his* gods.

The bell rings for the workmen to go to dinner, leaving the running-men behind, with the running-shed superior. Watching his opportunity, he timorously approaches him, and touching his hat he asks the 'mighty god' if he wants a boy to help to clean engines.

The lad has the locomotive measles, and the 'god' sees it in the little fellow's eyes – for he has it badly, and so, to bring him into form again, he is told to come again the next day at six o'clock.
– The start of the chapter 'Engine-boy: Early Struggles' from the Victorian Classic *Engine Driver's Life*.

Andes Survivor. One of two once derelict Andes class 2-8-0s (built by Hunslet of Leeds for the Central of Peru) now mysteriously back in working order (but not really one hundred per cent well) takes a special train out of Huancayo in the late autumn of 1985.
P. B. WHITEHOUSE

Guatamala steam. A Baldwin 2-8-2 No 205 built in 1947 takes a special train over the steep grades leading to Guatamala City in 1987. This is one of the very few steamable locomotives left in this extensive Central American railway system. P. B. WHITEHOUSE

the first town and the second water stop. Here it is time to eat from stalls of steaming food tended by felt-hatted Indian women, piles of bananas fresh or cooked, succulent bowls of soup side by side with whole roast pigs.

The train moves on climbing and criss-crossing the roaring Chan Chan river which has carved its way through the gorges and has been the cause of so many of the railway's problems. Over wooden trestles it goes, the sleepers misshapen and the girders rusty. Ahead is the great Chan Chan canyon and the fantastic obstruction of rock called the Devil's Nose at Sibambe, junction for the Cuenca branch with its bus-bodied railcar. After a lengthy water stop No 53 makes a spirited start out of Sibambe and within a few minutes has reached the spur before the first reverse. No sooner has it stopped than the locomotive is put into full reverse gear, the brakeman pulls over the single switch (there are no point locks or signals here!) and with a wave of his hand he guides the train up the grade. The sharp bark of the Baldwin echoes across the mountains as the train backs up the sheer face of the cliff rising 1,000ft and more above Sibambe station, now looking like a model far below.

At the top of the zigzag there is a smart application of the air brake by the engineer and the train comes to an abrupt halt on a stub end of track carved into the vertiginous mountain which seems to reach up into the sky. Below, deep down miniscule tracks appear on either side of a narrow glacial valley through which an apparently innocent river glistens

Almost the end in Turkey. Until recent years a mecca for the steam enthusiast Turkey has now succumbed to the throb of the diesel engine. Today there may still be a few 'Kreigslok' German built 2-10-0s in service but a very very few. In happier times (11 April 1985) one of this class, No 56523 leaves Afyon with a train for Usak. In the background is 2-10-2 No 57007. HUGH BALLANTYNE

Crosti survivor. Italy is one of the European countries to maintain a desultory selection of steam in working order including the 741 class of 2-8-0 some of which are fitted with Crosti boilers. One member of the class No 741 104 stands at Catania station in Sicily. P. B. WHITEHOUSE

Promotion Prospects

After an engine-man has been on the goods service for a number of years, and has become well acquainted with engines of various kinds, he begins to look for promotion. This is regulated in many sheds in the order of seniority, but sometimes a bad history keeps a man back; for every time a man figures on the fine-sheet for an offence, it is registered in the *continued opposite*

as it flows amid a myriad of small rocks. To the left and on the opposite bank the single track of the Cuenca branch winds round the hills, on the right a newly aligned road bed disappears into the distance towards Huigra. The Johnson bar is pushed forward and the final reverse made, the train perching on a ledge of rock which winds into the distance as far as the eye can see. One hopes that the train orders are not duplicated (as has been known to happen) and imagines a diesel appearing from behind a distant rock necessitating a quick reverse back to the spur to avoid what is known in the USA as a 'cornfield meet'.

The atmosphere is still crystal clear but by mid afternoon, and the approach of the great Alausi loop, the clouds will begin to threaten, heralding the possibility of a storm as the train climbs up the ever steepening grade towards Alausi town and the end of today's journey. This loop, spectacular though it may be, is only one of many, for the climb from Sibambe to the summit at Palmira entails a rise of 4,701ft in twenty-two miles. To gain these heights the Baldwin Consolidation will have rounded the equivalent of forty-five closed circles, many of the curves of three chains radius. The section from Alausi to Riobamba is still cut, and although restoration is in hand it is a long and costly job which rail traffic revenue will never to able to repay. If politics dictate that the line must go then the last steam operation in the Andes will cease – a sobering thought when one looks back at the once great days of over half a century ago when traffic was so good that they purchased three 2-6-2+2-6-2 Garratts.

Even higher in the Andes, Huancayo is the terminus of what was once known as The Highest and The Hardest – the old Central of Peru. Thirty or so years back, it was home to the famous Andes class 2-8-0. Miraculously one of these warriors is still extant and in working order (there are two very dead ones at Juliaca on the old Southern's line from Cuzco en route to Lake Titicaca at Puno) at Huancayo's standard-gauge depot. Adjacent is a row of defunct 3ft 0in-gauge engines once used on the narrow-gauge line out across the mountains to Huancavlica now worked by Wickham railcars with the help of a couple of diesel locomotives recently moved in to replace the ageing steam power. There is still one active steam survivor brought out for Indian market specials or an emergency – Hunslet 2-8-0 No 107 built in 1936. Until recently there was one other steam working remaining in the Andes, in Bolivia where the shed at Guaqui, that country's Titicacan port, housed a number of workable metre-gauge engines including a 2-10-2 Baldwin (64619/1942) which performed a desultory shunt in connection with the arrival and departure of the SS *Ollanta* from Puno, a steamship of vintage years (which no longer, alas, carries passengers on a regular schedule) and made infrequent runs over the high plateau to El Alto, the junction for La Paz.

The rest of South America has much more to offer. Brazil, for example, is home to the metre-gauge Dona Teresa Cristina, a busy coal carrier with its headquarters at Tubarao and ex-Argentina 2-10-2s. One can count on 1,000 ton trains running on weekdays from the mines to the Atlantic port of Imbituba. The shed and works at Tubarao are modern with all major facilities and, if one is very lucky there is the possibility of seeing a creaking survivor of a Baldwin or Alco Texas (2-10-4) type in steam. And, in the far west near to the border with Bolivia, there are the still working remnants of the Madeira–Mamore or the 'Mad Mary' – once called the Railway of Death. Uruguay has a few but still active British-built Beyer Peacock locomotives, and Paraguay the creeping FC Presidente Carlos Antonio Lopez, a standard-gauge line running from the capital Ascunción to Encarnación on the Paraná river bordering Argentina. This latter is a haven for any enthusiast. The locomotives are all of British manufacture (some ex-Argentina) and wood burners to boot. To see or ride behind the *International* train gently weaving its way over its grass-grown tracks across the pampas is an almost unbelievable experience.

Further south, the Ferrocarriles Argentinos has no steam on its standard-gauge tracks but it does run on two working narrow-gauge lines, both 750mm. The first is the Esquel to Ing Jacobbacci section, using the Baldwin and Henschel 2-8-2s with a passenger and freight service; its main workshops are roughly halfway at El Maiten. This is a fourteen-hour journey, most of which can be in the hours of darkness. Next, and of considerable importance, is the Ramal Ferroviario Industrial de Rio Turbio down in the far south east, with bitterly cold winds howling across the bleak plains and its seaboard terminus at Rio Gallegos almost opposite the Falkland Islands (Malvinas). Here are twenty modern, very modern, Mitsubishi 2-10-2s which fight against the Patagonian wind at the head of long rakes of coal wagons. Four locomotives

continued
books against him for the remainder of his term, and if he lets out a word about promotion, the 'history' is produced against him, and he may fare badly, too, if it should read thus:
Fined, one day's pay for choking a fire, and losing forty-five minutes.
Fined, one day's pay for hanging a hook upon the safety-valve lever.
Fined, two pounds, for locking the safety-valves of his engine.
Fined, one day's pay, for stopping on the road to clean the tubes.
Fined, one day's pay, for running through a pair of gates.
Fined, one day's pay, for threatening to throw his fireman off the engine.
Fined, one pound, for having a stranger on the engine.
Fined, half-a-crown, for smoke nuisance.
Fined, five shillings, for bringing a pig 150 miles without permission.
Fined, one shilling, for breaking a coupling.
Fined, a day's pay, for running over three horses, and not reporting it.
While an engine-man is on the goods service he is exposed to more temptations than dangers; but unless the guard is a confederate, there is very little chance of thieving. It has happened that two bottles of brandy have been found on the engine, or a lot of fish, or a new pair of boots. Men have been taken-up for having fowl, ducks, and green peas in their baskets. When fowls were missing, they generally 'walked off' in couples, as they did of old into the Ark. But, considering the amount of property in transit, and considering the facilities men have for helping themselves, while shunting in a siding to clear the way for passenger-trains, it must be acknowledged that they are, on the whole, a straightforward honest body of men. – *Engine Driver's Life.*

153

Baldwin Consolidation. Red painted 2-8-0 No 45 takes water at Bucay on a November day in 1988 prior to working the first section of the daily 'mixto' up to Sibambe and then over the Devil's Nose reverses to Alausi some 6,000ft and thirty five miles distant.
P. B. WHITEHOUSE

Opposite. Cuenca branch engine. From time to time Equador's 3ft 0in gauge Guayaquil & Quito Railway suffers from the ravages of the Chanchan river and other rainy season problems. Here, in 1985 the line was cut in several places and the only steam engine available on the Huigra to Alausi section was ex Sibambe & Cuenca Railway 2-8-0 No 17 (Baldwin locomotive works 61872). It is seen here with a train on the viaduct north of Alausi.
P. B. WHITEHOUSE

are actually named, one after the great Frenchman *André Chapelon* who pioneered modern steam locomotive design and whose development work has been extended further at Rio Gallegos by Ingeniero Porta making these narrow-gauge machines some of the most modern and efficient ever to run. Certainly this is the only place in the world where a steam train of up to 1,700 tons and nearly a kilometre long can be seen on 750mm tracks. Train services vary with mine output but there are at least two in each direction daily taking anything from eight and a half hours to ten. Very much an experience at a latitude of 52° south.

A decade ago Southern Africa was a steam enthusiast's paradise with the newly emerged Zimbabwe rehabilitating its Garratts and South Africa more than holding its own with the huge class 25NC 4-8-2s regularly working on many mainline services. This pattern has now changed for the worse on both sectors. Sadly the last classic African steam passenger may soon disappear with the dieselisation of the major portion of the nightly Bulawayo–Thomson Junction 'Mail'; true, the onward journey to Victoria Falls still uses Garratt power, but the image of one of these fine machines seen out of the windows of a regular long-distance train rolling through the bush past elephants and giraffes will then only be recalled from memory.

If one is very lucky it is still sometimes possible to see a Garratt-headed train crossing the great Victoria Falls bridge en route to and from Livingstone in Zambia. At the time of writing it is the exception, but there is hope, for there is talk of a small steam revival in Zambia with President Kaunda announcing that some fourteen locomotives (believed

154

to be 16th and 20th/20A Garratts) are to go south to Zimbabwe's ZECO in Bulawayo for overhaul. They are to be used for shunting duties. ZECO have overhauled and rebuilt much of the Zimbabwe fleet and been a major force behind that country's ability to keep steam on active service, including the branch lines such as the West Nicholson. Recently ZECO have also overhauled some locomotives from strife-torn Mozambique including a CFM 4-8-2+2-8-4 Garratt and a 2-8-2 tank. The other regular source of steam in Zimbabwe is the huge Wankie Colliery close to Thomson Junction which owns ex-19th class 4-8-2s with their typical torpedo tenders as well as a couple of South African Railways class 16DA Pacifics, though these two engines are little used. Welcome is the once-a-month Safari steam special which runs out of Bulawayo to Hwange, where tourists stay overnight at the Safari Lodge, continuing the next day to Victoria Falls for another overnight stop. Their passenger cars are attached to the rear of a regular train usually powered by a sparklingly clean class 16A Garratt.

But the decline in South Africa is real with less than five hundred steam locomotives left in regular service and the first withdrawals of the

Zambian decay. Engines belonging to the Zambian Sawmills Railway await their fate. Two have been rescued by courtesy of the well-known artist David Shepherd.
DAVID SHEPHERD

modern class 25NC 4-8-2s – a pointer to the future. The proposed total dieselisation of South Africa's last steam main line from Kimberley to De Aar may well have sparked a mutter of protest from railway enthusiasts but the Gods of General Motors and General Electric are not easily appeased. Indeed a new diesel locomotive plant has recently been installed by General Electric at New Brighton near Port Elizabeth, while General Motors licensed a South African firm to produce their products. The original intention had been to keep steam on the De Aar route until the advent of electrification and indeed a report had been prepared which advocated steam traction as the cheaper option. It was not to be. The sight of the huge class 25NC 4-8-4s at the head of long passenger trains and often double headed on freights of coal, minerals and even cattle was a stirring one albeit that the route could scarcely be called scenic. That Bible for the serious overseas enthusiast, the *Continental Railway Journal*, reported in early 1988 that only thirteen (an ominous number) of steam passenger trains were scheduled in the SAR timetable and these included the narrow-gauge *Apple Express* out of Port Elizabeth which only runs as a tourist train as required. Only five classes (25NC, 4-8-4, 24 2-8-4, 19D 4-8-2 and 15AR 4-8-2 plus the narrow-gauge NG15) are used on these services. Of those trains on the list most were freights with a coach or van attached. Soon even this meagre remnant may well have reduced by the removal of the class 25NC on the Kimberley–De Aar route. Steam will be in use for shunting and some freight plus the running of specials for some time yet, but the great days are gone.

The two countries which have kept steam in regular use on all types of service into recent years have been India and China. Though happily there is still much left, even here the decline is accelerating – in India as a general rule, and in China on the main line.

India has three gauges, 5ft 6in, metre and 2ft 6in. The broad-gauge lines link the great cities like Bombay, Madras, Calcutta and Delhi and serves the teeming Ganges valley whilst the metre gauge fills in the gaps leaving the narrow gauge to the very rural areas. Great mountain ranges have been pierced or surmounted and huge rivers bridged, deserts, floods and jungle have been encountered and subdued though most of the main trunk routes have been electrified or dieselised. The seeming myriads of non-standard engines once beloved of the enthusiast are now thin on the rails; this has left the comparatively modern standard classes such as the WP Pacific and the WG Mikado very much in charge on the 5ft 6in tracks and the YP Pacific and YG Mikado similarly so on the metre gauge.

Without doubt the hill railways are the most attractive of all. They include some notable climbs and engineering feats such as India's only rack-and-pinion line, the metre-gauge Nilgiri Railway which climbs from Meltapalayam near Trichinopoly in the far South up to Ootacamund: it uses the Abt system with a gradient of 1 in 12½. The Nilgiri line has Swiss-built 0-8-2 tanks though these days only three appear to be operable with rack gear. The engines work as simples when off the rack and as compounds when on it. But the most unique must surely be the 2ft-gauge Darjeeling Railway which uses remarkable engineering ingenuity to climb 6,000ft in just over forty miles (taking all day to do it) between Sukna, seven miles beyond its terminus at Siliguri and Ghum

Dead But Not Buried

Steam has lingered on in several parts of the Third World with many an enthusiast journeying thousands of miles to see the dying remnants of once-proud engines eking out their final years, kept alive by the cannibalisation of their less fortunate sisters, or perhaps working out the evening of their years in the sugar plantations of South America and the Spice Islands. But what happens to a dead engine in say central Java, or the mountains of Colombia, the steaming heat of the Ecuadorian coast or the jungle of Brazil let alone the fastness of the purely agricultural island of Negros in the Philippines? The answer is generally they are left to rot.

Sometimes the process takes a while. In Java at Cepu as far back as 1975 the shed contained perhaps six working engines and thirty dead ones but all were still kept clean and polished, their brasswork gleaming in the tropical sun. Now the men with sledge hammers are moving in, the once great Mallets at Cibatu have been broken up in this way; blow by blow each swing of the hammer makes its impact; labour is cheap, and the deformed hunks of metal have little value except at melting point – and there are few melting pots in Indonesia. Far into the Brazilian rain forest they built the 'Railway of Death' – the Madeira–Mamore whose metre-gauge Baldwins and Alcos plied their mosquito-ridden way towards the Bolivian border. When the time came for a road to replace the ailing steam railway, it was built by the army who took over the locomotive shed and shops at Porto Velho on the Madeira river, used the machinery for their own purposes, sold off some of the more easily disposable locomotive fittings – and tossed the rest into the rain forest. Well in the jungle, the machines now rest creeper-grown and almost invisible. They left the track where it was; it was
continued overleaf

Patagonian steam. One of Argentina's regular steam operations is the long 760mm line from Ing Jaccobacci using Baldwin (Ing Jaccobacci – El Maiten) and Henschel (El Maiten – Esquel) 2-8-2s. P. B. WHITEHOUSE

Opposite. 3ft 0in gauge in the Andes of Peru. Hunslet built (1936) 2-8-0 No 107 takes a train from Huancayo towards Huancavilica in the autumn of 1985. P. B. WHITEHOUSE

continued

just not worth taking it up. Here there is – unusually – a happy ending, for this end of the line has been resuscitated to take the town's inhabitants to a bathing spot on the river, though only a couple of engines are back from the ever growing forest.

It is a similar sight at the Flandes works of the Colombian Railways. Here a few engines are desultorily kept in working order, the rest dumped on the outskirts of the factory where they are gradually disappearing into the green landscape.

On Negros, where pilgrim enthusiasts from the USA and Europe go for steam's last rites, there are literally dozens of working or abandoned sugar mills where the once-active 'dragons' fuelled by wood or the pulped remnants of sugar cane lie derelict and overgrown. Mallets, Baldwins, Alcos, Porters and Shays, they are all there for the number specialist to list and record. Not for them the cutter's torch or the sledge hammer, it's just not worth spending the money. Maybe one day beyond the twenty-first century an explorer will come up against these unknown monsters and wonder what it was all about. – P.B.W.

four miles short of Darjeeling. Like a steam tramway, the track follows the winding road, now laden with lorries and buses, and by using spiral loops and zigzags plus some fierce curves it achieves it without the use of a rack – or even a tunnel. Heavy rains in the monsoon season play havoc with the light track; in this jungle area of the Terai, as much as 27in (London's annual total) can fall in one day. This and a lack of capital tend to make for an 'on and off' season and, sadly, a not very optimistic future. The locomotives of this remarkable railway are sturdy hill ponies in the form of 0-4-0 saddle tanks built mostly in Scotland by the North British Locomotive Company weighing about 14 tons and carrying a crew of six: driver, fireman, two assistant firemen who break and pass the coal from the bunkers and two sandmen riding on the front.

China is a very different story with new steam locomotives both standard and narrow gauge still under construction in 1988. The works at Datong on the borders of Mongolia has been using the consultancy services of David Wardale over the past three years, making use of this brilliant locomotive engineer's experiences of modernisation in South Africa where he developed the Porta principles of gas combustion on the now well-known *Red Devil* 4-8-2 and the smaller class 19D named *Irene* after his wife. Datong was due to cease manufacture of new QJ class 2-10-2 and JS 2-8-2s at the end of 1988 but it will be interesting to see how and if the development work continues. Now there appears to be no intention of ceasing to construct the SY class small 2-8-2 (used mainly for industrial purposes) at Tangshan or the standard 0-8-0 for the 760mm narrow-gauge systems.

The most ubiquitous class on China's railways is the huge QJ, used mainly for freight, but some of the SL and RM class Pacifics are still regularly employed on local and cross-country runs where dieselisation has not yet taken a firm hold. Add to these the older Japanese- and Chinese-built JF class 2-8-2s (which mostly perform trip working and shunting duties) and the modern-day steam scene in China is set. Up until a decade ago it was possible to see a number of foreign-built non-standard types, from the Russian FD 2-10-2 (precursor to the QJ) to some British- and American-built classes. Even now there are a few

US-built 2-8-0s supplied as part of the post World War II aid programme (Chinese Railways class KD7) at work on hump yard and similar duties in the Shanghai and Nanchang areas to the east.

Steam is spread widely throughout China although in the south and on all main lines it is mainly on freight and yard work. Certainly the constant sound of QJs rumbling over the great bridges at Wuhan and Nanjing is now a thing of the past. Most of the concentration is in the north east, taking in Manchuria with Jilin, Changchun, Harbin as excellent centres: this area is also home to many of the 760mm-gauge forestry lines which are mostly steam worked. There is a narrow-gauge steam locomotive factory at Harbin. Changchun also boasts a large locomotive-repair factory which today officially only overhauls QJ and JS classes, but some SLs plus a few RMs and JFs are also dealt with here.

The SL Pacifics are becoming rarer and tend, like men of an alien race, to have been pushed further and further into the wilder northern regions – though a number still work out of Jilin on long-distance locals plus the odd turn to Changchun which also sees some RMs with a degree of regularity.

Changchun is the one-time headquarters of the South Manchurian Railway and once the puppet capital of Japanese Manchukuo. The station has, as yet, not been rebuilt, and still retains a 1930s atmosphere with a solidly built entrance facade and low American-type platforms (the South Manchurian Railway was very much built on American railroad ideology). At one end lies a huge hump yard with reception and departure sidings fanning out from the small shunting hump almost at the platform ramp. Here there are constant comings and goings as trains are made up and dispatched. Something is moving every few minutes. The mainline services are all diesel hauled using DFH3 diesel hydraulics, but steam is constantly on the move whether it be light engines going to or returning from the shed, local passenger trains or freights (sometimes double headed) emerging from the yard. Traffic is generally very heavy and a count at the junction of the Harbin and Jilin lines north of the station produced a train every three and a half minutes.

Vietnam uses two gauges, standard and metre, with steam at work on the standard gauge in the northern areas, mainly French-built 2-8-2s that run as far as Vinh some 319km distant. There are also some French-built Pacifics as well as a number of 2-6-2 tanks. All still use French annotations such as 231.580 for a Pacific – a relic of the country's colonial past. North Korea also uses some steam but this too is hardly accessible to the enthusiast and can only be seen during the course of one of the standard package tours now in operation. Entry is via China by rail.

Even though steam there is very dormant and on the point of expiry, Indonesia continues to draw the discerning enthusiast. Once a thriving Dutch-built network, and pre-World War II almost certainly the finest 3ft 6in-gauge system in the world, the Indonesian railways fell into decay after independence. Then with a new influx of money and considerable modernisation the main line has come to life once again – regrettably not with steam. But this is only in recent years for even in the late 1970s there were as many as seventy – yes seventy – classes in stock comprising ten tender and twenty-one tank wheel arrangements ranging from 0-4-0

Left. Datong engines. Chinese QJ class 2-10-0s outshopped at Datong Steam Locomotive Factory. A sight no longer to be seen as the last engine to be built there was turned out in December 1988. The engines seen here are Nos 6813, 6810 and 6809. CHINA RAILWAY PUBLISHING HOUSE

Below left. One of the SL class 4-6-2s (normally fitted with smoke deflectors) No 629 taking water on Changchun shed, Manchuria in October 1984. In the background are (left) a QJ 2-10-2 and (right) a Japanese built 2-6-4 tank adapted as a 2-6-0 and used as a wash out engine. P. B. WHITEHOUSE

Engines Of Straw

The final class of locomotive to arrive in Tunisia under Bone-Guelma auspices came after World War I from Baldwin's and were an Americanised version of the 0-6-6-0 tank Mallet compounds. The engines carried Nos 681–90 and works nos, in order, 53322, 53323, 53334, 53352, 53353, 53365, 53420, 53389, 53419 and 53366; all were dated 1920. Originally the engines had bunkers with a straight back; later the bunkers were given rearward extensions slightly outside the buffers. While all very well when the engine was coupled to normal rolling stock, it occurred in the shed that two Baldwin Mallets met back-to-back on occasion. When this happened the bunker and cab acquired a severely bent appearance. Powerful whistles were fitted and the arrival of a Baldwin in the marshalling yards of Dubosville was well-advertised all round Tunis.

When first in traffic the American engines were oil-fired, but this apparatus was quite soon removed. During the extreme coal shortage of the war years these locomotives and the other Mallets were burning esparto grass, which *continued overleaf*

A modern Indian locomotive class. A WD Pacific No 1522 shunts at Agra Fort in front of the Jani Masjid mosque on 20 November 1984. The railway here is metre gauge and Agra is one of the stopping points for the Palace on Wheels luxury tourist train.
HUGH BALLANTYNE

continued

to outward appearance is a thicker and better form of straw. The central plain of Tunisia, the Sahel, is the principal world source of this grass from which the finest paper is made. During the war exports were stopped, but the Tunisians kept on growing and reaping their grass and some intelligent administrator conceived the idea of burning it in locomotive fireboxes in place of unavailable imported fuels. The straw gave a fine hot fire with very little ash, but was, of course, gone in a moment and constant replenishment was necessary. A certain amount of coal was required to provide a fire-bed and keep the firebox warm during stops.

To see a straw-fired freight start out of Tunis was a great sight; behind the engine were two or more bogie flat wagons stacked with trussed straw with a dozen or more firemen disposed along the top. As the regulator opened these men started pulling and pushing the trusses along to the open back of the cab where stood the opener, perilously balanced between engine and wagon, who hacked at the trussing cords before tipping
continued opposite

to 2-12-2T. Monster 2-8-8-0 Compound Mallets, rack tanks and steam trams were all at work on the three island PNKA (Perushaan Negara Kereta Api) system operating services on three gauges, the 3ft 6in predominating. In theory the Amberawa rack line continues to be open for spasmodic tourist trains but in reality the locomotives in the small shed beyond the large island-platformed station are unserviceable and dormant. But in Indonesia, you never can tell. Adjacent to the one platform edge is the 'museum', a collection of very deceased steam engines carefully placed in the open air each on its separate track and given a quick coat of paint. Sadly, tropical weather – August in Java is

continued

the straw on the footplate. On the footplate itself two more firemen pitchforked madly in a maelstrom of flying pieces towards the ever-open firebox door. What the scene can have been like at any speed on a stormy night baffles the imagination. It was the responsibility of the driver to close the firebox door before closing the regulator, a blow-back onto a crew knee-deep in straw would have been more than usually unpleasant.

In 1922 the Bone-Guelma and Prolongments came to an and and a new company, the CFT, Chemins de Fer Tunisiens, took over. New number plates were provided with the new initials and the numbers themselves were modified to the extent of adding the wheel arrangement in French style. Thus No 401 became No 130.401, No 754 changed to No 230.754 and so on. The Mallet compound classes became 2-2.451, 3-3.551 and so on. The same type of number plate was applied to the tenders but in this case the wheel arrangement was substituted by a figure giving the water capacity in cubic metres. – P. M. Kalla-Bishop

South African duo. Burgersdorp shed in March 1977 with 15AR and 19D class 4-8-2s. South African steam has dwindled with considerable rapidity during the 1980s. This picture can never be repeated. P. B. WHITEHOUSE

Java rack engine. Possibly but only possibly available for steaming is this 3ft 6in gauge 0-4-2 tank No B2501 based at Amberawa. The rack section is still extant and the large island platform station though isolated from any other trains has an open air museum opposite its other platform face. These B25 class engines are wood burners and No B2501, in better times, stands outside the shed on 26 December 1973. RON ZIEL/MILLBROOK HOUSE COLLECTION

the only month where you can be reasonably sure of a dry day – is not conducive to their welfare. There are still sugar lines in Java which use a little steam, and palm oil plantations in Sumatra which use a few locomotives, but the good days are gone forever. Even the Kediri–Pare tram which seemed to trundle on forever behind tiny 0-6-0 or 0-4-0 tanks (the pure tram engines have been long asleep) seems to be quiet and still. North Sumatra sees some desultory steam movements usually in the form of wood-burning 2-6-4 tanks at Tebing Tinggi and Dolok Merangir.

Fortunately there remains an affinity between sugar and steam and on estates, far and wide, ancient locomotives, mostly of American origin, work out their lives on a multiplicity of gauges far from the lines they were built to serve. There are three main centres of activity, Brazil (the plantations round Campos and Recife), Cuba, and the island of Negros in the Philippines where the cane fields can produce 'main lines' of considerable length. Steam is rapidly on the decline in Negros, on the wane in Brazil, but in adequate health on Castro's Cuba where Alcos, Baldwins and Porters can be found hard at work during the season, real descendants of the legendary locomotive factories of the USA. Some of the Cuban lines have immaculately kept engines, particularly the standard-gauge Marcela Salado system, which keeps a varied and venerable selection of steam power in superb condition using a black livery with yellow lining. They include a very stylish Baldwin 4-6-0 of 1911 and an Alco Consolidation. Many of the cane fields cover a wide area and it is not unusual to find engines working 25km away from their shed at the main mill. Some cane fields also have workmen's trains, while others have trains which run extensively over the FCC (national railways) trackage with round trip workings of over 50km. Just how long this will last no one can tell but there have been ominous deliveries of Russian-built diesels, both standard and narrow gauge, in recent years – so now is the time to visit. On Negros it is well beyond the eleventh hour, but some Dragons still lurch over the lightly laid tracks of Hawaiian, Philippines and other active mills, though most stand dead in the yards totally worn out and now just a part of the island's folklore.

164

Much has been written in recent years of steam's renaissance, old engines beautifully restored from scrapyard condition to glisten and gleam over enthusiastically preserved sections of railway the world over; for some there are even finer sights – mainline steam entering the landscape once again to hold the stage. In the hard cold light of railway economics this seems almost a resurrection rather than a renaissance; and that it has happened at all is due to a very few enthusiastic amateurs who refused to take no for an answer well over a generation ago. With so much happening, it is hard to believe that melancholy scene of the late nineteen-sixties when steam was a dirty word on many nationalised lines. On British Rail any railman daring to use it enthusiastically seriously risked passing over for promotion. Now even West Germany (one of the last western countries to maintain its steam locomotives in good working order who like BR said 'never again') has been converted to the attraction of steam tourism and limited charters.

Java Mallet. CC50 class No 5024 on the turntable at Cibatu in 1979. This was the last home for those huge machines which were in very poor condition. P. B. WHITEHOUSE

Shining Baldwin. 2-6-0 No 1530 (built in 1925) takes water alongside the locomotive shed at the Jose Smith Comas sugar mill, Matanzas Province Cuba on 17 February 1985. The engine is one of three used for main line services. P. B. WHITEHOUSE

Cuban consolidation. No 1549, belonging to the C Marcelo Salado mill, has just brought a heavy load of sugar cane down the system's main line and is about to go on shed. The date is 18 February 1985. P. B. WHITEHOUSE

Near the Mongolian border, modern steam power on the Datong-Vaston line in China around 1987.
CHINA RAILWAY PUBLISHING
HOUSE

Climbing out of Cuzco, a Henschel 2-8-2 heads for Machupicchu.
P. B. WHITEHOUSE

One of the pioneers to be remembered must be the late L. T. C. Rolt, not a man who suffered fools gladly but one whose determination was as strong as his character; fortunately a fine author as well as a staunch enthusiast for both waterways and railways, Rolt fought for the impossible, the acquisition and continued running of the 2ft 3in-gauge Talyllyn Railway in Wales, then the oldest surviving steam-hauled narrow-gauge railway in the world. This led to the formation of the Talyllyn Railway Preservation Society which lit a torch to show the way for so many to follow worldwide. Down in the southern hemisphere the Puffing Billy line, a 2ft-gauge one-time branch of the Victoria State Railway close to Melbourne, followed suit, the Strasburg in Dutch Pennsylvania, a standard-gauge railway, was not far behind, then came the French Vivarais metre gauge in the Massif, and so it has gone on. A glance at the *Steam Passenger Services Directory*, an annual guide published in the USA, establishes well over two hundred such operations there in 1989.

With the slow but sure rehabilitation of steam on the national systems using express and mixed-traffic engines restored at great cost and devotion, often by voluntary workers, to pristine condition, the dinosaurs once thought to be dead and buried have been raised from the grave. Today not a single continent fails to resound to the sound of this living machine, hauling hundreds of tons and an equal number of passengers over tracks which had heard nothing but the sound of diesels for a decade or more. From the far North West of Scotland to the shores of the Mediterranean, New Hampshire to Colorado, Brazil to Chile, out of Perth or Port Elizabeth there is a new era steam enterprise, albeit one of miniscule financial profit.

Steam may well be on its way out but it is a long time adying.

Below and opposite. Pioneer preserved railway. Enthusiasts rescued this 2ft 3in gauge line in 1951 achieving a world's first. Without the enterprise which saved the Talyllyn Railway in those early days one wonders just how much could have gone to the scrapyards before a further realisation dawned.
P. B. WHITEHOUSE

Horseshoe Curve

One of the great magazines of railroading is *Trains Magazine*. Here is a classic 1941 piece by Harry T. Sohlberg. It was sub-titled: 'Scenery and trains make the PRR near Altoona a mecca of railroad interest.'

The brakeman calls out, 'Horseshoe Curve on your right in a few minutes.' The deadheads don't even look up, but nearly everyone else in the coach crowds to the right hand side to get a good look, for this scenic wonder of the Pennsylvania RR main line is well known to every traveler and would-be traveler. That the curve is no less an engineering attraction is usually lost sight of, but this wide sweeping horseshoe allows the Pennsy's Pittsburgh Division line, four tracks wide, to breast the east slope of the Alleghenies with only 92 feet per mile grade.

What better spot than here for the man who likes to watch or photograph trains! Westerners can well be proud of their famous Cajon Pass in the San Bernardino Mountains, the fabled Moffat Tunnel in the Colorado Rockies, or Sherman Hill in Wyoming, but Horseshoe Curve has everything to make the true railfan happy. It is on the Harrisburg–Pittsburgh portion of the Pennsy main line, funnel for the traffic from Chicago and St. Louis to New York and Washington, a line which is never without the thrilling sound of locomotive exhaust.

Two engines on the front, two on the rear, the heavy freights roll up the line from Altoona, around the horseshoe, to the tunnels at Gallitzin, the crest of the Alleghenies. Light engines glide gracefully down to Altoona, there again to take up their task of helping to lift thousands of tons over the 2200ft summit. Long freights roll down, brake shoes telling the story of retainer-set cars helping to hold the immense potential energy in leash.

Day or night the story of heavy traffic railroading unfolds. The night owls can watch a show unequaled anywhere, as the great steel fleets of main line limited passenger trains from East and West cross and recross the center tracks, sparks flying from stacks of westbound locomotives, sparks from brakes of eastbound trains. The timetable reveals a delightful concentration of traffic. During the five night hours from 10.43 to 03.41, 27 named trains, including some of the most famous in the country, round the curve, and on fine Summer evenings nothing could be pleasanter than watching this parade from a car parked on the public highway below. Here are the heaviest hours listed in detail:

Time	Train No.*	Train Names
1043	49	The General
1049	69	The Red Arrow
1108	41	Cincinnati Limited
1109	52	The New Yorker
1123	59	Liberty Limited
1133	77	The Trail Blazer
1146	31	Spirit of St. Louis
1151	29	Broadway Limited
1232	22	Manhattan Limited
1254	16	Iron City Express
0112	66	The American
0116	23	Manhattan Limited
0118	76	The Trail Blazer
0136	50	The Statesman
0143	60	The Pittsburgher
0152	38	The Clevelander–The Akronite
0211	36	Philadelphia Night Express
0218	70	The Advance General
0225	40	Cincinnati Limited
0231	39	The Clevelander–The Akronite
0237	68	The Red Arrow
0243	67	The American
0245	58	Liberty Limited
0300	30	Spirit of St. Louis
0319	48	The General
0334	32	The St. Louisan
0341	28	Broadway Limited

*As is the usual practice, even numbers indicate eastbound trains, odd numbers westbound trains.

This is truly the great parade! But my associates and I came to this Mecca of railfans with our cameras, looking for daytime action. And there's plenty of that too. Start with us at East Altoona, the front yard of the big mountain workshop of the Pennsylvania RR. The

Pacifics on the Horseshoe Curve. A painting of a New York-Chicago express headed by two Pennsylvania Railroad 4-6-2s on the four tracked main line climbing into the Allegheny Mountains. WONDER BOOK OF RAILWAYS

engine house here is one of the largest of its kind in the world. It is a complete circle, with 50 engine house pits, and a capacity for handling 385 locos in a 24-hour period.

The same applies to Altoona itself. Bit by bit the entire plant unfolds itself. Juniata shops. Altoona machine shops. Altoona car shops. South Altoona foundries. The test department. The locomotive test plant. All of this lies directly at the foot of the main ridge of the Alleghenies, a true 'railroad town' of some 80,000 persons – beehive of super-activity and front door to the far-famed Horseshoe Curve.

Out of Altoona the average train adds another loco-motive, and, in the case of freight drags, two or three engines are added to surmount the heavy grade en-countered. From Altoona to Gallitzin, just west of the curve, Pennsy trains climb 1015 feet in 11 miles, nearly 1.8 per cent average gradient.

For about five miles the initial grade out of Altoona is pounded to the utmost, and further advance seems blocked by the lofty mountains until the train rounds the nose of a projecting spur and the picturesque station at Kittanning Point comes into view. We have reached Horseshoe Curve – 242 miles west of Philadelphia and 111 miles east of Pittsburgh.

⋆　⋆　⋆　⋆　⋆

Below us we see the Kittanning Valley and Burgoon's Run; above us tower the Alleghenies, dropping abruptly to line side, forming a giant amphitheater for our scene of action. At Kittanning Point the valley parallel to the road becomes a deep, wide gorge, the south side of which rises to a great height. To negotiate this gorge, after climbing steadily from Altoona, the construction eng-ineers built a line around the head of the gorge and along the side of the mountain in the general shape of a horseshoe, hence its name.

The toe of this horseshoe is a gigantic fill across Curve Center, or Burgoon's Run. The curve is what is technically known as a nine-degree curve and extends over a distance embracing 220 degrees. At a point 2000 feet on either side of Curve Center it is 1400 feet across Burgoon's Run. Visualize a real horseshoe and these figures are very easily assimilated.

The southern calk of the shoe is 1716 feet high, and the northern calk, Kittanning Point, is 1594 feet high. If the tracks were to be carried directly across the gap from calk to calk, without the sweep of the shoe and its subsequent fill, it would require an 8½ per cent grade, entailing the use of a cog wheel railroad.

Kittanning Point station, its sign still painted neatly in the familiar Pennsy red and gold, though no longer used for train stops, offers sanctuary from the boiling sun. Beneath its platform we await action – and it is not long in coming!

The sound of barking exhausts heralds the approach of a double-header moving west, and we turn our reflex cameras toward the nose of the point, expectantly, hopefully.

Hotshot freight!

Our catch sports a heavy I-1, 2-10-2 type, as a helper, with an M-1a, Mountain type, on the train. We notice that the I-1 is numbered 4527 as its front end reaches the correct position in our finders. As the helper rolls by we see that the Mountain type has road number 6768. We have time to count 110 cars before another pair of 'jacks', the pushers, loom up around the curve.

It is no trouble for the engineer on the first helper, over on the south shelf, to look across the valley and see his colleagues rounding Kittanning Point.

A smoke plume on the southern end of the shoe attracts our attention as we watch the head end of the freight disappear. Slipping gracefully around the bend, a long passenger train takes things easy as it moves toward Curve Center. This is in accordance with operating department orders, so that all passengers are afforded a good view of the curve, from beginning to end. Such courtesies pay real dividends!

With the signal bridge above the station for a frame, we click our shutters on a pair of K-4s proudly displaying the orthodox white feathers, a sign of intelligent firing. This train is the *Gotham Limited*.

During the morning a steady stream of freight and passenger trains keeps us busy changing film. During our two and a half hours' working time until noon we have cataloged 15 trains, four of which are passenger trains. This does not include returning pushers, merrily clank-ing down the grade to Altoona to pick up another drag and give it a helping hand.

Lunch is an ideal time to climb the steel ladder to the working platform of the signal bridge and capture a prize shot, both calks of the shoe on a single plane. It is a majestic sweep and should never be overlooked. But the question of permission creeps in. Properly supervised, the photographer has a wealth of material at his disposal.

After lunch we prepare to move with the sun, the better to catch Curve Center and the south slope. We have no sooner reached our chosen position, placed our equipment, and noted the position of the sun, than things begin to happen all over again!

Fast freight PG-7, hauled by two Decapods, swings around the point and slams it down for the roller-coaster ride across Burgoon's Run and up the west slope. As the loaded cars click by us, further assisted by another pair of I-1s, we are jolted into immediate action by the sight of two Mountain types rolling past Kittanning Point station.

With the freight on the outside iron, the *Metropolitan*, crack passenger flyer for the West, puts on a magnificent show as it rapidly overhauls the freight pushers. Exactly at Curve Center, before our very eyes and lenses, the two M-1a's run abreast of the I-1s; a true motive power parade!

The thunder of the two I-1s and the two M-1a's, abreast, all four engines wide open, will linger with us in memory for a long time to come. Would that we could record the sound of this action! The towering bulk of the mountains overhead acts as a giant sounding board, repeating the deafening echoes again and again.

Only Horseshoe Curve can furnish such drama!

Scarcely five minutes later passenger train No 24, powered by two K-4s, 3733 and 1339, slips down the

west slope into our awaiting cameras. Once again the white feathers bespeak of well trained firemen.

By 3.30 pm we have bagged 14 more train movements, including two mine-bound drags of empty gondolas, requiring no helpers. Following the advice of our guide, we decide to survey the situation at Gallitzin and Cresson for the next day's activities. Regretfully we take leave of our amphitheater, doubting if the other side of the mountain can offer us as much.

The three tunnels at Gallitzin break the continuity of main line, and are the gateway to the different gradients of the west slope, only 1 instead of 1.8 per cent.

A check on our records en route informs us that the Pennsy has placed a great deal of confidence in its Decapods, the I-1s; the Mountain type, M-1a; and its splendid Pacifics, the K-4s. Hauling freight over such torturous grades seems mighty easy for the prevailing Decapods, and we note that most of the drags boast of manifests covering 85 to 115 cars, with an exceptional

train hitting the 125-car mark.

Four main lines, all laid in the heaviest of steel, none of them idle for long, break the back of the Alleghenies, and stand as a tribute to those men who could foresee the future – the day when Horseshoe Curve was to be an important link in the defense program of the nation.

Above and right. Steam giants in the Allegheny mountains. What better spot could there have been for the steam enthusiast than the great Horseshoe curve on the four track main line of the Pennsylvania Railroads Pittsburgh Division? These two photographs show something of the evocative past glories of this fascinating piece of North American railroading. RAIL PHOTO SERVICES

10
BEYOND THE
SCRAPYARD GATES

IT was in the spring of 1958 that locomotive No 32424 *Beachy Head* – the last survivor of the hallowed Brighton Atlantics – arrived at British Railways' Eastleigh Works for scrapping, after a distinguished career spanning almost fifty years.

The cutting of redundant steam locomotives had been routine work at Eastleigh since the 1955 Modernisation Plan had rendered scores of steam veterans surplus to requirements; ordinarily to the fitters assigned to the task of stripping and cutting locomotives at Eastleigh, such an engine would represent just another week's work. When you were being paid to wield the acetylene torch, there was not much scope for sentiment.

Dick Mitchell and Eric Best, the only full-time locomotive dismantlers at Eastleigh at that time, were disposing of about thirty engines a year – but the arrival of *Beachy Head* at the Hampshire railhead on its final train – a thirteen-coach empty stock working from Brighton – provoked a certain stiffening of the sinews.

The Brighton Atlantics had always commanded a special affection amongst railwaymen, and for Eric Best, cutting up the last remaining example of the class seemed almost philistine. But for Dick Mitchell, the act was even more unpalatable; as a teenage apprentice fitter at Brighton with the London, Brighton & South Coast Railway forty-eight years before, he had helped build that very locomotive. How could he now destroy it?

'We talked about it for nearly a fortnight,' remembers Eric Best. 'We'd heard talk of preserving the engine, and we were loath to light the torch. After two weeks, when we could delay no longer, I started dismantling the loco. When the enthusiasts came round the Works, they called us "murdering bastards" – but in fact my sentiments were the same as theirs. I didn't want to see it go.' A typical sentiment of the nineteen-sixties, could be.

It would have been emotion on a very much greater scale though, if the flicker and spit of the acetylene torch had been more obvious to the outside world. As it was, the demolition of Britain's steam heritage was largely executed behind closed doors, away from the public gaze. Even the country's legions of railway enthusiasts, who had followed working steam frenetically to its last gasp, saw little of the disembowelling process. Access to the British Railways works, where the wholesale scrapping of steam was begun, and to the private yards of the scrap-metal dealers where the job was finished, was not always there for the asking; and anyway, for many the prospect of being a spectator at such post-mortems was just too morbid and too heartbreaking to contemplate. Thus, apart from occasional photographs of half-dismantled engines,

Eastleigh Works cut up the lion's share of 1960s Southern steam, Ashford coming a poor second. This view taken in August 1963 shows ex LB&SCR K class Mogul No 32341 in its death throes.
ROY HOBBS

and the growing lists of 'Locomotives Withdrawn' which appeared in the monthly railway-enthusiast press during the 1960s, publishers and enthusiasts alike bade their farewells to steam at the scrapyard gates.

It was not until the mid-1980s that a true picture of what really happened 'beyond the scrapyard gates' began to emerge in print. This, without much doubt, was inspired by the remarkable and much-publicised course of events at the Barry, South Wales, scrapyard of Messrs Woodham Bros, where some 213 steam locomotives which by rights should have gone to the melting pot back in the 1960s, survived and, one by one over a twenty-year period, were sold for preservation – in several cases to steam again in triumph on British Rail's own tracks.

Woodham's scrapyard was the final chapter of an epic saga which began with the Attlee government's Nationalisation of the railways in January 1948. The new British Railways regime inherited some 20,102 steam locomotives from the four main railway companies – 7,850 from the London, Midland & Scottish, 6,550 from the London & North Eastern Railway, 3,857 from the Great Western and 1,845 from the already extensively electrified Southern Railway. This vast stock of motive power ranged from tiny short-wheelbase four-wheeled docks shunters to 100mph Pacifics, from eighty-year-old goods engines to the

In 1959, rusting, dead locomotives were stored at six different locations around Derby works. This view shows Spondon, with Midland 4-4-0s and 0-6-0s in evidence.
R. H. G. SIMPSON

This view of Swindon works, taken on 30 August 1959, shows a typically unmanageable buildup of condemned engines. Far too many for C shop to cope with, they were sold to the pioneering South Wales scrapyards of Woodham Bros and Messrs Williams. Visible here are Churchward Moguls, 0-6-0PTs and 14XX 04-2Ts.
TERRY NICHOLLS

most modern express types, some of which, like the LNER A2s, were still in the process of being built. Alongside this were British Railways' own plans to build a new generation of steam locomotives – 999 of them – to standardised designs.

Clearly some 'thinning out' of the locomotive stock was needed, and during the first decade of nationalisation the whittling down began in earnest, well ahead of any serious dieselisation. It was quite usual for withdrawn locomotives to be broken up at the same works in which they had been built, and indeed, such an evolutionary process had been the norm during the days of the four large private companies. Ex-LMS engines invariably ended their days in the scraplines at Crewe, Derby or Horwich, and in Scotland at St Rollox (Glasgow) and Kilmarnock. Former LNER types succumbed at Doncaster, Darlington, Stratford (London) or Gorton, while north of the border Inverurie (Aberdeen) and Cowlairs took a share of the cutting. Brighton, Eastleigh and Ashford accounted for redundant Southern engines, while Swindon, with some assistance from Caerphilly, Stafford Road (Wolverhampton) and Barry, took care of the GWR breed.

In total, some twenty-nine British Railways works and depots shared the task of dispatching the unwanted, outmoded or accident-damaged victims of this early 'rationalisation', the cutters feeding off the

Hundreds of 'dead engine' movements were required to move condemned engines from works and sheds to the scrapyards. Preparation for these was thorough – rods were removed to free the motion and tenders were emptied. Virtually all such workings were classified 'out of gauge load' or OGLO and governed by a Special Notice issued by the Operating Department. Passing Bishton, near Newport, in the mid 1960s is 8F 48121 with a Saturday morning special comprising a standard 4, two WR 2-8-0s and a Hall. DEREK SHORT

scraplines of derelict engines, which were constantly being topped up with new withdrawals. Reusable parts – of which boilers were the biggest and most valuable – would be either stored or overhauled, to keep other, more fortunate locomotives in traffic. Because most of the works had their own foundries, the dismembered segments of steel were simply melted down on site, and used in the forging of new engine parts.

Then came – belatedly by world standards – the 1955 modernisation plan which among other things envisaged the total replacement of steam by diesel and electric power and when the plan was revised in 1958 'to achieve profit in five years,' the screw really began to tighten. As withdrawals accelerated, so the steam scraplines overflowed, and special arrangements had to be made to store withdrawn locomotives in sidings and railway yards away from the main works . . . anywhere where track space could be found for them. Steam dumps were established at strategic points throughout the country – from Bo'ness on the Firth of Forth to Newport in the Isle of Wight – and at scores of locomotive depots, sidings and disused lines between. But by 1958 however, BR's own cutting shops could no longer keep pace. To eliminate the complete steam fleet of sixteen thousand locomotives, it was subsequently estimated, would have taken one hundred men, working without a break, a total of six years and two months! So external scrap-metal contractors were invited to tender for redundant engines for the first time.

In March 1959 the first convoy of steam locomotives to be sold for scrap – four ex-GWR mixed traffic 2-6-0s – left Swindon Works, bound for the Barry yard of Messrs Woodham Bros. It was to be the first of countless convoys to the South Wales breakers' yards – but the special significance of Barry as a destination was something that would only be

The Newport yard of J. Buttigieg on a busy October day in 1967. The dismembered engines are Bulleid Pacific Nos 34005, 34009, and 34026 whilst the BR standard class 4 is No 76064. N. E. PREEDY

appreciated in the fullness of time. As even the new standard classes – BR built 999 of them from 1951 on! – were withdrawn, more than one hundred scrapyards were devouring steam engines. The plethora of scrapyards serving the steel industry in the South Wales and Sheffield areas became an obvious destination and steam enthusiasts who followed the month-by-month cull from the BR steam fleet in the railway press, soon became familiar with the names of the principal breakers: Cashmore's of Newport, Hayes of Bridgend, Birds of Risca, T.W. Ward of Beighton and Killamarsh, Buttigeig's of Newport.

But scrapyard geography was by no means restricted to the steel conurbations. Altogether 114 different sites were involved, the only common link being that they were all rail connected. The yard with the dubious distinction of having demolished the greatest number of engines was on the fringes of the Black Country. Cashmore's of Great Bridge, Tipton, Staffs, which became an abattoir for some 1,500 locomotives between 1961 and 1969. They included an astonishing 219 LMS '8F' freight engines – more than a quarter of the entire class – and 152 of the LMS 'all-purpose' workhorse, the Black 5.

Another notable valhalla was the former Hull & Barnsley Railway goods yard at Sculcoates, leased from BR by the Humberside scrap merchants Albert Draper & Sons. The first engine LNER B16 No 61420 – some 90 tons of metal, for which BR received the princely sum of £4,000 – arrived in December 1963.

179

Though Drapers employed forty men, none could be spared from their normal daily work of cutting redundant freight wagons – so the B16 became a weekend exercise, spread over six weeks. That did not deter Drapers from tendering for more engines, indeed in little over five years, a total of 732 locomotives were cut up, including, tragically, the last survivor of the much-loved LNER A1 Pacifics, No 60145 *Saint Mungo*.

The speed at which locomotives were scrapped varied greatly from yard to yard. At the height of loco-cutting activities, Cashmore's Great Bridge scrapyard had six two-man teams engaged in the practice, and were disposing of six complete engines a week. The policy at the Atlas Works yard of Airdrie breakers, George H. Campbell & Co, was to arrange for only one engine to arrive on site on a given date – and then liquidate it that same day. In November 1966, the *Railway Observer* reported that LMS 2-6-4 tank engine No 42264 arrived in the yard at 10.00 and by 16.15 that same afternoon had been entirely eliminated. On other sites, cutting would be a process spread over several weeks, alongside other dismantling jobs, or, as in the case of R. S. Hayes of Bridgend, locomotives which the company bought in 1962 and 1963, languished at various BR depots, until at length in 1964, Hayes called them all in for cutting. Hayes, incidentally, earned a special place in scrapyard history by being the only yard to put a withdrawn engine to work, as its own yard shunter. Enthusiasts travelled from far and wide for a glimpse of the former GWR pannier tank No 9642, rather incongruously painted in Hayes' own gaudy green livery, shunting its hapless relatives into position for the cutting gangs.

The fickle hand of fate caused several engines to benefit from a stay of execution. One of the last convoys of condemned locos to reach a private breaker's yard, left Bolton on 27 September 1968 – nearly seven weeks after the official 'end of steam' on BR – bound for George Cohen's yard at Cransley, near Kettering. On arrival at Gowhole Sidings, near

180

New Mills, the convoy's driver decided that his eight hours of duty were up, and refused to work any further. Thus the engines – Black 5s 45104, 45290 and 45312 – were parked in the up goods loop line. Local police caught vandals armed with sledge hammers having their own crack at their demolition, and when the engines were inspected by BR they were deemed 'unfit to travel'.

However, on 6 December, the first two were collected by diesel, and in company with an LMS 8F freight engine, No 48467, which had languished at Patricroft locomotive depot in Manchester, resumed their journey to Kettering. It was more than a month later that the lone No 45312 was finally dispatched to Kettering – in company with sister engine No 44816, which had been lying rusting in the open at Lostock Hall engine shed, near Preston. Thus the last of the trio reached its destination some three and a half months after the journey began. It had ceased to exist within a month of reaching its valhalla.

To the enthusiast world, the elimination of steam through the 1960s fostered mixed emotions: the race against time to hunt out the last survivors was enthralling – yet the whole exercise was undeniably depressing too. The most regrettable – some would say shameful – instance of a steam locomotive being devoured by the fiery torch, occurred in June 1966, when the former Highland Railway Small Ben class engine No 54398 *Ben Alder* was sold to, and hurriedly devoured by, Motherwell Machinery & Scrap Co. The special significance of this act was that the engine, a veteran built in 1898, had been withdrawn for preservation some thirteen and a half years earlier. No satisfactory explanation has ever been given for this piece of 'official vandalism', although it is believed by some observers that the shortage of exhibition space in the original Glasgow Museum of Transport, where four other classic Scottish steam designs found sanctuary, prompted the unforgivable act.

Engines were sometimes dispatched to parts of the country where, in normal circumstances, their presence would have been considered rare, or even impossible. Thus LNER A1 Pacific No 60129 *Guy Mannering* reached the Norwich yard of Messrs A. King, while several of the Southern Railway's Schools class 4-4-0 express engines, traditionally associated with passenger train workings between London (Victoria) and the Kent coast, or between Waterloo, Basingstoke and Southampton, found their way to Cohen's yard at Kettering. The locomotive cut up furthest from its home territory was perhaps the diminutive Great Western Railway 0-6-0 pannier tank No 1646, a former Croes Newydd, Wrexham loco which met its demise in BR's Cowlairs, Glasgow, works, after spending its last few years working the very unfamiliar territory of the Dornoch branch, on the north-east coast of Scotland.

Actual cutting of the locomotives tended to follow much the same pattern, wherever the work was done. Non-ferrous parts (mostly brass and copper) such as cab fittings, safety valve bonnets (GWR engines) and bearings which could be easily removed were stripped away, usually followed by the cab assembly. Then, with boiler cladding plates

Java ghosts. A scene at Cepu shed, Java in 1975. Only a handful of engines were in daily use but every single one on the shed shone like a new pin. In Java one never knew when the next call to duty may come. These two engines were really on the scrap line – it was only a matter of time. P. B. WHITEHOUSE

Biggest and most destructive of all the locomotive scrapyards was John Cashmore's of Great Bridge, Staffordshire, which cut up nearly 1,700 ex BR steam locomotives including 36 GWR Castles, 152 Black Fives, 219 8F 2-8-0s and 107 2-6-4Ts. This 1965 view shows a Cashmore's employee turning his sledgehammer on a pile of blast pipes and cylinder blocks.
SUNDAY MERCURY

Things That Go Bump

Mansfield is a town which depended on the coal industry, and its residents were invariably within earshot of a labouring steam engine hauling coal from one of the numerous local mines or bringing in empty wagons for loading.

One day in 1947, listeners were surprised when the throaty bark of an ex Midland '3F' 0-6-0 dragging a heavy coal train against the grade was interrupted by a loud bang and alternate beats changed into loud roars up the chimney. The train came to a stand, the engine too weak to proceed. Superficial examination showed no cause, so the crew ultimately opened the smokebox door. To their surprise they found the inside of the smokebox blasted clean as a whistle, and to the side of the blastpipe a jagged hole about 6in across through which they could see the piston head. Years of corrosion in the smokebox bottom had thinned the cylinder wall to about ¼in, though elsewhere it was ¾in or more. Under the heavy working it had given way.

American scrap. What appears to be a 1918 USA Alco built 2-8-2 JF, at Lanzhou locomotive repair works in north west China in 1984. It was cut up by 1986.
P. B. WHITEHOUSE

Opposite. Also at MM&S, but in the previous October, an ex LMS built Black Five No 45082 has its tender gutted. The crane hovers ready to load the pieces into a waiting lorry. This was the busiest of the Scottish engine breakers.
KEITH ROMIG

removed, the boiler barrel would be cut by acetylene torch, at the point where it joined the smokebox at the front, and the firebox at the back. Boiler tubes could then be easily removed and discarded, to leave the real prize – the copper firebox – easily accessible within the engine frames. For a scrap-metal dealer, this was where the profit really lay. A firebox could constitute some 2½ tons of prime copper, and in the early 1960s, with the price of copper almost doubling within the space of two years, it was not difficult to see why demand for redundant engines eventually exceeded supply.

In 1964–5 however, BR put a damper on the proceedings by insisting that copper fireboxes would have to be returned after dismantling. Most found their way to BR's Derby Works, where, melted down, they were to re-emerge as copper wire, used in the mid-1960s electrification of the West Coast main line. Sometimes BR had to buy back certain parts, in order to keep surviving engines in traffic! Messrs Hughes Bolckow of Blyth, Northumberland resold parts from 9F 2-10-0 freight engines to BR at Crewe, while an 'unofficial' exchange of engine parts took place between Hughes Bolckow and the BR locomotive depot across the road, to keep serviceable the dwindling numbers of former North Eastern Railway J27 freight engines.

A disturbing aspect was the indifference – or perhaps ignorance – shown by the cutters and by BR alike to the potentially lethal blue asbestos lagging which insulated thousands of locomotive boilers. Though there was ample medical evidence then to suggest that the inhalation of fine asbestos particles could promote forms of cancer, boilers were cut – and asbestos particles flew – without any safeguards.

186

Left. Cashmores operated a second yard, at Newport, South Wales. Only slightly less busy than Great Bridge they concentrated mainly on GWR and Southern engines, and cut their way through 51 Halls, 165 57XX pannier tanks, 38 Bulleid light Pacifics and no fewer than 73 standard Fives. The yard's most notable feature was the 40ft high mountain of 'engine bits' which rose and fell as withdrawals ebbed and flowed. REX CONWAY

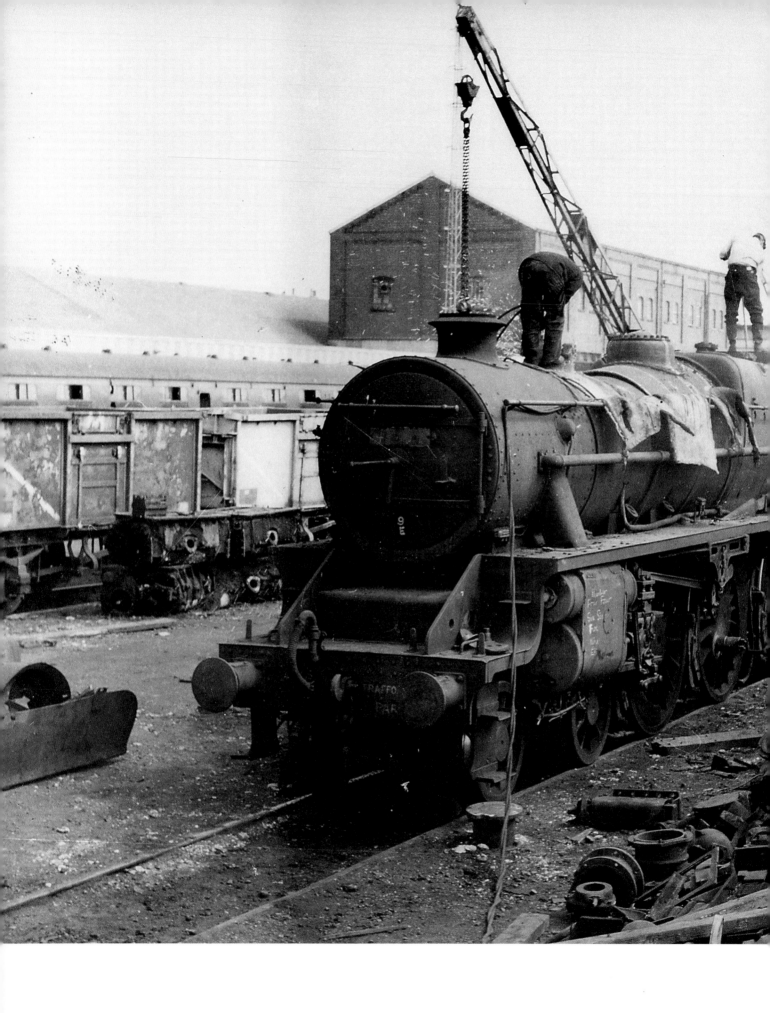

A classic photograph of steam for scrap. Draper's scrapyard at Hull was one of the leading purchasers of condemned steam, disposing of many hundreds of engines, including 156 8Fs and 111 Black Fives. This June 1968 view shows No 44665 of the latter class being disposed of in a ruthlessly efficient manner. TIM EDMONDS

Narrow Lines

It was not every day that you received a message like: 'Engine No 45654 has just come on to the depot and a wheel has dropped off.' It took a little while to establish that one's leg at Leeds Holbeck shed was not being pulled.

Examination showed that the leading bogie axle had developed a fatigue flaw close to the wheel boss; in the way of such things it had started slowly, gradually accelerated its progress to a gallop until about 70 per cent of the area was flawed, causing the remaining sound area to snap. The bogie wheel fell flat on the ground approaching the coaling plant. The engine had just worked an express from London to Sheffield, 159 miles, and a stopping train the thirty nine miles to Leeds. If the break had come half an hour earlier . . .

Not even protective masks were worn.

It is estimated that more than seven thousand steam locomotives were liquidated in private scrapyards between 1958 and 1969, when the last few stragglers were cut, amounting to more than two million tons of metal. Most found its way into UK furnaces, to re-emerge as hair grips, garden swings, bridge girders and a multitude of other applications. But intriguingly, the remnants of at least a small part of Britain's steam heritage was shipped abroad. The Derbyshire contractors Albert Loom of Spondon, exported a large quantity of railway scrap to Japan (to return to Britain, perhaps, as Honda and Datsun cars?), while Messrs Birds Commercial Motors received an order from South America for more than £2 million worth of scrap. The first train-load of 500 tons of mostly sliced-up steam locomotives, left the company's Long Marston, Warwickshire, depot on 24 November 1966, bound for Cardiff Docks.

The final locomotives to be cut in the great steam purge, succumbed to the torch in May 1969, LMS Black 5s Nos 44894, 45017 and 45388 being the last to go, at Draper's yard, in Hull. Save for the two hundred or so ex-BR locomotives rescued for preservation, the vast majority from Woodham's yard at Barry, the steam fleet of sixteen thousand locomotives had been eliminated in a little over ten years – a devastation unparalleled before or since in the world of railways.

Greatly mourned until the last – the penultimate day of steam at Rose Grove shed, 3 August 1968. In the previous decade over 16,000 BR steam locomotives had been taken out of service and cut up.
T. G. FLINDERS

INDEX

Page numbers in *italics* refer to illustrations.

Location names include depots, stations, works etc.